CRESCENT

Acclaim for Homer Hickam

"Classic science-fiction storytelling in the style of early Heinlein, humor, and grand adventure permeate every page of this first book in a trilogy. Boys in particular may be inspired to bring back the time-honored tradition of reading by flashlight under the covers."
—School Library Journal review of Crater

"Long-haul trucking on the Moon . . . with raiders, romance and a secret mission. . . . High adventure on the space frontier."
—Kirkus Review, regarding Crater

"Crater shows what it would be like to live on the Moon: to work there, to struggle and to triumph. A fine piece of work by Homer Hickam."
—Ben Bova, author of Leviathans of Jupiter

"Readers will be caught up in Homer Hickam's thrilling novel of life on the moon! Plenty of twists and an admirable, spirited hero in Crater who takes us on an adventure filled with intrigue and excitement that leaves us wanting more."
—Donna VanLiere, New York Times & USA Today bestselling author of The Good Dream and The Christmas Shoes

CRESCENT

SECOND IN THE HELIUM-3 SERIES

HOMER HICKAM

THOMAS NELSON
Since 1798

NASHVILLE DALLAS MEXICO CITY RIO DE JANEIRO

Published in Nashville, Tennessee, by Thomas Nelson. Thomas Nelson is a registered trademark of Thomas Nelson, Inc.

Thomas Nelson, Inc., titles may be purchased in bulk for educational, business, fund-raising, or sales promotional use. For information, e-mail SpecialMarkets@ThomasNelson.com.

Scripture quotations are taken from the Holy Bible, New International Version®, NIV®. Copyright © 1973, 1978, 1984, 2011 by Biblica, Inc™. Used by permission of Zondervan. All rights reserved worldwide. www.zondervan.com

Publisher's Note: This novel is a work of fiction. Any references to real events, businesses, organizations, and locales are intended only to give the fiction a sense of reality and authenticity. Any resemblance to actual persons, living or dead, is entirely coincidental.

Library of Congress Cataloging-in-Publication Data

Hickam, Homer H., 1943-
  Crescent : second in the Helium-3 series / by Homer Hickam.
    pages cm. -- (A Helium-3 novel ; 2)
  Summary: "They said she wasn't human. They were wrong. A seemingly endless war against the insurgent Crowhoppers keeps the people of Moontown fighting when they'd rather be mining valuable Helium-3. Crater Trueblood's valiant efforts against the genetically-manipulated beings weighs heavily on his mind. What is he really fighting for? In the midst of a deadly battle, Crater captures an enemy Crowhopper. But this one he refuses to kill. "It" is genetically more human than not and its gender seems to be female. She calls herself Crescent. Crater takes her to Moontown as a prisoner of war, but treats her kindly. However, at the hands of Moontown residents Crescent experiences prejudice and even cruelty. Soon Crescent is imprisoned for a murder she didn't commit. Crater comes to her aid, and the two become fugitives, escaping into the vast expanse of hostile terrain called "the big suck." For Crater, it turns out the cause most worth fighting for may be right by his side"-- Provided by publisher.
  ISBN 978-1-59554-663-0 (pbk.)
  [1. War--Fiction. 2. Prejudices--Fiction. 3. Prisoners of war--Fiction. 4. Fugitives from justice--Fiction. 5. Moon--Fiction. 6. Science fiction.] I. Title.
  PZ7.H5244Cu 2013
  [Fic]--dc23
                                            2012051410

Printed in the United States of America

13 14 15 16 17 RRD 6 5 4 3 2 1

To Deborah Underwood, Chuck Lewis, Ken Smith, Steve Noneman, Jerry Richardson, John Thomas, Harvey Shelton, Tony O'Neil, and all my NASA supervisors and co-workers. You understood.

There is no death! The stars go down
To rise upon some other shore,
And bright in heaven's jeweled crown
They shine forevermore.

—J. L. McCreery

Part One

CRATER'S CREATURE

All things bright and beautiful,
All creatures great and small,
All things wise and wonderful:
The Lord God made them all.
—Cecil Alexander

::: ONE

A full tide of glittering stars and fluorescent galaxies washed across the darkness of eternity, the flood of heaven a welcome distraction to Crater Trueblood, who lay in a crumbling ditch waiting to kill or be killed. Actually, it wasn't a ditch at all but an ancient rille that had fallen inward between two faults in the moon's crust, but the Colonel had called it a ditch and Crater supposed it didn't matter much what it was called, considering it was just a place to hide before a battle began.

To his left and right, thirty heel-3 miners-turned-irregular-soldiers gripped their electric railgun rifles and lay in the gray, gritty dust, waiting for the signal to attack. Crater brought his helmet scanner down to the crater-pocked plain that fronted the dustway, the main heel-3 convoy road that crossed a thousand miles of the moon from Moontown to Armstrong City. To the west, snaking around a low hill, a convoy of heel-3 trucks was trundling along toward a feature on the dustway known as the Sinking Ship, a big, brown rock that looked like the prow of a ship sinking into the dust. The convoy was bait for the enemy. If all went according to the Colonel's plan, the convoy would be ambushed by the crow-hoppers, who would then be ambushed themselves. Crater saw the glint of something metallic on the other side of a low hill. The Colonel's plan was working. The crowhoppers were coming.

"Crater!" the Colonel snapped. "Have a look at the battleputer."

Crater didn't understand why the Colonel wanted him to look at the battleputer, but he slid back from the ragged lip of the rille and had a look over the shoulder of the battleputer operator, a fellow who went by the name of Cat Tramon. The view was a signal from a flying drone. In the light gravity of the moon, the drone, no bigger than a small Earthly bird, pulsed along using laser bursts to keep it aloft while it scanned the ragged surface below. Cat gave the hand signal for *enemy approaching* to the Colonel.

Colonel John High Eagle Medaris, in dust-covered coveralls and an old scarred helmet, nodded his approval. Infrared signatures showed the creatures moving across the plain, threading through a crater field. "I count twenty moving into position to ambush the convoy, Colonel," Cat said. "No evidence of spiderwalkers."

Crater was glad they weren't going to have to face the eight-legged war machines the crowhoppers sometimes rode into battle. In past battles, he'd fought these mechanical beasts with artificial intelligence and snapping pincers and thought himself lucky to have survived. The crowhoppers on foot were tough enough.

Crater studied the battleputer screen and saw the signature of a jumpcar parked a mile to the rear behind the rim of a large crater. Its landing two weeks ago had been reported by a Lunatic—one of those hardy moon pioneers who lived alone in the wayback—which caused the Colonel to send out the drone, then call up the Moontown Irregulars who, like Crater, were Helium-3 miners employed by the Colonel's company. The crowhoppers were part of an invading force mostly destroyed by Lunar Council forces over a three-year period. The genetically tweaked troops, sent by the Unified Countries of the World to take over the lunar Helium-3 supply, were reeling after a series of setbacks. This group, then, was a desperate remnant of a defeated army.

Crater saw the glowing figures on the battleputer begin to disperse. "They're fanning out," Cat warned. "Moving into ambush position."

"Tell me when they're set," Colonel Medaris answered. "Then we'll go at 'em."

Crater glanced back at the Colonel. The old man's expression was intent, even eager for the coming battle. The Colonel was undeniably a great man. He'd pioneered the Helium-3 scrapes on the moon, founded Moontown, and built many companies large and small. But he was also a man who did not seem to mind the blood and stink of war. General Robert E. Lee, the "Gray Fox" of the American Civil War, said, "It is well war is so horrible else we would become too fond of it." Crater wondered what General Lee would make of the Colonel. He was well fond of war and did not seem to mind its horrors, nor the body count of friend and foe, as long as he was victorious.

"All right, Crater," the Colonel barked. "You've seen enough. Get back in line."

"Here we go again," Asteroid Al said to Crater as he

crawled back into the rille, then added, "I hope this is the last battle."

Crater gripped his old friend's shoulder. "There can't be many crowhoppers left, Al."

"We keep thinking that, then we're called up to fight some more. I've had it, Crater. I'm a heel-3 miner, not a soldier. I can't take much more of this."

"Today you're a soldier. You've got to think and act like a soldier to stay alive."

"Silence in the ranks!" the Colonel growled.

"Get scragged, you old reprobate," Asteroid Al muttered.

"What did you say, Al?" the Colonel barked. "Keep your focus, man."

Al shook his head, gritted his teeth, and clutched his rifle. Crater looked down the line and saw one of the Irregulars climb out of the rille and crawl back toward a small crater. Since he was in charge of that section of the line, Crater moved to stop the man.

"Crater!" the Colonel snapped. "Who told you to go anywhere?"

Crater ignored the Colonel and kept crawling. He stopped the retreating trooper by putting his gloved hand on his shoulder, but then Crater saw it wasn't a man at all but a boy. "Get back in line," Crater said.

The wild-eyed boy stared back at him.

"What's your name, soldier?" Crater demanded.

"F-Freddy Hook," the boy croaked.

"Hook? Are you Liu Sho Hook's boy?"

"Her eldest."

"Your mom's the best blue banger—I mean foreman—on the scrapes. What are you doing out here?"

"V-Volunteered. I came in by jumpcar just a few hours ago with the other new fellows. Mom didn't want me to go but I thought it was my duty."

Your duty, Crater thought, *is to grow up and be a good man.* But he didn't say that. The boy was here, he had a rifle, and he was needed to fill out the ranks. "You're going to get back in line now, Freddy."

"I'm scared," Freddy said.

Crater made the necessary eye movements toward the heads-up display screen on his helmet to turn his do4u to the private frequency of an experienced fighter named Doom. Before coming to the moon, Doom, once a citizen of the Republic of North India, had been a mercenary in several Earthly armies. "Doom, I need you," he said.

Doom crawled over and Crater pointed at the boy. "Someone needs to look after Freddy. I'd do it but I think the Colonel's got something planned for me. He's been on my case all day."

"With pleasure," Doom said and moved to lie beside Freddy. He patted him on the back, then pointed at the power setting on the boy's rifle. "Move that to the highest level. You must not wound a crowhopper. You must kill him or he will kill you."

The boy fumbled with the setting, then looked up for approval. Doom smiled at him. "We are going to get back in line now. You will be fine, Freddy. Just stay with me."

"Y-Yes, sir." Freddy gulped.

"Crater," the Colonel hissed. "Stop playing around and get back up here. I want you to take charge of the attack."

Crater clambered over to the Colonel and switched to his private channel. "Why me?"

"Why not you? My orders are simple. Kill them all. Remember it's only crowhoppers. It isn't as if they are real humans."

Crater couldn't argue with the Colonel's opinion. Crow-hoppers were a foul bunch, fond of killing, and it didn't matter if they killed enemy soldiers or innocent civilians, including children. The moon needed to be rid of them. He switched to the Irregulars' battle frequency. "All right, you scrag heads. The Colonel's ordered me to lead this lashup." He looked left and right and saw grim smiles. His eyes landed on Captain Mike, who'd once been an officer back on Earth for one side or the other. "Mike, you take the right side on my signal. I'll keep the left. You good with that?"

"Let's just get this over with," Mike growled.

Crater checked the battleputer one more time and saw the crowhoppers had settled into an ambush line along a series of craters near the dustway. "Let's go, you apes," he growled. "You want to live forever?"

He clambered out of the rille, the rest of the men in the line peeling off and following single file. He led them through a field of broken rock, then dropped to one knee. The others did the same, their rifles at the ready. He waved Mike's line to move to the right to set up the pincer movement. A few minutes later there was a flash in the direction of the dustway. "They're attacking the convoy," Crater said. "Mike, are you in position?"

"I'm go for battle," Mike replied.

"All right, on my count. Three-two-one. Attack!"

Crater stood up and ran toward the dustway, his rifle at his hip. In the gravity of the moon, each stride carried him ten feet. He leaped over a small crater and saw the black-armored crowhoppers had come out into the open. A spray of their flechettes slammed into the convoy trucks abandoned by their drivers and several of the heel-3 canisters were struck, triggering spouts of gas.

Crater shot a crowhopper who clutched his side and fell. A crowhopper beside him brought his rifle around. Crater bounded forward and slammed into the creature with his shoulder, knocking it down. Kicking its rifle away, he put his boot on its chest, jammed his rifle muzzle into the vulnerable spot beneath its spiked helmet, and fired. The Irregulars waded into the crowhoppers, picking them off.

One of the crowhoppers jumped up and made a run for it. Crater followed. The creature turned and fired its rifle, the flechette ripping through Crater's body armor deep enough that its point nicked his chest. Snarling, Crater pulled the black flechette out and tossed it away, trusting the biolastic pressure sheath that covered his body to heal itself. Crater leaped and landed behind the fleeing crowhopper and jammed the muzzle of his rifle into the creature's neck and pulled the trigger. Reacting, it threw its head back, then fell, rolled in the dust, and died.

Crater spotted another crowhopper running away. He followed it through a maze of small and large craters, then saw that it was running toward a black jumpcar, a bullet-shaped suborbital vehicle that landed tail-first. Reaching the jumpcar, the crowhopper climbed its ladder. Crater went down on one knee, aimed, and pulled the trigger three times. The flechettes, each flying at eight hundred miles per hour, zipped through the vacuum. One struck the crowhopper in its right leg, one in its back, and one dented its helmet. It recoiled from the triple impact, then kept climbing until it reached the hatch where it tried to pull itself inside, then seemed to lose heart, let go of the ladder, and fell slowly back into the dust. After crawling a few feet, it leaned its back against one of the jumpcar's landing fins.

Crater cautiously approached the creature. It sat with its legs outstretched and turned its black helmet toward him. Its face could not be seen, although the eyes in its view slit burned with hatred. Crater activated his do4u helmet communicator and chose the frequency he knew the crowhoppers favored. A language savant, Crater knew its language, a variant of Siberian. "Are there any more of you?" he asked.

"I am in pain," the crowhopper replied in the guttural voice all crowhoppers seemed to possess. "Kill me."

"Are there any more of you?" Crater asked again.

"I think you have killed us all, my lord, except me," it replied, this time in English. "Now it is my turn. Shoot me and be done with it. Death is life, life is death. There is little difference. This the Trainers teach us. This we know as truth."

Crater lowered his rifle. This one was talking, which was unusual. It might give away valuable information if he could keep it talking. "Have you ever considered your Trainers might be lying?"

"What do you care? Kill me. Savor your victory."

Crater's eye landed on disturbed dust nearby. In the shadow of a small overhang of brown fractured rock, he saw what appeared to be a tunnel. "Is this your hideout?" he asked.

The crowhopper glanced at the overhang, then turned back to Crater. "I ask you again by the gods of war and blood, kill me." It stretched out a hand toward its rifle which had fallen just outside its reach, then fell back with a groan. "Hand me my weapon and I will take care of myself."

"What's in that hole?" Crater demanded. "Tell me the truth and I promise I'll kill you if that's what you want."

"We lived there," the creature answered. "It's empty now but is wired to explode."

"Why did you set up camp here?"

"Why not? We had to go somewhere."

"You're certain that hole is empty?"

"Yes."

"Then why did you wire it to explode?"

The creature fell silent. After a moment of indecision, Crater picked up the thing's rifle, removed the flechette magazine, jacked out the final round, then threw it into a nearby crater. The crowhopper's eyes softened. "I don't understand. I am sure you have killed many of us before. Why not me?"

Crater planned to interrogate it but he kept silent on his intentions. First, he wanted to find out what was in that hole. He walked to the overhang and knelt down and saw an embedded hatch, probably covering a dustlock.

The crowhopper called out, "Come back! I have secrets I will tell you!"

Crater ignored it and inspected the hatch. Briefly, he considered calling up support, then rejected the idea because he knew the Colonel would strap a detpak to the hatch, blow it, then throw in more detpaks until there was nothing left inside except dust. The crowhopper's attempt to divert him away from the hole made Crater determined to find out what was in there.

Not for the first time, Crater wished he had his gillie. He tried to recall its face, although it had no face, and its voice, although it had no voice, and the way it looked, although it didn't look like anything. The gillie could have scanned through the hatch and told him what was behind it. But the gillie was dead. It had sacrificed itself to save Crater during another battle against the crowhoppers. Though the gillie was only a clump of slime mold cells made into a biocomputer, Crater still missed it, almost like a lost friend.

Crater studied the hatch. It was a standard portable dust-lock design. He grasped the lever, swung it over, and then pulled the hatch open. Since he was still alive, he assumed that at least the outer hatch hadn't been wired. He stepped inside, pulled the hatch closed behind him, switched on his helmet lamp, and looked around until he found the button that activated pressure into the chamber. He pushed it and the dustlock filled with air, a meter on the hatch counting until it reached one Earthian pressure. Crater inspected the internal hatch, saw nothing suspicious, and threw the lever to open it. As soon as it swung open, he saw the crowhopper. It sprang away, just avoiding the flechettes Crater sent flying in its direction. He climbed through the hatch and kept firing, but the crowhopper's shadow was all he hit as it scurried around a corner of the hole.

Crater took a moment to notice that he was in a small lava-tube. His eye caught sleeping bags and empty ration cans and water bags on the dusty floor. There were glowing biolume lights hanging from the roof of solid rock. He had entered a crowhopper nest.

Crater eased toward a curve in the tube. He took a breath, dived to the floor, and rolled. When he brought up his rifle, he found it pointed at the crowhopper which was quietly squatting on its haunches, its hands empty of weapons. Crater's finger stroked the trigger of his rifle but he didn't pull it. He stood and beckoned the thing out of the shadows. "Come out where I can get a look at you. Come on, I won't hurt you."

When he lowered the barrel of his rifle just fractionally, the thing leaped, its spiked helmet aimed at Crater's chest. He moved aside, grabbed it by its backpack, and threw it across the tube. Crater followed it, kicked it, then drew it up, a forearm across its throat. That was when he realized how small the crowhopper was. He'd never seen one under six feet. Seven was the norm. This one was barely five feet tall, if that. Crater took away his arm from its throat, shoved it down, and put a boot on its chest. A knife suddenly appeared in the hand of the crowhopper, probably drawn from a camouflaged leg holster. It swiped at him but Crater dodged, seized the creature's wrist, and wrenched the knife out of its hand. He tossed it away, then struck the creature on the side of its helmet with his gloved fist. It cried out, and Crater dragged it across the tube and penned it against the wall. It glared at him, then said in a shrill voice, "I will kill you as sure as the summer sun rises above the tundra."

"The battle is over," Crater replied. "You lost."

"The battle is never lost," it replied, switching to English. "And the Legion never loses. Life is death. Death is life."

Crater grabbed the thing by the neck of its armored torso and pushed it toward the hatch. "Move."

"I am going because I want to go," it said. "It will give me time to consider how best to kill you."

"Just keep walking," Crater growled. He punched it in its back with his rifle and it staggered ahead. In the dustlock, he left the inner hatch open and bled out the air, depressurizing the lavatube. He doubted there were more crowhoppers hidden inside, considering how small the tube was. But exhausting the air would kill anything alive or, if they had a pressure suit, force them outside. Crater prodded the small crowhopper to the jumpcar. The other crowhopper was still there although its situation had somewhat changed. It had managed to acquire a big knife, the kind that Earthian warriors called an elk sticker, no doubt from some hidden recess in its armor.

The small crowhopper, ignoring Crater, walked up to the other one. "You are dying," it said without emotion.

"Yes, I am dying but too slowly," the crowhopper said, equally without emotion. "And you are a captive."

"I will kill this one soon," the little creature answered. "And then I will get away."

"That is good." The dying crowhopper glanced at Crater. "Will you give me your name?"

"Crater Trueblood," Crater answered.

"Ah, Crater Trueblood, life is death."

Crater shook his head. "Death is death, you vile creature."

"You have power over me, do you not?" It nodded toward Crater's rifle. "But when I do this, you have none. Death is life." And then the crowhopper used the elk sticker to cut its own throat with a horrific swipe that at the end of it also included tossing the bloody knife to the little crowhopper, which grabbed it and plunged it into Crater's calf. A slow-motion spray of blood, instantly turning to pink vapor in the vacuum of the moon, burst from the wound.

Alarms cried out in Crater's helmet. *Suit failure! Suit failure!*

The little crowhopper cheered. "I knew I would kill you!"

::: TWO

Maria Medaris concluded the meeting called to review the new inventory procedures for her jump-car factory in Armstrong City. On her reader screen were six black-rimmed squares, each containing an individual image of one of her corporate officers, including her father, vice president for Central European sales and marketing. Maria led each manager through the action items the meeting had produced, but when she reached him, her father was on a do4u call, a casual one based on his smile and relaxed demeanor. "I'll talk to Dad later," she said to the others, doing her best to tamp down the resentment she felt for the disrespect toward her he was clearly showing.

It was typical of her father. While her grandfather, the Colonel, believed in her and gave her every opportunity to excel, her father had ridiculed her from the moment she'd expressed an interest in joining the Medaris corporate empire. Her father's dream was to be a sculptor, a dream squashed by the Colonel, who'd threatened him with the loss of his inheritance. How unlike her father she was! Maria lived for business, especially the business of making the Medaris brand the strongest on Earth and the moon. When the Colonel removed her father from the presidency of the Medaris Jumpcar Company, he had replaced him with Maria. Since then, she'd taken the company her father had nearly run into the ground and made it prosperous by moving manufacturing to the moon, a solution he had ferociously opposed. The latest balance sheet more than proved her position. Manufacturing jumpcars in Armstrong City, using local labor and materials, was a remarkable success story.

"There's no time to lose," Maria said, summarizing her business philosophy. "You have your action items. Get going on them and hit your deadlines. If you run into snags, let me know. Otherwise, I trust you to get everything done on time."

Maria touched each of the squares to end their participation except her father's. "Dad, get off your do4u. We need to talk."

Her father raised his eyebrows but completed his call. "Well, Maria," he said, "you no longer say 'please' to your old man? You just give me orders?"

"I'm sorry," Maria said, "but I need your support during these meetings. Going offline to take a personal call is disrespectful. Please don't do it again."

Her father leaned back, contempt flickering across his face. "How can I be respectful when everything you're doing shows your inexperience? You've had a run of luck with your factory, but over time, it'll all fall apart. The moon simply has too many drawbacks to be a good manufacturing area. Maybe in a decade or two but not now. So this is what I think you should do—"

"Dad," Maria interrupted, "my moon factory is running rings around the plant you set up in Shanghai. As for what you call drawbacks, I foresee them and plan for them. If you'd listened to the actions I gave out, you'd know that. Speaking of actions, the sales in your sector have slumped by three percent. What's the explanation?"

Her father sighed. "Of course they've slumped, Maria. I laid off four of our sales staff."

"You did what?" Maria demanded. "By whose authority?"

"My own, of course. I am still a senior officer in this company."

Maria's voice went cold. "Yes, you are, but this is *my* company. You are responsible for marketing and sales in Central Europe and that is the extent of your authority. Hiring and firing is done by me and me alone. Who did you fire?"

"McCoy, Tsing Hai, Tanner, and Bohannon."

"Four of our best salesmen! I hired them myself."

"I didn't like their attitude," her father replied with a shrug.

"Hire them back."

"Excuse me?"

"Hire them back. Increase their salary if you have to, but hire them back today! Do it, or I will do it myself. Understood?"

"Really, Maria, I simply will never understand how you got to be so much like your grandfather. Your mother and I—"

"Leave my mother out of it," Maria interrupted. "You really don't want to bring her into any conversation you and I might have."

Her father pursed his lips, then shrugged. "I was only going to say she and I had hopes you might become a ballerina. You were such a good dancer. I'm sure she would be disappointed to know you would throw away your talents to become a mere businesswoman."

"If so," Maria said, "it would be only one more disappointment on top of all the others she had because of you. Would you like me to list them? Let's start with the booze, then we could talk about the hard drugs, and after that, the women—"

"That's enough, young lady!" her father snapped.

"Or what? Are you going to send me to my room? Dad, this conversation, such as it is, is over. You have your orders. Either comply with them or I'd be more than pleased to accept your resignation."

Before he could reply, Maria touched his square, sending it spinning into digital oblivion. Afterward, she realized she was trembling. Her father had that kind of effect on her. He not only didn't respect her as a businesswoman, he simply didn't like her. Why that was, she had no idea, but she'd sensed it her entire life. Growing up, it seemed he always went out of his way to belittle her accomplishments or anything she wanted to try. Nothing was ever good enough. Her mother tried her best but she was weak and never defended Maria or even herself. There was a palpable tension in the house anytime her father was in it. He would blow up over the smallest pretext and go storming around, even getting violent. Once, he'd pulled from the wall a display case that was filled with glass figurines her mother had collected from around the world. They were all smashed to bits and he never apologized. "I don't apologize," she heard him say once. "It is a sign of weakness."

When her mother lost her life in a boating accident, her dad had not mourned her, at least as far as Maria could tell. Maria sat back and put her hand on her belly. Whenever she thought about her childhood, her stomach hurt. She was relieved when her assistant came in with a reminder that she was already late to join the committee formed by Armstrong City businesses to save the old Apollo landing sites. Called ARC for Apollo Restoration Committee, its charter was to assess the landing sites and make recommendations to save and restore them in perpetuity. Today they were visiting the Apollo 12 site.

Maria pressed her thumb to three decision papers on her reader, approving one, rejecting the others, then grabbed her flight jacket and hustled out of her office. Her secretary, a fussy little man, followed her into the street outside the Medaris Enterprises building where her fastbug waited for her. "One more thing, Jarvis," she said as she climbed into the four-wheeler. "Check in with the Colonel. Provide him with the minutes of my meeting and let him know where I'll be for the rest of the afternoon."

"Should that include your post-meeting discussion with your father?"

Maria thought about that, then said, "No. I'll talk to him about it myself."

"Yes, ma'am. Have a nice flight."

Maria nodded her thanks, pressed the accelerator, and drove toward the landing field where her corporate jumpcar was kept in a private hangar. On the way through the narrow backstreets, she thought over her latest encounter with her father. She loved the man—he was her father, after all—and tried hard to understand the resentments he'd built up over the years. She knew instinctively that it was his frustration with his own father that caused him to be petty and vindictive toward her and her mother. But was that a reasonable excuse? Maria knew it wasn't. She would forgive him as best she could, but she wasn't going to forget he had a streak of cruelty a mile wide. She would stay wary around him and, if need be, she would fire him. He could go whining to the Colonel if he didn't like it. Somehow Maria doubted that would happen.

Her jumpcar was a beautiful burnished copper, a color that was proving to be very popular with the customers of the Medaris Jumpcar Company. It was an innovation she'd started, allowing customers to pick from a myriad of colors, even combinations of colors. It made the setup a little more complex in the factory located in Armstrong City's north maintenance shed, but it was worth it. That was another thing she and her father had clashed over—basic black and silver had served them well for decades. Why confuse things by offering a rainbow of colors? "Because our customers like colors," Maria explained to him while he rolled his eyes. Even the simplest of all sales techniques escaped him: give the customer what he wants.

Her party of three committee members was waiting for her. She pulled up beside them and got out. "Sorry to be late," she said. "My meeting went a little longer than planned."

She led them to the ramp up to the jumpcar entry hatch. Amy Bandas of the Lunaradar Company, Lauralei Osinski of Floridamoon Sports, and Jessica Gaskin, Armstrong City Lunar Optics, took their seats in the passenger compartment while she climbed into the cockpit and turned on the control console. The panel lights burned brightly, then automatically dimmed to her preferred level. She called up the puter and went through the checklist, then called the hangar crew. "Ready for rollout," she said. Within seconds, the big inner hangar doors swung open and the mobile pad trundled into the airlock. Once inside, the inner doors swung shut, the air was bled out of the chamber, and the outer doors were swung open. Perfectly synchronized, the mobile pad crept through the doors into the dusty vacuum. When it was in position, the pad stopped and Maria called up Armstrong Control.

"You have clearance," came the crisp reply.

"Roger that, and thank you," she said, then looked over her shoulder. "All ready?" she asked her passengers, and received nods and thumbs up from them.

"Okay, baby," Maria whispered while putting her hand on the throttles. "Let's show them what you've got."

Flames spurted at the base of the jumpcar and it rose majestically as Maria nudged the throttles with the base of her hand, holding the g-forces to a minimum. Below, Armstrong City receded, its three huge domes glittering in the sunlight. At five miles altitude, she lowered the nose and aimed it westward. The Sabine and Ritter double craters slid by to the north. Ahead lay a tortured crater field that marked the approach to a relatively small lava field known as Sinus Medii, which had the distinction of being the closest feature on the moon to Earth.

A light on the panel flared, followed by the voice of Armstrong City Control. "High Eagle One, be advised that you need to shift southwest immediately. Recommend a vector of one hundred and twenty degrees."

Maria switched to the secure channel. "Armstrong City, why the course change?"

"Military situation, Miss Medaris. You should be fine if you'll fly a hundred miles south before continuing to your destination."

"Understood," Maria replied and began her turn. She made it as smooth as she could so as to not disturb her passengers. A glance at the map display confirmed her suspicion. The only thing north of her was the dustway, the road the Helium-3 convoys used from Moontown to Aristillus and, ultimately, Armstrong City. A military situation there likely meant a convoy was being ambushed, and if that was so, the nearest military force was the Medaris Irregulars, the company of militia the Colonel maintained in Moontown. The Irregulars were likely in battle, and that meant the Colonel and other Moontown citizens were too.

Including Crater Trueblood.

She guided the jumpcar along its new vector, every minute taking it farther away from whatever was happening up north. Worry furrowed her brow. The worry was not for her grandfather, who could take care of himself—he always had and she believed he always would. But what about Crater?

Her heart almost physically hurt when she thought of him. Three years before, she and Crater—both sixteen at the time—were scouts on a convoy across the moon. They had fought crowhoppers together and then were launched into space aboard a Cycler, there to collect a special package for the Colonel. During all this, though she had not wanted to, she found herself more and more attracted to the orphan boy. He was smart, filled with the potential for greatness that she admired, and he was a nice-looking, good boy too. Maria admittedly had always been more attracted to the bad boys, the ones who were smart and capable and poised but a little dangerous. Crater was a bumpkin in almost every way, kind and honest, yet when she wasn't paying attention, somehow that dusty bumpkin had stolen her heart.

The days they'd spent aboard the Cycler, however, had not gone well. It had been up to her to keep the secret of what was in the package from everyone, and that required her to lie to Crater. And then the Demons, genetic monsters who wore red armor and carried axes, ten times worse and vastly more maniacal than the crowhoppers, had swarmed aboard the Cycler to steal the Colonel's secret package. They had been defeated but only after Maria had suffered a terrible wound exposing her to the vacuum in space.

Weeks later, after she was well enough for visitors, the Colonel came to her and told her Crater had taken his great horse Pegasus north with the package and delivered it to the Russians. Since it was meant to go to the Czarina anyway, the Colonel did not blame Crater, but Maria blamed him for not coming to see her or making the slightest attempt to communicate with her. As the weeks turned into months, now nearly three years, she'd finally accepted that he hated her. She had recently written him a note of farewell. It was a business-like note and she wondered what he would make of it, or if he would even read it—and if he did, would he care?

Now she looked north, wondering what he was doing. Would he live through the day? Her eyes filled with tears. She missed him! "You are the ruin of my life, Crater Trueblood," she muttered, then pushed the throttles forward as if velocity could tear the pain from her heart.

When she realized the little spacecraft was rattling from the fiery jets at full throttle, she pulled them back, then kept the jumpcar steady, giving her passengers the best ride possible. Thirty minutes later, with Frau Mauro off to the right, Maria eased the jumpcar into a slow rotation, then began to back down to a landing using the Montes Riphaeus mountain range as a reference. She touched down three hundred meters from the Apollo 12 landing site at Mare Cognitum, Latin for The Sea That Has Become Known, a place explored robotically by Surveyor 3, Ranger 7, and Luna 5 before Apollo 12's *Intrepid* had landed. Two American astronauts, Pete Conrad and Alan Bean, had spent over a day exploring the lava flow basin. They had also cut a piece of tubing off Surveyor 3 to carry back for analysis. It had been an exciting mission and only the second to carry humans to the moon.

Maria climbed down from the cockpit and opened a viewport that allowed a perfect view of the site. The base of *Intrepid* was all that was left of the lander, the upper portion flown to a rendezvous with the Apollo capsule *Yankee Clipper*. The remnant of the lander looked dull and dusty. The American flag erected nearby had turned white, the red, white, and blue colors long since blasted away by the fierce sunlight that swept the moon, unhindered by a protective atmosphere.

Maria provided her passengers with binoculars. "The site seems to be in good shape," Amy said. "No sign of any visitors at all. The boot prints are all Apollo treads. We're lucky to find it still so pristine, considering the lunatics."

"And no truck tracks around either." Jessica grinned. "Immaculate. Amazing after all these years no one has come visiting."

"Since there are no hills nearby," Lauralei said, "we'll need to build a tower for observation. Maybe a hundred feet high."

"Several towers," Jessica said. "And a fence to surround them."

"Too expensive," Amy replied. She caught Maria looking northward where there were no Apollo 12 artifacts. "Maria? Are you paying attention?"

On one level Maria was listening, but her mind was also wandering. She wanted to get on the comm unit and get an update on the military situation up north. She forced herself back to the business at hand. "It's expensive, yes," she said, "but it isn't our charter to worry about where the money comes from, just what needs to be done to protect the site. A fence with a security system is without a doubt required, although I don't think we need more than one tower if it's placed where most of the activity area can be seen and studied."

Amy nodded. "Agreed."

"Let's talk about it on the way back," Maria said.

"I'd like to study the site a little longer," Jessica said.

Maria tamped down her frustration. "Of course," she said, then said a silent prayer for the men who were out there fighting. Especially one of them. *Please keep Crater safe!*

"Did you say something, Maria?" Amy asked.

"Just a little prayer for somebody," she said. "An old friend who may be in trouble."

"What is that thing up there?" Lauralei asked.

Maria followed Osinski's point and saw a small black spacecraft coming in from the west. It stopped, its jets funneling downward so it could hover, stirring up a cloud of dust. Electrostatically charged, the dust hung above the surface, a portion moving ominously toward the Apollo 12 site. Then the craft flew straight at the jumpcar, passing overhead so close Maria could see its seams before it zoomed straight up, its jets turning from two bright orange bursts to twinkling amber stars in seconds.

"What was that?" Amy shouted.

"A warpod scout," Maria replied as she clambered up the ladder to the cockpit. "Robotic and likely unfriendly. Belt yourself in. We're in for a chase."

::: THREE

tack the bodies over there," the Colonel directed his Irregulars, and silently they did his bidding, placing the lifeless creatures into a crowhopper pyramid. Asteroid Al wasn't with them. He sat crouching in a small, deep crater gouged out of the Sea of Rains a billion years ago. He hadn't fired his rifle once during the short battle. He'd tried but just couldn't do it.

Al took a breath of biosoup oxygen, stood up, and began looking for Crater. His search led him into a field of craters where he found Freddy Hook lying alongside Doom. The boy was on his back, clutching his stomach. Doom was dead, his helmet shattered, his face turned purple. Al knelt beside the boy and checked his suit. It was holding normal. The boy's eyes were hollow, his lips pale. "What happened, Freddy?" Al asked.

"Three attacked us, sir. Mr. Doom got two of them but then his helmet exploded. I felt like something puffed up inside me and I got sort of tired and had to lie down."

Asteroid Al felt helpless, incompetent, and worthless. Not

only was he not much of a soldier, he was certainly no medic. He barked at his do4u, demanding a direct connection to the medics which, because of the color of the suits they wore, were called greenies. "Al here! Need a greenie now!"

It was the Colonel who answered. "Let's show a little professionalism, Al, and calm down. Why do you need a medic?"

Asteroid Al felt a surge of resentment against the Colonel. Why had that old fool let a mere boy get involved in a dirty battle? He choked down his feelings, took a breath, and answered, "It's Freddy Hook, Colonel."

"Freddy who?"

"Mrs. Hook's boy. I think he's hurt bad."

"What is he doing out here?"

"I don't know. All I know is he's been shot. Doom was with him, and he's dead."

"Greenie on the way," the Colonel answered.

Al took Freddy's hand. "It will be all right, Freddy," he said. "Help's coming."

The boy didn't respond. Blinking occasionally, he just kept looking at the sky. "Are you looking at the stars?" Al asked.

"No, sir. I'm looking at the darkness between them," Freddy said.

"Why?"

"Because I know what stars are. I don't know what the darkness is."

Al wiped at a tear, only to brush his glove against his helmet faceplate. The moon was a tough place to cry.

Then Crater came limping up with the smallest crowhopper Al had ever seen. "Sit!" Crater said to the creature, pointing to the ground. When it didn't move, Crater shoved it down.

Since its hands were tied behind its back, it had nothing to catch itself and fell heavily on its side, its helmet thumping on the dust.

"What's that?" Al asked.

"A problem I've decided to create for myself," Crater replied. "Don't ask me why."

"May I ask why you're limping?"

Crater demonstrated his leg and the knife sticking from it. "It got me with an elk sticker. I'll need a few stitches. The biolastic membrane is holding so far."

Then Crater noticed the two Irregulars in the dust. "Doom's gone," Al said. "Freddy . . . well, there he is."

Crater knelt beside the boy. "Hey, Freddy. How you doing?"

"I'm burning up," Freddy said. "There's a fire inside me. It hurts everywhere."

Crater gently peeled Freddy's gloved hands from his stomach, revealing a stain of blood on his gray coveralls. The biolastic membrane had healed itself, but the flechette that had caused the wound had clearly gone deep.

"Help's on the way," Al said, just as one of the green-suits arrived along with the Colonel plus two Moontown Irregulars carrying a stretcher.

The greenie made a cursory inspection, then said, "Let's get him to the popup." Freddy was gently placed on the stretcher and carried off.

"What about Doom?" Al asked the Colonel.

"We'll pick him up later. By the looks of the dead crowhoppers in this crater, Doom was a good soldier to the last."

The Colonel turned to Crater and the black-suited figure lying on its side with its knees pulled up. When he saw it twitch, he demanded, "Why isn't that thing dead?"

"It seems to be a young one," Crater answered. "I thought somebody ought to look at it."

The Colonel squinted. "All right, I've looked at it. It is a biological monster. Dispose of it."

Crater's expression remained neutral. "Do you want me to shoot it or slit its throat?"

"What difference does it make?"

"Since it'll be an execution in cold blood, I just wondered what your preference was."

The Colonel's eyes went hard. "Don't hand me that scrag, Crater. I can assure you that thing is at this very moment plotting your death."

Crater shrugged. "Life is death. Death is life. That's their mantra."

"Charming," the Colonel growled. He pondered the small crowhopper, then said, "I don't care how you do it, just as long as you do it."

The Colonel stalked away, Crater glaring at his back. Al watched Crater and wondered what he was thinking. Only nineteen, Crater was an astonishing young man. He was not only a fine soldier but a language savant—the latest count was eighteen languages—and an accomplished musician—expert on the violin, guitar, piano, and drums. He was also the best engineer Al had ever known. Crater's inventions included a sensor that regulated electrical output in biofuel cells, and a device that found water molecules in the lunar dirt and gathered them into pools that could be tapped. Both were revolutionary, the sensors increasing the range of moon vehicles using biofuel cells by twenty-five percent. The water device, although not in production, might very well make the moon a home for hundreds of thousands of people, rather than the seven thousand or so who presently lived there. Up until now, Al was certain any decision Crater made was based on facts and physics, but the little crowhopper still alive in the dust didn't make sense. Had Crater finally snapped? Al had seen it happen before. The moon, especially under the dictatorial hand of Colonel Medaris, was a place where any man could break beneath the strain.

Crater turned toward Al. "What are you looking at?"

"I was just trying to figure out if you'd finally lost your mind," Al said.

"Why?"

Al nodded at the crowhopper. "Yeah, well, maybe I have," Crater acknowledged. "But what's done is done. Keep an eye on it for me, will you, Al? I need to get my leg looked at and have a few more words with the Colonel. You got some mine wire on you?"

Mine wire, thin cable on a spool, was common equipment for miners and handy for a lot of things. Al fished a spool from his pack and handed it over. Crater wrapped it around the crowhopper's boots, ran the wire up and around its gloves, then wrapped it tight. "That ought to hold it. But if it gives you any trouble, shoot it."

"I didn't pull a trigger once during the entire battle."

"You're not much of a soldier."

"I told you that."

"Are you soldier enough to defend yourself?"

"I guess so."

Crater shrugged. "Well, I guess I'll find out when I get back."

"Thanks for your vote of confidence."

Crater raised his thumb to Al in a hopeful gesture, then shoved off. Al sat down on the rim of a small crater and rested his rifle in his lap. He watched the mutant for a few minutes but boredom set in and he looked up, ignoring the pinpricks of light that were the stars and searching the darkness between them. He recalled Freddy thought there were answers there, but Al saw nothing but the absence of light. He looked toward the little crowhopper and noticed its boots were against a boulder and it had gathered itself in a ball. He wondered why it had gotten itself into such a contorted position, just before it launched itself like a spiked guided missile. Al promptly stepped aside and the spike on the little crowhopper's helmet slammed into the crater rim where Al had been sitting just moments before. Crumpling, the creature slithered to the base of the rim. *Maybe it killed itself,* Al thought with some hope, but was disappointed when it moved its head, then sat up.

Al considered putting the thing out of its misery. It would be so easy. All he had to do was insert the muzzle of his rifle anywhere along the base of the creature's helmet and pull the trigger. What kind of life could it possibly have, after all? Most likely, if the Colonel didn't kill it, it would be locked up somewhere, maybe even tortured. Crater had not done the thing any favors by making it a prisoner.

The creature looked at Al. Its eyes, all he could see of them through the slit in its helmet, were filled with hate. Al had not fired his rifle once during the entire battle. If he was ever going to do it, maybe now was the time. He walked up to the thing and was astonished when it raised its head, offering the sweet spot at its throat. When Al pushed the muzzle of his rifle there, the creature's eyes softened as if begging him to go ahead. Al pulled the trigger.

::: FOUR

rater caught up with the Colonel at the popup surgery. The greenies had Freddy stripped of his biolastic membrane and were working diligently on his wound. When Crater entered through the airlock, he heard the conversation the surgeon was having with the Colonel. "We can't save him, Colonel."

"I provide you the best field hospital money will buy," the Colonel growled, "and you let this boy bleed out?"

"There is nothing we can do. The flechette splintered inside him. His liver, kidneys, spleen, and intestines are shredded."

The Colonel noticed Crater. "Why are you here?"

"I have a medical situation," Crater answered.

The Colonel's eyes drifted down to the knife protruding from Crater's leg. "I can't believe you'd be so careless as to get stabbed. Did you kill that thing?"

"Not yet."

"Why not?"

"I didn't want to."

"Your insolence is beginning to irritate me."

"Next time you have a battle, leave me behind and you won't have to deal with it."

The Colonel's eyes turned brittle. "You're going too far, Crater."

Crater shrugged. "All I want is to get back to work on the scrapes."

"You're a smart fellow, Crater, but you just don't know what's good for you. Work on the scrapes? You're far too good for that. You've invented a way to recover water from moon dust! It's revolutionary and worth millions—but you refuse to sell it to me."

"That's because I think I can make it better."

"Sell it to me and I'll make it better. You can just count your johncredits."

Crater shook his head. "I don't work that way."

"No, you don't, and it's a shame."

"Colonel?" It was the surgeon. "Freddy's leaving us."

Colonel Medaris walked over to where the boy lay and took his hand. "Well, Freddy," he said, "we have the enemy beaten. Congratulations. Your valor won the battle."

Freddy's eyes fluttered. "Sir? I didn't do anything. I just got shot."

The Colonel forced a chuckle. "That's the drugs they give you. Makes you forget things. You're going to get a medal, Freddy. The highest one it's possible for me to award a soldier. The Medaris Company Medal of, um, Supreme Honor. How old are you?"

"Twelve, sir."

"Well, there you go. The youngest recipient of the Medaris Company Medal of Supreme Honor ever. Your mother will be proud."

Freddy moaned. "I need my mother. Can you call her for me, sir?"

"We're a little out of comm range, Freddy, but I'll call her up in just a minute."

Freddy twisted his head, his eyes fading. "Mom?"

The surgeon recoiled, but at a curt nod from the Colonel, she came forward and took the boy's hand. "I'm here, Freddy."

"Did you hear I'm getting a medal?"

"Oh, yes, Freddy. You're a hero. I'm proud of you."

The boy smiled, but the light in his eyes was almost gone. "Love you, M-Mom . . . tr-tried to be good."

"I love you too, Freddy. You're the best boy there ever was."

Crater watched Freddy Hook, the youngest recipient of the Medaris Company Supreme Medal of Honor, die. Disgusted with the Earth, heaven, and the moon, he impulsively reached down and pulled the knife from his leg and angrily threw it on the deck. "That's great, Colonel. Was this battle worth Freddy's life?"

The Colonel turned and gave Crater an angry glare. "What's wrong with you?"

"That boy should have never been out here." He gazed dumbly at the gush of blood that was flowing from his leg. "And now I've done a stupid thing."

The Colonel stared at Crater's wound. "Yes, you have, Crater. Yes, you have."

The surgeon untwined the boy's fingers from hers. "There's no such thing as that medal, is there?" she asked the Colonel.

"There wasn't," the Colonel answered, "but there is now."

When Crater hit the floor, both the Colonel and the

surgeon turned to stare at his crumpled form. "What's wrong with him?" the surgeon asked.

"A little nick in his leg," the Colonel replied. "I'm sure it's not serious. He's just being dramatic. Patch him up and put him back on duty. No bed rest, you hear?"

::: **FIVE**

Maria pulled her seat belt tight, then gave a count-down for her passengers. "On my mark, hang on, five-four-three-two-one . . ." She pushed the throttles forward and the jumpcar thundered aloft. She throttled back and smoothly arced it over on its back, her view the gray and black rilles of the Known Sea. Leveling out, she rotated the jumpcar so she could have a view of the sky, then turned up the gain on the radar. No blips appeared but warpods were stealthy. They were also well equipped with long-range, heat-seeking missiles. She aimed the nose of the jumpcar at the stars and firewalled the throttles, this time holding them there. Up and up they soared. Then a klaxon sounded and a light flared on the console. *Unknown craft on collision course.*

The jumpcar was not a military vehicle. Its radar did not know what to make of an incoming missile except to call it an unknown craft. Maria fired up the verniers and auxiliary jets and put the jumpcar into a torturous loop. One of her passengers produced a small shriek.

She checked the radar. The blip was gone. She aimed the

jumpcar's nose straight up and held it there until the vibrations became too intense. Abruptly, she shut down all jets and coasted, praying that the cold soak of space would drain the thermal signature away before the invisible warpod unleashed another missile. To help, she pumped supercold unburnt propellant through the rocket nozzles.

Unknown craft on collision course.

The jumpcar shook violently. A flash of orange light filled the cockpit. Dazzled, she blinked at the console lights. One engine was dead. The rattling jumpcar was holding together, but just barely.

Maria groaned when the radar showed another incoming missile. The jumpcar hadn't cooled enough. She relit the jets, flipped the jumpcar nose down, and put it into a dive. *Pull up! Pull up!* the puter cried as the moon reached out for a final embrace.

The dive had defeated the missile, but getting out of it was the new problem. Maria coolly went through her options. One engine was out. The other engine was intact. It was also gimbaled, meaning it could be used to maneuver. She pushed the engine bell over, then fired up the nose verniers. The nose rose abruptly, nearly putting the jumpcar into a deadly tumble. Maria cut the verniers and eased the engine bell over until the nose stayed level. A line of hills loomed ahead. Maria skimmed over them, then roared aloft, heading eastward.

She checked the propellant load. There was a leak. The numbers were flipping downward. "Puter, do we have enough propellant to return to Armstrong City?"

Negative.

"Maintenance program, please."

Maintenance.

"Detach engine number two propellant lines. Release engine number two clamps."

This cannot be accomplished during flight.

"This is a red-level security override. The security code is Crater2112."

Maintenance procedures initiated.

There was a horrific scraping noise as the useless engine was dropped out, falling and spinning away. "Puter, initiate mass calculations to compensate controls for lost engine."

Mass calculations accomplished. Controls compensated.

"Do we have enough propellant for Armstrong City now?"

Affirmative.

A shadow swept over the cockpit and Maria looked up to see a big warpod with missiles hanging on each wing. The communications light flashed. Incoming message. "Pilot, you are to land immediately," a man's voice said. "Land or be destroyed."

Maria fought for time. "My controls are shot!" she called back. "I cannot maneuver."

"Cut off your jet. Dead stick a landing. There is a flat plain five miles ahead."

Maria was confused. Why did they want her to land safely, even going so far as to give advice? Then it hit her. This was a capture mission. That explained why the missile that hit the jumpcar hadn't destroyed it. The warhead had been set for a low order explosion. And of the four people on board, there was only one person who would warrant a capture mission.

Maria knew a great deal about warpods. They were built to take off from Earth. That was why they had wings and scramjets. In other words, a lot of useless hardware once in space. Medaris Spacecraft built some of the best warpods in the world. This wasn't one of them, but certain design features were the same and she knew they had blind spots. They were designed for long-distance warfare, not dog fighting at close range where everything was visual.

Maria throttled her engine back, falling behind the warpod until she had faded into one of its blind spots, then used the verniers to raise the jumpcar nose. She pushed the throttle forward and swept up over the warpod, the fiery cone of the remaining jumpcar engine washing over its fuselage. She rained fire across the starboard wing and an undeployed missile, its nosecone jutting from beneath the forward edge of the wing. It did not explode but its rocket motor cooked off. There it burned, still hanging on the wing, while Maria maneuvered away. Then the missile broke free of the clamps on its launch rail and raced away before turning in an arcing loop that carried it into the warpod's starboard engine. Still, it did not explode, its warhead apparently made inert by its software, but that didn't keep it from tearing the engine apart. With debris trailing it, the warpod hauled up and limped skyward, its remaining engine burning bright.

Maria didn't have time to savor her victory. Even a wounded warpod was dangerous. She knew it could make lunar orbit on one engine and engage her from there. The only chance was to lose the jumpcar in surface clutter. She pointed its nose toward the east, dropped down to just a few feet above the surface, then jinked and juked her wounded craft across the tortured hills and cratered plains of the moon.

::: SIX

The newbie Irregulars in the back of the truck would not stop talking about the battle. They told and retold how they'd fought the crowhoppers, and their stories got more colorful every time. Crater, sitting on the hard plaston slat bench amongst the newbies and veterans, the latter mostly sleeping, just wished they'd shut up.

But they wouldn't shut up. They were too excited. One of them, a fellow from Calimexica called Frisco Larry, leaned over to show a dent in his helmet. "Knocked me silly," he said. "When I turned around, there was one of them holding its rifle by the barrel. It had whacked me with the scrag thing so I didn't do nothin' but take my rifle by the barrel and whack it back."

"Why didn't it just shoot you?" a newbie who called himself London Bob asked.

"Don't know. Must have run out of ammo. Or maybe it was just crazy."

"You're the one who's crazy," Bob said. "You had ammo, you shoulda just shot it."

"If I get clubbed, I'm gonna club back."

Bob laughed. "Good thing I came along and shot it for you. That big creature would've torn you from limb to limb."

"Naw, I'd have shot it pretty soon. I ain't that crazy."

Crater held his head, or tried to but failed since his helmet got in the way. As far as he was concerned, *everybody* involved in the war was crazy, from the foot soldiers on up. On one side was the Lunar Mining Council (LMC) headed up by the Colonel, which included the independent mine owners plus the Russian Czarina who controlled the mining towns in the Sea of Serenity. On the other side was the Unified Countries of the World (UCW), an organization of nations that had gotten together and decided to break the LMC Helium-3 monopoly by terrorizing the mine owners with crowhopper mercenaries. Their plan had been a dismal failure. Not only had the LMC fought back, it cut off all Helium-3 shipments to the world. This caused other Earthian nations, their fusion plants starved, to band together and attack the UCW. After that, the war on the moon became a backwater while the larger war on Earth went ahead to resolve everything, another of a long series of wars to end all wars, the foolishness of mankind on display for the universe.

Crater had reached a point where he almost didn't care who won as long as somebody did and it would be over. Ever since the war had started, nearly three years ago, he'd been a Moontown Irregular and he was sick of it. The Colonel kept promising every time he pulled his miners off the scrapes to fight that it was going to be the last battle, but somehow it never was. This time in what was supposed to be just a mop-up action, poor Freddy Hook and Doom had been killed and Crater had nearly been bled white from an elk sticker wound before the greenies got around to patching him up. For a reason he didn't understand, they had released him back to duty as soon as he'd come out of the anesthesia. He'd not taken too many steps out on the dust before he'd passed out, waking in the back of the truck where Asteroid Al had dragged him and propped him up on the bench.

At Crater's feet was the little crowhopper wrapped in mine wire. It was alive even though it had attacked Al, who had responded by pushing the muzzle of his rifle into its neck and pulling the trigger. Nothing had happened because Al had neglected to charge the railgun's pulsed power supply. After he'd turned the necessary switch, Al found he just didn't have the heart to pull the trigger a second time. When told the story, Crater had responded with a shrug. Al, sitting quietly beside him, was obviously never going to become a proper soldier.

"What you got there, Crater?" Bob asked with a smirk. "A pet? Is it house trained? You gonna walk it around Moontown on a leash?"

"No, Bob," Crater said. "I'm going to train it to kill anybody I don't like and, right now, I don't much like you."

The newbie Irregular nervously chuckled. "You wouldn't do that."

"What *are* you going to do with it?" Al asked Crater on their private channel. When Crater didn't answer, just kept holding his helmet, Al suggested, "Why don't we just roll it out the back?"

"Why don't you just shut up?" Crater growled. "You had a chance to kill it and you didn't."

"So did you."

Crater didn't want to talk anymore. His head was killing

him from whatever drug the greenies had given him in the popup and his leg, the numbness of the anesthetic wearing off, was starting to hurt. He thought he should be in an ambulance, not shoved in the back of a cargo truck. He looked down at the crowhopper and it looked back at him through the slit in its helmet. Its eyes were filled with questions that Crater didn't want to hear or even imagine.

The truck slowed, then stopped. "The Colonel said I should let you fellows walk around some," the driver called into their helmets. "Shake the dust outa your joints."

The Irregulars climbed down except for Crater, who took the opportunity to stretch out on the empty bench. He closed his eyes, and the next thing he knew Al was shaking him awake. "They're playing with your crowhopper," he said.

Crater groaned, then sat up. His head felt like the devil was pounding on it with an ax and his leg felt like another devil was stabbing it with a spear. He came close to throwing up. When he didn't, mainly because there was nothing in his stomach, he looked out the back of the truck and saw that London Bob and Frisco Larry had cut the mine wire holding the creature and had taped its eye slit over. It was furiously lashing out with its fists and feet, lurching this way and that trying to get at its tormenters who were taking turns poking at it with a scragbar. When Bob tripped it, the others joined in to kick it when it fell in the dust. Crater drew his sidearm and dropped into the dust. He pushed through the Irregulars and stood over the crowhopper, which was lying on its side, its legs pulled up, its arms over its helmet. "Next scraghead touches my crowhopper gets a slug through his helmet." He raised his pistol. "Don't believe me? Give it a try."

"It killed Freddy and Doom," Bob said.

"It didn't kill anybody," Crater replied. "I captured it in a lavatube. It was unarmed except for a knife and I, um, took that away from it."

"Yeah, with your leg," an Irregular hooted.

"You won't shoot," Bob said and demonstrated his conviction by kicking the little crowhopper.

Crater nodded, then holstered his pistol before grabbing the scragbar from Larry and smacking Bob with it a little harder than he meant to. "You broke my arm!" Bob cried, holding the afflicted arm.

Crater was in too much pain to care about anybody else's. "Tie my crowhopper up," Crater said to Larry. "And put it back on the truck. Treat it gentle as a baby or you're next." He patted the scragbar in his hand. "You get me?"

Larry and the other Irregulars got Crater very well and did as they were told, carefully placing the crowhopper into the truck. Bob watched, still holding his busted arm. "What about me?" he demanded. "I need a greenie."

"You're not going to get one," Crater said. "You're going to get on the truck and shut up. Somebody wants to put a splint on you, give you something, I won't stop them."

Bob looked around but the others were trying not to look back. "Ain't somebody gonna help me? My arm is killing me. Anybody got a pain injector?"

Nobody did and Bob whimpered and complained all the way back to Moontown. The others muttered amongst themselves, saying Crater should have actually shot Bob, not made him and them so miserable. Crater heard them but pretended he didn't. Mostly, he thought about how much his leg hurt and how glad he'd be to see old Moontown. The crowhopper had stopped moving. Maybe, he thought with some hope, it had died.

::: SEVEN

Maria tossed her gear to the landing tech, then turned to gaze fondly at her battered jumpcar. "Thank you," she said to the machine as her three passengers wobbled past, their stricken expressions reflecting the ordeal that had been the battle and chase.

"Give her a new engine and a bath. She'll be fine," she told the jumpcar maintenance crew, all of whom were staring with awe at the smoking rocket ship.

Maria's do4u beeped. It was her grandfather. "Maria, thank God," the Colonel said. "What happened? I heard you declared an emergency landing."

The Colonel, of course, had spies everywhere. There was little of importance that happened on the moon he didn't know about. She gave him a brief description of the encounter with the warpod and the perilous flight back to Armstrong City. He was silent for a moment, then said, "They wanted to take you alive."

"Yes, sir. The question is why?"

"Ransom," the Colonel immediately said in a clipped

voice. "The price—we sign contracts to deliver lots of cheap heel-3 to the UCW."

"Something you wouldn't agree to, in any case," she said.

The Colonel was quiet for a moment, then said, "I want you to be very careful during the coming days, Maria. Stay in Armstrong City. No flying jumpcars or going outside for any purpose. Understand?"

Maria crossed her fingers. "Yes, sir. News came in on a battle up north while I was flying out. Did you win it?"

"Yes, and for the answer to your real question, Crater Trueblood received a small wound. Nothing serious. He did something stupid afterward but we'll clear that up. He's a brave lad but ultimately foolish. Why you care about him, I don't know."

Maria resisted asking for details, saying, "It doesn't matter since I'll never see him again."

"Sometimes I wish I could say the same. Just remember. Stay under the domes of Armstrong City until further notice!"

The Colonel clicked off. Maria stood on the streets of the city, its busy people flowing past her. With a word, she could connect with Crater on his do4u, hear his voice, find out everything, perhaps even discover that he still cared, but she didn't say the word. Instead, she endured the stinging tears, then headed for the Medaris Building where there was no Crater, and where a heart of stone had value.

EIGHT

Moontown sat on a sparkling plain of dust in front of the corrugated, shadowy walls of the Alpine Valley. Although most of the town was beneath the ground, there were eight observation towers a hundred feet high and painted in patterns of black-and-white stripes, diamonds, and hexagons. One glance at the patterns by incoming jumpcar pilots oriented them to the dustlocks and landing pads. Two large maintenance sheds were set east and west of the town, their sloped roofs covered with glittering blue-green tile made of a special blend of mooncrete and anorthosite. Various vehicles were parked nearby: scrapers, loaders, heel-3 trucks, flatbed trucks, and fastbugs. Moontown looked like exactly what it was, a working mining town.

In the observation rotunda atop the nearest tower, Crater could see Moontown tubewives, tubehusbands, and their children waving as the victorious troops came home. Then Crater spotted Q-Bess, the woman who had adopted him fifteen years ago when he'd been orphaned a second time, his adoptive parents killed on the scrapes when he was four. When she saw him, she waved. Her wave was, of course, a regal one since Q-Bess claimed she was the rightful Queen of the British Isles and associated islands. For all anyone knew, she might have been exactly that, not that it mattered much in Moontown. There, she was just another refugee from Earth.

The grimy Medaris Irregulars piled off the trucks and headed for the dustlocks. The biolastic sheaths were wonders of biological science that allowed people to stay outside for days, but they were not entirely self-cleansing. A fellow could get a little smelly inside one when he was hard at work on the scrapes or tracking down and fighting crowhoppers. As anxious as the Irregulars were to climb in the dustlock showers, they waited respectfully for the dead to be carried inside first. The Irregulars saluted, all but London Bob, who held his splinted arm.

Crater and Asteroid Al stood back. "Let everybody else go inside," Crater said. He nodded at the little crowhopper they'd shoved into the dust. "We're going to have to get this thing out of its body armor. No use having a bunch of gawkers around."

"We can't take it inside," Asteroid Al said. "For scrag's sake, just let it loose and be done with it."

"He's right," the crowhopper said in a raspy voice. It struggled to its knees and held up its hands, tied together with mine wire. "I have no food, no water, nothing to survive with. Let me go and be done with me."

Crater and Al exchanged surprised glances. "I thought your communicator had stopped working," Crater said.

"I had nothing to say and even if I had, no one intelligent to say it to."

"The first thing I'm going to do after we get your helmet off," Crater said, "is strap some duct tape across your mouth."

"Take my helmet off now," it said, "and you won't have to. I will be dead. That should amuse your troops."

"That was a bunch of newbies. I regret they tortured you."

"Making me a captive is worse than any torture."

"Let this thing go, Crater," Al pleaded.

"Maybe it can be studied or something," Crater said.

"You are the stubbornest fellow I've ever known," Al said. "But all right, I'll help get your creature inside. After that, you're on your own."

"Thank you," Crater said. "You're a friend."

Al laughed. "After Moontowners get a look at this thing, I'm likely to be your only friend."

When the dustlock was clear, Crater pulled open the hatch and climbed inside. After a brief struggle, Al pushed the little crowhopper through the hatch far enough that Crater could get a grip on its armor and haul it the rest of the way in. When Al climbed in behind it and pulled the hatch shut, Crater said, "Moontown standard," and the first chamber of the dustlock, which was technically an airlock, responded with a hiss of air.

The next chamber was a true dustlock where helmets, coveralls, biolastic sheaths, and waste-disposal plaston girdles were removed. A dustlock technician, called a dustie, appeared. He stopped in his tracks when he saw what Crater and Al had with them. "Why is that thing alive?" he asked.

"Crater thought it was too little to kill," Al said with a grin.

"I didn't know there was a size limit," the dustie said, scratching up under his cap before handing Crater the wand that provided the electricity that caused their biolastic sheaths to unroll. Crater applied it to his neck, then pulled his helmet off, happy to be free of it. Al took the wand and, when the biolastic material parted, pushed his helmet up and off and breathed in fresh, clean Moontown artificial air.

His knee on its chest to pin it down, Crater pulled back the armor from the crowhopper's neck. "Looks like pretty much the same rig as ours," he said and applied the wand to the base of its helmet. The biolastic material unraveled and Crater lifted the helmet off. A musty smell filled his nostrils as he got his first look at the creature's face. It had the pug nose, narrow eyes, flat lips, high cheekbones, and coarse hair peculiar to crowhoppers, although its features seemed somehow softer.

"Ugly thing," the dustie said.

"They weren't bred for looks," Al remembered.

"In that case, they succeeded," the dustie said, wrinkling up his nose. "And it stinks too. Get your suits and sheaths off, then we'll tackle this thing together."

The dustie handed filter masks to Crater and Asteroid Al and clamped one over the mouth and nose of the crowhopper. Removal of suits after being outside meant dust was going to get spread around. Although there were powerful suction fans, there was still a chance the dust would get breathed in. Moon dust wasn't like Earth dust. It was more like powdered glass.

Crater and Al pulled off their coveralls and boots, deposited them into a laundry bag, then peeled off their biolastic sheaths and plaston girdles. Normally, they would have walked naked into the next dustlock where the water showers were located, but to get the crowhopper out of its suit, they put on clean coveralls, provided by the dustie.

While Al held it down, Crater pulled off its boots. There were armored greaves on its legs and arms and Crater removed them, then figured out the zippers and latches holding the armored upper torso. He untied the mine wire from around its wrists and began to pull the armor away. The crowhopper silently struggled, but Crater and Al worked diligently until they had the black upper torso and pants off.

Underneath was a plaston girdle and an opaque biolastic sheath. Crater unlatched the girdle and handed it to the dustie, who treated it like toxic waste, depositing it in a blue tub and sealing it. Then Crater rolled the crowhopper over on its stomach and used the wand to open up the back of its sheath. He peeled the sheath off, slicing it along the legs and arms and pulling it away in pieces, all of which went into another blue tub. When they rolled the creature over, they saw it had legs thick as mooncrete posts and heavy, muscular arms, slick with sweat. There was also something else they noticed. Crater looked away while Al laughed. "At least now we know why you didn't kill it, Crater."

"That thing is a girl!" the dustie cried. "And the ugliest girl in the history of the universe."

"Cover it with something," Crater snapped.

"It needs a shower," the dustie said, after draping it with a blanket. He thought for a moment, then said, "Let call in some other dusties, female ones. This is going to be tricky."

Crater was grateful beyond words but managed two. "Thank you."

"There's another alternative," the dustie said. "We can haul it into the airlock and depressurize. It wouldn't feel much pain."

Crater glanced into the airlock. He could feel the words forming on his lips. *Do it.*

::: NINE

She did not fight the humans because they were going to do what she wanted them to do. They were going to suffocate her and then she would fly to the promised nothingness where her brothers waited for her, their voices raised in greeting: *Life is death! Death is life!*

She felt the strength of the Legion fill her as she was carried to the airlock and oblivion, the righteous fate of every Legionnaire.

Her name was Crescent Claudine Besette, her name selected by the Trainers for its grandeur and nothing to do with her ancestors, who did not exist. To be part of the Legion Internationale, Crescent had hiked across the tundra through a blizzard, climbed a sheer-sided mountain in a lightning storm, swam across a three-mile lake littered with ice floes, and run across a frigid desert carrying an eighty-pound pack. She was well trained on nearly every pistol and rifle in the world's arsenal, and knew how to improvise bombs out of junk and household chemicals. She knew how throw a knife, sling a sling, shoot a bow and arrow, set a variety of booby traps, and choke until dead an enemy with her bare hands. She was fluent in Siberian, Russian, Mandarin 1.0 and 2.0, English, French, Hebrew, Calimexican, Greek, Español, and Latin, and knowledgeable of other dialects. She could quote from the works of Aristotle, Socrates, Shakespeare, Twain, Tolstoy, Steinbeck, and other writers and philosophers. She had absorbed the poetry of the masters and learned to appreciate the music of the classical composers. She had listened diligently to the Trainers and studied everything they gave her to learn. The proudest day of her life was when she was formally inducted into the Legion. On that day, she carried the guidon flag of her new century, a band of brothers and one sister, a fighting force without equal anywhere in the world. They were known as the Phoenix Century, their symbol, an eagle surrounded by flames, emblazoned on their armor and on a pendant they wore around their necks.

Crescent had no mother, no father, and no sisters although she had thousands of brothers. Legionnaires were a product, no more or less than soap or fertilizer, created for customers who required warriors to fight their battles. Crescent was intent on being as good a Legionnaire as any of her brothers. She had scored high marks on everything except survival swimming and that was only because she was afraid of fish.

When the word came down that the Phoenix Century was under contract, they gathered on the cold, windswept parade ground of Legion Training Camp #3 to be addressed by Tribune Henri Victor DuBois, the highest ranking Legionnaire in the force. He stood before them in his heavy black armor while Crescent and her century shivered in their light tunics.

"Hear me," he said. "You have been leased by the Unified Countries of the World. Under this contract, five centuries of your brothers have already been deployed to the moon. You are the sixth century. You will gather here on the morrow to begin your transport to the lunar surface. I am confident you will fight with all the skill you have been taught by the Trainers, and with steadfast devotion for the Legion and for the details of our contract. Go to your quarters and prepare your gear. When you reach the battlefield, fight and die well. That is all."

The chant rose from the century and Crescent had joined in until her voice was raw. *"Life is death! Death is life!"*

It was the second proudest moment in her life even though she, like her brothers, knew the other five centuries sent to the moon under the UCW contract had been killed to the last man. It was therefore no surprise that when they landed on the Sea of Serenity, the Russians turned their arrival into a blood sport. Eventually, they ran from the battlefield in stolen trucks and jumpcars until the survivors, whittled down to twelve, finally holed up in a camp a hundred miles from the Alpine Valley. When their leader, a centurion named Artur Velos Trabonnet, noticed a convoy passing nearby, he told them to prepare for battle. Other than don their pressure suits and their armor, there was little to do except to chant the pre-battle chant of the Legion:

> *Where does our spirit go after we die?*
> *It goes to glory.*
> *Where does the spirit of our enemy go after we kill them?*
> *To a place of darkness.*
> *When will we die?*
> *When we so choose.*
> *When will our enemy die?*

When we kill them.
What is our secret?
Life is death! Death is life!

As they were climbing through the hatch into the dust, Trabonnet barred Crescent's way. "You will stay here," he said.

"Why will I stay?" Crescent demanded. "I can fight as well as any Legionnaire."

"You will stay because I command you to stay."

"And what is the logic behind this command?"

Trabonnet did a strange thing. Legionnaire officers did not touch enlisted men, but he placed his hand on her shoulder. "There is no logic. It comes from me wanting you to live."

"But if I die and you die, we will meet in glory."

He smiled, or struggled to arrange his facial features into the grimace that Legionnaires used as a smile, and said, "Live, Crescent. If the humans come, and come they will, live. Return to the Earth and breathe the clear air of the Steppes and feast your eyes on the land beneath the mountains and swim the cold, clear lakes of our youth."

"I am afraid of fish," she said.

His grimace broadened. "I am sorry. I forgot. But do the other things."

"But death is life. We above all others must believe this."

"Perhaps, but not today. Not for you. Give me your rifle. If you are armed, they will kill you. You must surrender and bow your head before them. I know this is a hard thing, but it is necessary if you are to live. I do not know how you will make it back to Earth, but I trust your training to get you through. Do not go to the Legion. Just live out your days in peace." He noticed something. "You've lost your pendant."

She touched her neck. "I'm sorry. The chain broke."

He took the pendant from around his neck. "Take mine. Wear it in memory of me."

After he'd gone, she looked at the pendant—an eagle wreathed in flames—then put its chain over her head and sat down and waited. Unlike Trabonnet, she believed the humans would kill her whether she had a rifle or not. But the young human named Crater had not killed her but instead made her a captive. Outside the lavatube, she saw that Trabonnet was also alive, though badly wounded, sitting against the fin of their stolen jumpcar. By killing himself and tossing her a knife, he had done what he could to set her free. But then she had been trucked across the moon, tortured by the humans, and disgraced in one of their dustlocks. Finally, she was promised death, for which she was ready.

They laid her naked on the cold lunasteel deck where she waited eagerly for the air to be drained away. Instead, the hatch opened and four women came inside carrying a water hose. "Let her rip!" one of them yelled, and a spout of cold water struck Crescent like a battering ram. She rolled and cried out, trying to get away, but the water pressure was too strong. Finally, the water stopped and the women fell on her with mops and sponges until she felt as if she'd been rubbed raw. Afterward, they wrapped her in towels. "Put these on," one of the women said and handed her a gray tunic, black leggings, and black boots. "If you don't, we'll put them on for you."

Trembling with shame, Crescent complied. After she dressed, one of the women brought her the pendant they'd taken. "Here," she said gruffly. "We're not thieves."

Crescent placed the chain and the symbol of her century

around her neck, then looked at it, remembering Trabonnet as he'd asked, before dropping it beneath the neck of her tunic.

The women tied her hands and put a wire around her ankles and pushed her out of the chamber into another one where her captor, Crater, sat on a bench. If she read his features right, human expressions being difficult for her, he was unhappy.

"What are you going to do with me?" she demanded. "Torture? Death? Or are you going to put me on display like an animal in a zoo?"

The answer he gave was not helpful. "I wish I knew," he said. "I suppose you're my prisoner of war. If you're smart, you'll make the best of it. We're going into the main tubeway. You can be carried, in which case you may be dropped and hurt, or you can cooperate and walk with dignity."

Crescent looked down at the wire between her ankles. "The wire the females tied on me is too short."

"That is so you can't run."

"I believe your promise of dignity was a bit exaggerated."

Crater raised his eyebrows. "You have a sense of humor!"

"Of course I do. For instance, it will amuse me when I kill you."

Crater's grin faded and the other human, the one called Asteroid Al, laughed. "She's pretty saucy!"

"If she stays saucy," Crater said, "I'll cover her mouth with duct tape."

"You will not do that," Crescent said.

"Why not?"

"Because you do not have brains enough to operate a roll of duct tape."

Al laughed again. Crater stood up, roughly clutched her shoulder, and pushed her toward a hatch. "Let's go."

Crescent sat on the rim of the hatch, swung her boots through, then stood in a large cylindrical mooncrete tube. Humans apparently going about their daily errands stopped and stared and some of them even screamed.

"It's all right," Crater said. "It can't hurt you."

Crescent raised her tied hands. "I will kill you and then eat you!"

Crater shushed her. "Kindly stop scaring everyone."

"It amuses me," she said.

A fat man in a khaki uniform arrived. There was a brass star pinned to his tunic. "What's this, Crater?" he demanded. "A monster, but what kind?"

"She's a crowhopper, Sheriff, and my prisoner."

"Crowhoppers are trained killers," the sheriff said.

"She knows that," Crater replied.

The sheriff pushed his face close to Crescent, his breath blooming with alcohol. She backed away, wrinkling her nose.

"If this thing is a female, it is without a doubt the ugliest female of any race, creed, or nationality I have ever seen. Deputy Zageev, take it into custody."

"Don't touch her, Deputy," Crater growled. "She's my prisoner."

Crescent was surprised the humans were fighting over her. She had often wondered how humans interacted. She studied their faces, trying to understand what their expressions meant.

"I am the sheriff of Moontown," the sheriff said, "and you are a part-time soldier. I have the authority to keep order in these tubes and arrest anyone I wish, including you. Deputy, I told you to take this thing into custody."

The deputy drew what Crescent recognized was a nine

millimeter moon-standard pistol. "Do what I tell you," he said to her and waved the pistol down the tube. "One wrong move and I'll put a bullet in your ugly head!"

Crescent studied the sweating deputy and determined he was afraid. "I am not going with you," she said. "Shoot me and I will do my best to bleed in copious fashion, which I imagine you will have to clean up." She raised her heavy eyebrows. "Well? I'm waiting."

Crater and Al grinned. Crescent wasn't certain, but it appeared they were proud of her.

Then a big woman dressed in scarlet robes pushed through the crowd. On her head was a mountain of silver curls. She was the grandest and gaudiest person Crescent had ever seen. "My boy!" cried the woman, then took Crater in her arms. "I am so glad you survived!"

"I am too, Q-Bess," Crater said, his voice muffled in the folds of her robe.

The woman released him, then stepped back and peered with twinkling blue eyes at Crescent. "And who do we have here?"

"A crowhopper, ma'am," Crater said.

Al added, "A female crowhopper."

"Of course she is. But why is she with you?"

"I captured her," Crater said.

Q-Bess smiled. "You could not bring yourself to kill a girl."

"I don't think that was it," Crater mumbled. "I don't know what it was."

The woman turned and played to the crowd in her regal manner. "My boy Crater has brought this creature to us to civilize, however impossible that may be." She turned to the sheriff and his deputy. "And why are you here?"

"To take Crater's creature into custody," the sheriff answered.

"Nonsense," Q-Bess said. "I claim this creature as mine."

The sheriff rolled his eyes and said, "What are you going to do with it, your royal highness?"

"I will put it to work. It looks strong."

"I imagine it is very strong, but it will cut your throat with a kitchen knife the first chance it gets." The sheriff turned back to Crater. "I notice you're limping. Battle wound or did you fall in a ditch?"

Crater nodded toward Crescent. "She stabbed me."

This earned a hearty laugh from the sheriff.

"What is your name, girl?" Q-Bess asked.

Crescent proudly raised her chin. "I am Crescent Claudine Besette of the Legion Internationale."

"A lovely name," Q-Bess said, "and appropriate too, a crescent being the arc of the moon often admired and written about in poetry and a lovely aspect of our small planet. Well, Crescent, will you work for me?"

Recalling Trabonnet's advice to live, Crescent said, "Yes, Madame. I will even kill for you. You need only ask."

Q-Bess cast an eye toward the sheriff. "Perhaps I will."

The sheriff shook his head. "All right, your majesty, take it. I don't have any place to lock it up anyway. I will consider it on work release until the Colonel decides what to do with it."

Q-Bess waved her hand, her many bracelets jangling, and walked away. When Crescent hesitated, the sheriff shoved her in the queen's direction. "Well, follow her, you foul thing!"

Crescent stumbled, the wire between her feet tripping her. Crater caught her and raised her up. "I would not have fallen," Crescent said, though she knew she would have.

"The proper response is 'Thank you,' to which I would reply, 'You're welcome.'"

She recognized that she had just been trained in a basic human interaction. She tried it. "Thank you."

"You're welcome."

Crescent walked, her steps little stumbles while chanting under her breath, "Where does our spirit go after we die? It goes to glory."

Crescent hoped Trabonnet's spirit was in glory with all the brothers of her century. She also hoped they would watch over her as she plotted her escape from the ugly underground town. She raised her head and began to study everything.

::: TEN

The Medaris Irregulars were given one day off, then sent back to work on the scrapes. Crater was assigned as a scraper driver. Over the following days, he did his job, although those miners who knew him well—such as Asteroid Al—knew that there was something bothering him. One day, during a break, he wandered off alone and sat cross-legged on an outcropping of basalt, lowered his helmet into his cupped hands, and stared balefully at whatever there was to stare at, which, considering where he was, was mostly gray dust and black sky.

Crater was trying to work through something that would not leave him alone. Once, so long ago it often seemed more like a dream than reality, he and Maria Medaris, the Colonel's granddaughter, had crossed the moon together as convoy scouts and then gone into space to complete a mission for the Colonel. At the end of their adventure, Crater learned that Maria had spent the entire time lying to him. This had not kept him from falling in love with her. When Maria was wounded and taken away by her family, Crater had completed their task.

After that, the war had come and Crater had been fighting it ever since. Now that the battles seemed over, he thought he might find Maria and see where they stood.

But that was not to be.

Amongst the piles of bills and messages he found in his room there was also a memory puter plug that contained a letter from Maria. He'd read the letter a dozen times, and every time it felt as if an elk sticker were stabbing his heart. Still, he kept wanting it to say something other than what it said. That was why, while sitting on that basalt outcropping, Crater got out the memplug and inserted it in his do4u to read it again. To his disappointment, it was exactly the same.

July 22, 2131
Medaris Mining Company
Building #1
Armstrong City, Luna

Dear Crater:

I hope this letter finds you well. My grandfather tells me that you have served valiantly in the battle to clear our planet of crowhoppers. For that, you have my heartfelt thanks.

In the absence of any query on your part pertaining to my present health, I shall nonetheless briefly apprise you of my condition. I have healed and the doctors have discharged me from their care.

It is not the intention of this posting to stimulate any response or communication of any kind from you. In point of fact, it is my preference that there not be any now or in the future.

Be certain I valued our time together. I bid you adieu,
good-bye, good fortune, and a worthy life.

With conviction,

Maria High Eagle Medaris

Crater had no notion of what he should do in response to
Maria's letter or if he should do anything at all. He hadn't con-
tacted her during the intervening years because he supposed
that she was fully engaged in getting back her health. Besides
that, he had spent much of it fighting crowhoppers and trying
to stay alive. Still, in retrospect, he could see he probably should
have kept in touch and not assumed that he could just turn up
some day. He thought maybe he should go to Armstrong City
and beg her for forgiveness or perhaps he should write her a
letter and pour out his feelings. He considered calling on his
do4u and singing her a song of love and longing or something,
but any and all of those things he suspected would only make
things worse, if that was possible.

The Earth hung in the lunar sky like a big blue eye and
seemed to regard him with interest, as if it knew the turmoil
in his heart. Crater tried to think of something else. He looked
out and admired his scrape. He ran a straight scrape, none
straighter. The shift was only half over and he'd already piled
up enough dust tents for a full day. No one could pile tents
as fast as he. He also knew all the tricks of picking rocks out
of tracks, levers, and rollers that slowed most scraper drivers
down. In fact, they usually stopped to let the scrag pickers
come and get the rock out. Not Crater. He picked out his own
rocks.

This took Crater's mind off Maria for only a few seconds
and then he sank back into the despair of the lovelorn. That

was when Asteroid Al, who was working as a loader operator, walked over. "Is something wrong, Crater?"

Crater wished Al would just leave him alone. "There's nothing wrong," he said. "I'm just resting."

"Is this about the letter from Maria?"

Crater wasn't surprised that Al knew about the letter. There were no real secrets in Moontown. By the time that memory plug had gotten to him, there was no telling how many people had read it. "It's nothing I can't handle," Crater said.

"You can't be earthing around out here," Al said. "You've got to keep your mind on business or you'll get hurt."

"My mind is on my business, Al. How about you minding yours?"

Crater put the memory plug in his pocket, climbed off the outcropping, and shoved past Al. He went back to work and his scrapes stayed straight and he kept piling up the tents and he didn't need anybody to feel sorry for him while he did it. And he sure didn't need to talk.

After the shift, Crater gathered with the other miners at the dustlock hatch for the end of shift prayer. The oldest miner on the scrape, by tradition, said the prayer. In this case, it was a woman named Sally Murdock, a puter-order bride from New Scotland. Sally bowed her head and said, "Lord, thank you for not letting any of us get killed today and thank you for giving us the strength to meet the Colonel's production schedule. Help us do the same tomorrow."

"Amen," came the chorus, and everybody headed into the dustlock to remove their dusty coveralls and boots, peel off their biolastic sheaths and plaston girdles, and hand them over to the dusties for cleansing. Afterward, they showered, put on their tube clothes, and headed for their home tube or, if they were bachelors, the Dust Palace. Asteroid Al fell in step with Crater but kept his peace. If Crater didn't want to talk, that was fine with him.

Al peeled off for his tube while Crater went to the cafeteria looking for a freshly baked cookie or two to take the edge off his blues. He also wanted to check on the progress of the crowhopper. He had seen little of her since Q-Bess had put her to work, but he'd heard from the cooks and servers she was a willing trainee. In fact, it seemed at times she worked harder than necessary. The creature was curious about everything, Kurto, the Dust Palace's chief cook, said. Kurto, once a celebrated chef on the European continent, added, "She has quick temper but she try very hard. I think she make fine cook someday."

When Crater climbed through the cafeteria hatch, there were no cookies to be found, mainly because the big mooncrete cylinder, normally sparkling clean, was in complete and utter disarray. Tables and chairs were turned over. Food trays littered the deck. The aluminum sliding tubes were bent, the lunaglas covers cracked, and food was strewn everywhere. Kurto was standing behind the wrecked service line, sorrowfully contemplating the ruin of his kitchen. Q-Bess was sitting disconsolately on a bench, her head bowed. In the back of the cafeteria shrank a contingent of miners, their eyes wide. And then there was Crescent. She was standing amidst the ruin with a man held over her head. "Crescent," Crater said in a quiet voice. "What do you think you are doing?"

Q-Bess raised her head, then dropped her chin in her hands. "Yes, Crescent, what indeed are you doing?"

The man Crescent was holding over her head appeared to be unconscious but at least he was breathing, which Crater took as a hopeful sign. "Put him down," he said. "That's an order, Crescent. I'm your captor. Do as I say."

Crescent snarled, then tossed the miner all the way across the cafeteria, making the miners huddled there dodge the flying man who bounced off the wall, then fell to the deck. Crescent put her hands on her hips and faced Crater. "As you commanded, Master, I put him down."

"That's not how I meant," Crater said, "and you know it."

"He said I stunk. I do not stink."

Q-Bess nodded. "That much is true. I make her take tub baths and use perfumed salts."

"Baths are not new to me," Crescent vowed. "During my training, after every fifty mile hike, we chopped a hole in the ice and washed in a lake."

"I don't think that's entirely pertinent, dear," Q-Bess replied in a tired voice.

Crater saw a medical greenie arrive and kneel over the miner Crescent had tossed. He was a man Crater recognized as Classy Amos, a low fellow of poor character prone to cheating, lying, and stealing and not very classy at all, hence his ironic name. Crater was relieved when the greenie helped Amos sit up. He was apparently going to be all right.

"So what happened?" Crater asked Q-Bess.

"After Amos said what he said, Crescent leaped across the serving line, grabbed him, then started swinging him around by his boots."

"You're a bad crowhopper," Crater said to Crescent.

Crescent stiffened to attention, raising her chin. "If I have done wrong, Master, I await my punishment. You may beat me and I will not resist."

Q-Bess managed a wan chuckle. "Go for it, Crater."

Crater didn't go for it. Instead, he said, "Don't call me Master again. I am not your master. My name is Crater and that's what you should call me."

"Then you should not call me a crowhopper. I am a Legionnaire."

Crater didn't want to argue with Crescent about the fine points of a proper title for her band of vicious killers. He was thinking about what would happen when the sheriff found out about the altercation and, more importantly, what the Colonel would do. He surveyed the miners cowering along the back of the tube. "Fellows, I apologize for Crescent. She felt threatened, that's all. I would appreciate it if you wouldn't spread this around. How about it?"

One of the miners, a bearded fellow who called himself Memphis Smith, called out, "Well, I ain't keeping my mouth shut about this. She's a danger and she don't belong here. I say get rid of her."

Chief Cook Kurto answered, "Ha! If you afraid, Smith, you go live somewhere else."

"Where would that be?"

"Marry that schoolteacher you be seeing and go live in own living tube."

Smith shifted in his boots, then said, "Reckon I'll stay."

This prompted laughter and back slapping and shoulder thumping from Smith's fellow bachelors. "Okay, Crater," a miner called Dogwood said, "I guess we fellows will keep all this secret. Anyway, it was pretty entertaining, right, Amos?"

Amos had managed to get to his feet, mainly because two big, burly miners had hauled him up. "Whatever you boys say," he said, warily eyeing the two manhandling him before they let him go, whereupon he slithered to the floor.

Everybody got busy moving the cafeteria furniture back into position and repairing the serving line. Crescent helped Kurto pick up pots and pans and, by herself, set to rights an overturned dishwasher. "That girl, she is strong," the chief cook said.

"She was designed that way," Crater said. "Thanks for taking up for her."

"I come from a place where many people killed for being different," Kurto replied. "I know too well her trouble." He surveyed his cafeteria, then added, "But would be nice if she not do this again."

"I will talk to her about it," Crater promised.

Later, over dinner, Q-Bess joined Crater at his table. "I have an idea," she said. "Why don't you let Crescent help you with the scattering tomorrow? You could spend a little time with her and talk about things." Before Crater could object, she waved Crescent over. "Dear, would you like to go outside with Crater tomorrow?"

Crescent's eyes narrowed with suspicion. "For what purpose?"

"Crater has volunteered to perform a very important duty," Q-Bess explained. "He is going to scatter the ashes of our Moontown citizens who have died during the past month."

"If she doesn't want to go, she doesn't have to," Crater said.

Q-Bess smiled. "You want to go, don't you, dear?"

Crescent provided a small shrug, then lowered her eyes. "If you wish it, ma'am."

"Do you see how well I've trained her?"

"Was that an example earlier?"

"Pish-posh," Q-Bess said. "A mere incident. A trifle. Not representative at all."

Although Crater suspected Q-Bess just wanted to get rid of the little crowhopper for a while, he didn't want to upset his mother, so he said, "She can help me."

"Splendid! Now, back to work, girl, and let Crater eat his dinner." After she'd gone, Q-Bess patted Crater on his shoulder. "Thank you. The girl will learn something and you can talk to her about her temper."

"I was hoping you would do that."

"She'll take it better from her brother."

"I'm not her brother. I captured her. She's a prisoner of war. And you're not her mother."

"I could adopt her," Q-Bess mused, "the same as I did you. She is, after all, an orphan."

"She was born an orphan," Crater pointed out. "Look, I don't want anything bad to happen to her, but ultimately she can't stay here. She needs to be taken somewhere to be studied."

"Now listen to me, Crater," Q-Bess said. "She is not going anywhere. You brought her here because you couldn't bear to kill her. Well, all right, that was a noble thing you did, but it also made her your responsibility, which also makes her mine, and we can't give her to some white-coat to be turned into a lab specimen. We have to look after her."

"For how long?"

"From now on."

"Q-Bess—"

Q-Bess raised her finger in warning. "From now on!" she vowed, and stood up and marched into the kitchen.

Crater sat before his dinner, rapidly cooling, then got up and dumped it in the trash. He was no longer hungry. "From now on" sounded like a very long time to look after a creature born to kill.

::: ELEVEN

aria Medaris signed with her finger the holo-papers Jarvis, her secretary, placed before her. "These production reports were due this morning," she growled.

"Sorry, ma'am. Power was down on the transat." Jarvis touched the pages with his boss's reader, sucking them inside. "I'll get these in the system right away."

"Anything else? If not, I'm late for my game."

"Nothing else, ma'am," Jarvis replied, then quickly exited.

Maria walked down the hall but didn't get too far before her public relations manager appeared from a side office and released a holo-document from her reader that hovered in the air. Maria recognized it as the society page of the *Armstrong City Bootprints* social page. "It's a good one, Maria," she said. "Congratulations."

Maria knew the woman liked to talk so she absorbed the paper in her reader and kept going. Outside, her chauffeur was waiting with the limobug. Maria settled in and then took a moment to glance at the article, which showed her sitting with a young man dressed in a fashionable black tunic and leggings. His name, the article said, was Eric Stanley and he was described as "handsome and fresh from Earth with all the latest news, gossip, and fashions." Maria was described as "our true moon goddess, the lovely and elegant young lady of fair skin, crisp gray eyes, and a delightful smile whom we all know as Miss Maria Medaris. Her silk red dress turned every head."

The article went on to say the event was to raise money for the Colonel John High Eagle Medaris Hospital and Maria had made a passionate plea for funds. Maria was pleased that the photograph accompanying the article showed her and the "fresh from Earth" young businessman sitting close together. Her grandfather, always hopeful she would find a suitable husband, would like that. As for her father, she supposed he might be pleased as well. If she married and had children, he might hope to maneuver her out of her job while she was distracted.

Of course, the reporter did not follow Maria and the young businessman back to Maria's apartment. If she had, she would have seen him put one hand on the door and lean in to kiss Maria. She would have also seen Maria turn her head and mutter, "I don't think so," and slip inside, leaving the disappointed suitor outside.

It wasn't the first time Maria had played that scene. She knew very well she was attractive and desirable, but she was, after all, only nineteen years old, even if she did hold a doctorate in economics from John Wesley Clayton University, the most prestigious academic center for such studies on the North American continent. She was in no hurry for romance. Her focus needed to be completely on the Medaris Jumpcar Company.

She snapped the reader off. Thinking of the young man she'd disappointed had inevitably led her to think about

Crater. What was he doing at that very moment? Who was he with? Every day she had to battle with herself to keep from calling him. She detested her weakness. She wished with all her might she had never heard of that stupid, stupid boy!

The other players had already gathered at the Christopher C. Craft, Jr. Park near the east wall of the Neil Armstrong Dome. The game was called Butterfly, a gentle name for a brutal sport. To play the game required the players to first climb the interior of the dome to its top where there was a round platform hanging on cables, placed there to hold huge sunlamps.

In the privacy of the limobug, Maria changed out of her business tunic and drew on a silver jumpsuit. Outside, the chauffeur removed the flimsy wings from the trunk and handed them to her. "I will call you when I need you, Derek," she said. The chauffeur touched his cap, climbed in the limobug, and drove away.

Six men and two women were in various stages of preparation for the game. She recognized all but one, a trim, muscular young man with a determined look on his face. He introduced himself. "Levi Malenkov," he said. "Last year's Butterfly Champion in the Russian Province."

"Maria Medaris. Butterfly champion here in Armstrong City."

"I know who you are," Malenkov said. "I came here to knock you down."

"Good luck on that."

"We Russians are known for our chess. You North Americans for your poker. Chess will win tonight. You see, I have studied your moves."

It was true Maria played poker. In fact, she was very good

at it. But chess was a game she was good at too. She always made a point of knowing who'd signed up for Butterfly. When she'd seen Malenkov's name, she had searched out vids and studied his moves.

The players began to climb the great curved lunasteel buttresses that supported the dome. It was an arduous task, hand over hand, step after step, up the curve until each player was clinging to the buttress upside down. One missed handhold or boot placement and down they would plummet. They would not die, presuming their parachute worked, but if they fell, they were automatically out of the game.

Two players, one man and one woman, slipped on the way, leaving Maria, Malenkov, and five others still climbing. When they reached the platform, they swung up on it. "I'm glad you made it," Malenkov said to Maria.

"I'm glad you made it too," Maria answered. "I like to play against people who know what they're doing."

"You have the reputation of being vicious in this game," Malenkov said.

"I do what it takes to win."

"So do I."

Maria smiled. "Good. I wouldn't have it any other way."

The players donned their wings, counted down, and then simultaneously threw themselves over the edge. Maria folded her wings back, dived straight down on one of the other players, slammed into him, tore off his wings, then pushed him away. She looked between her boots and saw Malenkov was after another player. The Russian was a nimble player, brute force not his style. He kicked out, caught his spurs in one of the man's wings, and tore it to shreds. The player fluttered downward until he was forced to deploy his parachute.

Maria slammed into another player and kicked him in the helmet, tore off his wings, pushed him away, then deployed her wings. She gained lift and soared upward, found one of the other players trying to avoid Malenkov, and used her spurs to tear away her wings. When the woman tried to fight back, Maria kneed her in the stomach. She gasped, then fell away, clutching her midriff, before finally deploying her parachute. Maria's helmet mirror revealed a flier coming at her. She arched her back, pulled in her wings, and spiraled away. The flier went past and Maria dived after him before stretching out her wings again. Slipping in close, she lashed out with her boots, kicking him in the head. She pulled in her wings, then wrapped her legs around her foe. The man desperately tried to punch her but she dodged his fists. A well-aimed elbow to his face stopped him and his nose spurted blood. She pulled off one of his wings before pushing him away. Another parachute deployed.

Malenkov swooped away from her, gained lift, then flew back. She flitted away toward the side of the dome, coiled up her legs, then pushed off hard to gain altitude. Malenkov circled beneath her. To get at him, she tucked in her wings and went into a vertical dive. He looked up and tried to get away, but Maria had the advantage. She crashed into him, kicked him in the chest, battered his helmet with another kick, then tore off one of his wings. After he deployed his parachute, she flew down and circled him while he looked at her with a puzzled expression.

The players met back at the green. The man she'd elbowed in the face was sitting in the grass, holding his ruined nose. The other players were giving him sympathy. Maria ignored them and concentrated on packing her wings. Malenkov came over. He studied her, then asked, "What are you so angry about?"

"I'm not angry about anything."

"To you, this game is not about winning," he replied. "It's about getting even. Tonight I understand why you are always victorious. Who is it you are trying to get even with?"

"I beat you," Maria said. "That is all you need to know."

She turned away from the Russian, folded her wings, and stowed them in the trunk. The limo driver opened the door and she climbed inside. There, she slumped down in the seat, then put her hands to her face. Bitter, hot tears leaked between her fingers. What was she angry about? Perhaps a father who disliked her and sabotaged her every ambition. Or maybe it was a certain young man she'd once cared for, maybe even loved, who had not come to see her when she lay sick and injured in a hospital bed. "I hate you, Crater Trueblood," she said, focusing her anger. "I really do."

::: TWELVE

Crescent followed Crater along the main tube. She was scuffing her boots on the floor like a petulant child. Crater looked over his shoulder and said, "If you don't want to go, why don't you go back to the Dust Palace?"

"I told my queen I would serve you," Crescent answered, "and I will."

"Then pick up your feet."

"Yes, Master."

"I told you to stop calling me Master."

"Perhaps I would remember better if you didn't treat me like a slave."

Crater recalled he was supposed to talk to Crescent about her temper, but he was having trouble containing his own. He'd lain awake half the night worrying about Crescent. It certainly had not been his intention to adopt the little crowhopper, but Q-Bess had now made it clear Crescent was part of the family. The Colonel had more than once accused him of being soft. Maybe, Crater thought, that was the reason he'd brought Crescent to Moontown. He muttered to himself, "Soft!"

"What was that, Master?"

"Nothing. And stop dragging your feet!"

"As you wish." Crescent started running. She threw herself against the ceiling, flipped off it, then built up enough velocity to run along the side of the tube.

"Stop it!" Crater shouted.

Crescent slowed until she was walking, then started scuffing the soles of her boots on the floor again. This time Crater didn't say anything. He just shook his head and kept going until they arrived at the east dustlock where not only his equipment was stored but he also knew a female dustie was on duty. After they'd climbed inside, the dustie—a woman named Annie—came out, her eyebrows rising at the sight of Crescent. "Annie, I'd appreciate it if you would measure her for a biolastic sheath," Crater said.

Annie frowned in disbelief. "I heard you'd brought one of those things to town."

"Annie," Crater said, "this is Crescent. Crescent, say hello to Annie."

"Hello," Crescent said.

Annie's frown turned into a scowl. "How many of our troops did it kill?"

"She didn't kill anybody," Crater replied.

"That is true, to my shame," Crescent said.

"If you want it outfitted, Crater, do it yourself," Annie said. "I have no intention of touching it."

This attitude confused Crater. "But it's your job," he said.

"Then you can take this job and shove it in the scrag pile," she replied and left the dustlock.

Crater thought the situation over and came up with no good solution except to go ahead. "Look," he said to Crescent, "before we go outside, you'll need to be measured for a biolastic sheath. Do you know what that is?"

"A biolastic sheath," Crescent answered, "is a film of microorganisms genetically programmed to apply one Earthian pressure on the human or other body wearing it. When attached to a helmet, usually in conjunction with coveralls and boots, the human or other organic body may safely enter an area of low pressure, such as the surface of the moon, and return without fear of decompression sickness or the need to undergo a lengthy decompression regimen."

"Word for word, right out of the book," Crater admired. "Do you know how to use the apparatus to make your sheath?"

"Of course I do. I am well educated in most technical matters. The Trainers believe the more a Legionnaire knows, the more likely he is to survive. I assure you I know many things that might surprise you."

"It is well known crowhoppers lie," Crater pointed out.

"Legionnaires, you mean, but you are correct. We are trained to lie if required to complete our mission. However, I have no present mission and I presume my contract was voided when you captured me. Therefore, I have no reason to lie at present. Do you understand?"

Argumentative people wore Crater out. He knew what he knew and he saw no sense arguing about any of it. He nodded toward a locker that held coveralls, boots, and helmets. "Find what fits and take them in with you. After you get your sheath made, put everything on, then come back into this chamber."

"Aren't you coming with me?" she asked.

"No. You can do everything yourself."

"But I will need to input my measurements to the puter so it can make my sheath. It would be much easier if you helped."

"To make the measurements requires you to be naked."

"What does that matter?"

Crater sighed. "Just do what I tell you."

"Yes, Master," she answered, looking triumphant. She chose her coveralls, boots, and helmet, picked up a backpack, then climbed inside the dustlock with the gear.

After closing the hatch behind her, Crater waited until he heard the spray of the biolastic shower, then quickly undressed, pulled on his sheath, coveralls, and boots, donned a backpack, then sat down and impatiently waited. Ten minutes passed, then fifteen. "Aren't you ready yet?" he called.

"Have a little patience," she replied. Her tone was grumpy.

It took another ten minutes, but finally Crescent emerged, fully suited. Crater ran through the suit checklist. "You're all set," he said.

"I am quite capable with the technical requirements of most dustlocks," she replied. "Although, as I correctly pointed out, it would have been much easier and faster if you would have helped."

"Everything would actually go easier and faster if you weren't constantly griping," Crater said in exasperation.

"Yes, Master."

"Fine. Call me Master, just as long as you do exactly what I tell you to do."

"I await your various ill-considered commands."

"All right. Here's my next ill-considered command. Let's go outside."

"I can't get out there fast enough, oh masterful one."

Crater chose to ignore Crescent's insolence, mainly because he didn't know what to do about it. Once they were inside the airlock chamber, he pulled the inner hatch closed, pressed the necessary keys on the control panel to depressurize the airlock, and heard the hissing of air as it was emptied into a holding chamber to be cleansed and recycled. When the dustlock puter announced pressure had reached essentially zero, Crater checked his and Crescent's gauges. They were in the green so he climbed through the outer hatch onto the well-trod dust.

Crescent followed him and stood in the dust, the first time she'd been outside since arriving in Moontown. The Earth hanging in the black sky attracted her attention. "When I first went into space, I was surprised at how blue the Earth is," she said. "Where I grew up, the dirt was brown, the water gray, and the trees green. I never saw anything blue."

"What else do you remember of Earth?" Crater asked as he pushed the hatch shut.

"Wooden barracks, cold days, colder nights, weapons training, crawling through the mud, mush for food," she said.

"Anything good?"

"That *was* good."

"What do you consider bad?"

"Losing," she said.

"That's it?"

Crescent thought it over. "I don't like being laughed at. I know I'm ugly. That is no reason for amusement."

Crater had a natural urge to tell the little crowhopper she wasn't ugly but he didn't, mainly because he was certain she wouldn't believe him. Her flat face, coarse hair, gray skin, thick torso, and heavy legs were different enough that the human brain, trained to recognize feminine beauty in a much different way, was judgmental. Instead, he asked, "Considering that standard humans are proportionately different from Legionnaires, do we look ugly to you?"

"Some do. The sheriff to me is as ugly as a dirty pistol."

Crater chuckled. "He's ugly to most folks. How about me?"

"You are a well-formed human male, reasonably pleasant to look at," she said. "Understand that the Trainers are human and we naturally admire and honor them. Perhaps for this reason certain human faces and forms are recognized as attractive."

"Thank you, I guess," Crater said.

"You're welcome, I suppose," she replied, rewarded by Crater's pleased smile. "Why do you smile?" she asked.

"Because you said 'You're welcome.' You've learned!"

"Of course I've learned! Does not the slave learn from the master?"

"I'm sorry," Crater said. "I didn't mean to insult you."

"However, you did, and it is not the first time."

Crater started to apologize further, then thought better of it. It was clear Crescent liked to argue, almost as if it were a game, one at which she was far more skilled than Crater. "Let's go to work," he said, then led her up a well-worn trail to the sun-powered furnaces.

Inside the control building was a shelf that held three burial urns made of mooncrete. One of them was marked *Frederick J. Hook*, another *Doom*, and the other *Argentina Mike*, a miner who'd been running from several wives and had managed to live less than a year on the Moontown scrapes before being run over by a loader.

Crater carefully placed the urns in a plaston crate that he handed to Crescent. "Don't drop this."

"What are these things?"

"They're urns, containers that hold the dust of the people whose names are on them."

"How did they get turned into dust?"

"Solar furnace. That's why they're here."

"What are we going to do with them?"

"We're going to a special place and scatter them."

"Why?"

"Because the human body doesn't decompose on the moon. It becomes a mummy."

"Ah. Like the ancient Egyptians."

Crater didn't want to get off talking about ancient Egyptians. Crescent probably knew a lot about them and it might be difficult to get her off the subject. "Get aboard the mini-scraper," he said, pointing at a small tracked vehicle with a blade up front.

Holding the urn box, Crescent sat in the passenger's seat while Crater got behind the wheel and drove north. A little over an hour later they arrived at the rim of a large crater. Crater parked, then trudged up to the rim, Crescent following with the crate of urns. To the north, a vast plain of brownish-gray dust spread to the horizon from which rose the ebony blackness of space. "What is this place?" Crescent asked. "The Trainers never taught me much about the geography of the moon. That was specialty training for the navigators."

"It is a crater called Trouvelot," Crater answered. "It is where we place the remains of our dead."

"I don't understand why a special place is needed."

"It's just our way, Crescent."

Crescent looked northward. "What is out there?"

"Mare Frigoris. The Sea of Cold."

Crescent considered Crater's answer. "Why did the ancients call it a sea when it is plainly a desert?"

"They didn't know what it was," Crater answered, "but they

thought it might be an ocean. In a way, they were right. It's an ocean of dust. But enough questions. Let's see to the urns."

"I'm sorry I ask so many questions," Crescent said, "but may I ask one more?"

"No," Crater said. His head was beginning to hurt. "Let's take care of these people."

Crater took Doom's container and waved it over the steep wall, releasing the dust within which fell into the chasm. Then he did the same with Freddy's dust and then Mike's. "From dust to dust, ashes to ashes, amen," Crater said.

"What is this word 'amen'?"

"We end our prayers with it."

"Why?"

Crater confessed he didn't know, then, to forestall another question, he asked one of his own. "Do you want to drive the mini-scraper back to Moontown?"

Crescent's face lit up. "Yes!"

"It's all yours."

Crescent cocked her head, then said, "I think it might be informative if I told you I find you pleasant to be with."

After hesitating, Crater replied, "I find you pleasant to be with too."

"It is not necessary to patronize me. My comment was simply to confirm that we are communicating well."

"Humans call that being friends," Crater said.

Crescent pondered Crater's response and might have replied had not a shadow flitted over the gray dust, a shadow that was like a huge bird where no birds had never flown. Crater and Crescent looked skyward and saw a delta-winged ship. It was going slower than orbital velocity, using its rocket jets to maneuver.

"It's a warpod," Crescent said.

"It sure is," Crater replied, unable to keep the awe out of his voice. "But what's it doing here?"

"There's something else following it, silvery and torpedo-shaped."

Crescent's eyes were obviously better than Crater's, perhaps part of her genetic tweaking. He zoomed in with his helmet optics and spotted the craft she'd seen, a type he'd never seen before. It was descending on the warpod, its jets glowing. Something bright streaked from it, and the warpod began to fall until it disappeared beyond the horizon. An orange glow rose from that point, then faded away. Crater looked up and saw the silvery ship accelerate, then curve upward and disappear.

"I hope that thing is on our side," Crater said. "Drive us back, Crescent, quick as you can. Likely they saw this in Moontown, but I suspect we got the better view."

Crescent pressed the accelerator down, the tracks dug in, and she steered them across the dust. One thing certain, Crater thought as they roared along, the war was not yet over. The question was who had just won the aerial battle over Moontown—and did it mean an invading force was about to land?

::: THIRTEEN

The scrapes were empty of miners, the machinery abandoned, and the conveyor belts unmoving and piled
high with dust. The battle in the sky had apparently
chased the miners off the dust, presumably inside the tubes.
Crater and Crescent stripped off their gear quickly, showered,
and dressed in their tube clothes. When they stepped inside
the main tubeway from the dustlock, they found it was also
empty. Following a low thrum of voices, they found much of
Moontown's population crowded into the various observa-
tions decks and towers. Crater led Crescent to the observation
tower nearest the Dust Palace. Most of the hotel residents were
there, buzzing over the space battle they'd just witnessed.

Crater and Crescent wormed their way into the crowd
until they reached Asteroid Al and Q-Bess, who were standing
together. "What did you see?" Crater asked.

Al's face registered relief at the sight of them. "We were
worried about you two. What did we see? A warpod was being
chased by some kind of ship. Silver-colored thing, never seen
anything like it. The Colonel evacuated the scrapes."

Q-Bess clutched Crater to her bosom, tears freely flowing slowly down her cheeks. "Oh, my child. I was so worried! Thank God you're safe!" She reached out an arm to pull Crescent in close too. Crescent stiffened, her eyes going wide, but she allowed herself to be enveloped in the queen's arms.

When Crater got free, he took Al aside. "We had a good view," he said. "The silver craft blasted the warpod, then lit its jets and took off."

"Never heard of a ship like that. Hope it's on our side."

"That's exactly what I said to Crescent."

Heads in the assembly began to turn toward Crescent. "This is her fault," someone grumbled.

"She brought them here!" another voice rang out.

"Where I come from, we'd string that little rat up by her toes," another citizen said.

Crater positioned himself beside Crescent. "Leave her alone. She had nothing to do with this."

"How do you know, Crater?" someone called. "I say we put her in an old jumpcar and blast her across the Sea of Cold!"

There was a rumble of voices agreeing with the idea. Then the sheriff arrived. "All you folks disperse," he ordered. "You miners, back to work."

"What about that creature, Sheriff?" a citizen demanded. It was Classy Amos, the man Crescent had tossed around in the cafeteria.

"It ain't none of your business, Amos," the sheriff snapped. "Now, I said for all of you to get gone. You got ten seconds."

Grumbling, the Moontowners descended the staircase to the main tubeway, leaving behind Crater, Crescent, Q-Bess, and Asteroid Al. The sheriff frowned at Crescent, then shook his head. "This thing has been nothing but trouble."

"Crescent didn't do anything," Crater said.

"It's breathing," the sheriff replied. "That's trouble enough. Anyway, your little monster ain't why I'm here. The Colonel wants to see you."

"What about?"

"For some reason, he forgot to confide in me."

"Take care of Crescent," Crater said to Q-Bess and Al.

Q-Bess put a protective arm around her and Al said, "We'll get her inside the Dust Palace safe and sound."

"Thank you," Crescent said.

Q-Bess and Al smiled at her. "You're welcome!" they said in unison.

The sheriff rolled his eyes. "Monkey see, monkey do. That thing would still cut both your throats in a heartbeat. Let's go, Crater. The Colonel is waiting."

Crater walked with the sheriff down the tower steps and along the tubes. "You ever miss that blob of slime mold cells that used to sit on your shoulder?" the sheriff asked.

"I don't think about it much," Crater replied.

"You really are a terrible liar," the sheriff said. "That gillie sure could hack a puter. Good thing it was illegal."

"It knew that."

The sheriff laughed softly. "So you have said, Crater. So you have said. And here we are."

They were there, all right, but not where Crater expected, which was the Colonel's sumptuous office. Instead, they stood before the hatch to a dustlock marked Private. No Access Without Permission.

"Your gear is waiting for you there," the sheriff said. "I had it moved."

"But I just came in from the big suck," Crater said.

"It appears you're going out into it again. Hurry up."

For a brief moment, Crater considered telling the sheriff he wasn't going anywhere but then relented. He was curious what the Colonel was up to. He climbed into the dustlock, took off his tube clothes once more, wearily put all his gear back on, climbed into the airlock, depressurized, then went outside. There, he beheld the Colonel's jumpcar, its silvery hull glimmering in the sunlight. No one was around so he climbed the ladder to its hatch and went inside where he found the Colonel sitting on a couch, studying a reader. Two technicians were in the aft control room, manipulating a bank of instruments. "Glad you could make it, Crater, although you took your time," the Colonel said, glancing up from the reader before placing it in a hold net. "Join me in the cockpit."

The Colonel climbed the short ladder to the cockpit and sank into the right seat. Crater climbed into the pilot's seat, looking over the familiar controls. He'd been flying jumpcars since he was ten, trained by Rocket Rob, a Dust Palace resident and one of the best jumpcar pilots on the moon before he'd slammed into the dust several years ago, a victim of a clogged fuel valve.

"North," the Colonel said, without preamble.

"Sir?"

"Fly this machine north."

"You want me to pilot?"

The Colonel yawned. "Take her up, Crater. I don't have all day."

Crater tried not to act pleased, but the truth was he loved flying jumpcars and there was not a sweeter one on the moon than the Colonel's. He checked the instrument panels, then ran through the engine checks, talking with the jumpcar puter.

"Engines."

Go.

"Pumps."

Go.

"Servos."

Go.

"Propellants."

Go.

"Navigator."

Go.

"Puter."

Go.

"Guidance."

Auto or manual?

"Manual."

All systems go.

Crater set the initial engine thrust. "Everybody belted in?"

"We're all belted in, Crater," the Colonel growled. "Take us aloft."

Crater wound the engines up, his eye on the panel gauges, then increased the thrust so that the jumpcar began to rise. Working the verniers with the stick, Crater made the liftoff as smooth as possible, limiting the number of Gs everyone aboard had to endure, then arced the rocket to the north. "Where to?"

"The techies will guide you."

Crater took the jumpcar up to an altitude of twenty-five miles. When the Colonel and the techies didn't say anything, he went on up to fifty, then began to fly along a northerly heading.

"We need to gain altitude for the scanner," one of the

techies called, so Crater climbed to seventy-five miles, the surface of the moon wheeling beneath them. He leveled the jumpcar out and the techie reported that he was happy with that altitude.

Crater wished he could wring the little rocket ship out but he held it steady. "We have acquired the target, sir," a techie called. "Sending the pilot the LPS numbers now."

"Take us there, Crater."

Crater keyed in the Lunar Positioning Satellite numbers sent to him by the techie, then made a course correction. When he was near the target, he rolled the jumpcar over and put it into a steep dive. The cratered surface filled the lunaglas dust-screen and then began to grow larger. "Easy, boy," the Colonel said. Out of the corner of his eye, Crater could see the Colonel gripping the armrests of his seat. This pleased Crater for a reason he suspected was not good for his soul. He popped the nose of the jumpcar up, then hit the retros and, while checking the rearview vid, smoothly decelerated until the jumpcar landed gently on the dust between two medium-sized boulders.

"A fine landing," the Colonel said, "but I didn't need the roller-coaster ride."

"Just blowing out the scrag in her jets, sir," Crater said. Then he looked through the cockpit lunaglas and saw the reason for the landing. Less than a shovelball field's distance was the wreck of the warpod.

Crater followed the Colonel down the cockpit ladder, then outside and down the exterior ladder. It was a small warpod, coated in the deep black radar-absorbent material of its kind. Its delta wings—needed to give the vehicle lift when its scramjet engine carried it to Earth orbit—were still attached, although one of them had a big crack in it. Its cockpit cover was open and from it sprawled its pilot. By his contorted posture, Crater could tell the pilot was dead.

While the Colonel took pix with his helmetcam, Crater walked around the wreck, then climbed on one of the warpod's wings to have a better look at the pilot. A human male, it was in a black pressure suit with no markings or patches.

The Colonel spoke into his do4u. "Jim, would you and Miguel come outside?"

The techies dutifully arrived, and the Colonel ordered them to carry the pilot's body to the jumpcar and place it in stowage. "The sheriff and the docs will figure out where that gentleman came from," the Colonel said.

"Surely he came from the UCW," Crater said.

"Probably," the Colonel answered.

"How could they get a warpod here without us noticing it?"

"We did notice it. Our Russian friends, who have a network of obs-sats around the Earth, alerted us that it was on its way. You may take a great deal of satisfaction over that, Crater. After all, it was that package you picked up for me that allowed me to make common cause with the Czarina."

Crater watched the techies carry the pilot toward the jumpcar. "Do you know why he was here?"

The Colonel sniffed. "Probably to have a look at Moontown. The UCW has lately been resorting to such thuggery as kidnapping. When the Czarina was visiting Earth, they tried to kidnap her. Fortunately, she escaped. Now I suspect they have their sights on me."

Crater reflected that there were a few Moontown folks who would have been delighted if the Colonel was kidnapped, but he thought it best not to point that out. Instead, he asked, "What was that silver craft that fought them off?"

"An asset of mine."

"It is very fast. Fusion powered?"

"One of a kind," the Colonel replied. "A warpod doesn't have a chance against it."

"So the war continues."

"Yes, so it seems. By the way, there was a kidnapping attempt on Maria too."

"Maria?"

"You recall my grandaughter, surely. You crossed the moon together."

Crater frowned. "What happened?"

"A warpod attacked her while she was piloting a jumpcar near Frau Mauro."

"A warpod! How did she escape?"

The Colonel chuckled. "Surely you of all people know my granddaughter is a survivor. She used the wash from her rocket jets to cook off a missile beneath the warpod's wings. It looped around and flew up one of its engines. If the warhead had been armed, the warpod would have been destroyed. As it was, Maria sent it limping home."

Crater whistled. "Impressive."

"An excellent description of Maria."

The pilot's body was loaded up, and Crater and the Colonel climbed back into the cockpit. Crater ran through the check-list with the puter, then blasted off and arced over, heading south. "You mind if I blow more scrag out of her jets, Colonel?" he asked.

"Be my guest," the Colonel said and pretended to be bored while Crater swooped and zoomed the jumpcar through a series of acrobatic maneuvers. Below, the techies did their best not to turn green. After Crater smoothed the rocket ship out, the Colonel tuned to Crater's private channel. "Starting today, I want you to be my jumpcar pilot."

Crater was astonished and thrilled at the same moment. A jumpcar pilot! It was a dream job.

"What do you say, Crater?" the Colonel demanded. "Don't just sit there with your mouth open."

Crater hesitated. "Sir, with respect, why are you offering me this job?"

"For three reasons. First, you're a good pilot. Second, I like you. Always have. I want to see you get ahead."

"And the third reason, sir?"

"There's a lab in the hangar. I thought you might like to work on your moon dust water extraction system."

"It's true I haven't had much time to work on it."

"There you have it! You can piddle around in the lab when you're not flying me hither and yon. What do you say?"

"Thank you, sir," Crater said. "I'd like nothing better."

"Good. Consider yourself hired."

Crater smoothed the trajectory of the jumpcar and silently took possession of the ship. *Jumpcar pilot.* He couldn't wait to tell Q-Bess. And Asteroid Al. And, oddly enough, he wanted to tell Crescent too.

Sweeping over Moontown, he turned the nose up and backed down to a perfect soft landing. The Colonel left the cockpit while Crater sat there, savoring for a few moments his new position. "Hello, ship," he said quietly. "My name is Crater Trueblood. I'm your new pilot."

Crater felt almost as if the ship answered, whispering, *Let's go. Let's go. Let's go.*

In the entire history of his life, Crater had never felt better except for perhaps the time he'd kissed Maria and she'd kissed him back. He wished she knew about his new job, but then, after he thought about it, he realized she would find out—and probably right away. After all, she was part of the Medaris empire. Maybe he'd even get to see her when he flew the Colonel to Armstrong City. If so, what would he say to her? And what would she say back?

Crater leaned back in the pilot's seat and imagined what that moment would be like until he noticed a flickering red light on the console. He called up the jumpcar's puter. "Check and verify servos," he said.

The servos are overdue maintenance.

"Noted. What is the thirty-day maintenance schedule for all other systems?"

The puter listed all maintenance required. It was a long list. Crater got on the horn, calling up the jumpcar techies for a word. He planned on putting some steel in their backbones. Maintenance would never be overdue on the Colonel's jumpcar again, not while Crater Trueblood was on the job.

::: FOURTEEN

Except for having to endure her exile from Britain's throne, Q-Bess was content. Her contentment was derived from her certainty that her son Petro, the Prince of Wales, was alive. The source of her certainty rested with an empty paper envelope, the kind used in olden times to hold letters. This particular antique had been carried by a heel-3 convoy trucker across a thousand miles of dusty wayback and handed to Q-Bess with the explanation that a stranger had paid him a hundred johncredits to deliver it.

Q-Bess had carefully studied the envelope on the outside and found no markings of any kind. But when she tore it open and turned it inside out, she found a small dot of ink in a corner. Under a microscope, she'd discovered the coat of arms of the royal family. So Petro was out there somewhere, doing who knew what. It almost didn't matter. The prince was a man of destiny. In fact, both her sons, Petro by blood and Crater by adoption, were men with glorious futures. She was certain of it.

Q-Bess prayed a silent prayer for Petro, then worked her

way toward further contentment by savoring the fact Crater was also still alive, the survivor of many battles. Of course, his heart had been broken by the Colonel's granddaughter but no matter. He was young and there were lots of moon dust girls in the craters. He had also recently taken a job he loved as the Colonel's jumpcar pilot. It was amazing to see how Crater had thrown off the darkness that seemed to cover him after three years of combat. He was a new person, cheerful and optimistic.

Q-Bess was also pleased with the little crowhopper Crescent, whom she now considered her daughter. Every day Crescent was proving herself with her diligence and her willingness to learn. Q-Bess was beginning to think being raised as a genetic mutant super-warrior wasn't such a bad thing for a child if the militant spirit bred into her was channeled into productivity. Nobody could tuck a hospital corner on a sheet tighter than Crescent, and she scrubbed the lunasteel pots and pans with coarse moonsoap until they glittered like polished silver.

Thinking of Crescent's torture of the pans reminded Q-Bess she needed to get her staff to make more moonsoap. Two workers could turn out a thousand bars in a day but orders were still piling up. The soap was much coveted on Earth since nothing had the scouring power like moon dust mixed with glycerin, water, lye, and faux coconut oil. It was called Colonel Medaris's Mighty Moonsoap, and even with the occasional blockade mounted by the UCW, Q-Bess sold tens of thousands of bars every year at twenty johncredits apiece, often carried through by blockade runners.

Savoring her contentment, Q-Bess sat at the table reserved for her in the Dust Palace cafeteria and watched the day shift devouring her food. But then her contentment evaporated when she noticed at a table in the back one of the sheriff's deputies, a new man down from Earth. Tattoos of a military nature crawled up his thick arms and he sported a walrus-moustache that did little to hide the scars on his face. Q-Bess noticed the deputy's small, black eyes never left Crescent as she worked at the food line. When she left the line, Q-Bess saw the deputy rise, casually stroll through the cafeteria, then climb through the kitchen hatch.

Q-Bess threaded her way through the tables and went into the kitchen where her staff was busily preparing meals for the next shift. Kurto, the chief cook, was looking anxious. "What's wrong with you?" she asked.

"Nothing," he said, then added, "That deputy, what name does he use?"

"Jones," she said and looked around. "Where's Crescent?"

Grace, the sous-chef, glanced up from her chopping board. "Sent her to the biovats to pick up some protein."

"Which one?"

"Chicken's what I need so I'm guessing she went to biovat 12. It's been the most productive lately."

Q-Bess searched the kitchen and the pantries. When she didn't find Deputy Jones, she headed to the biovats. Biovat 12 was in a deep tube, one of the first installed in Moontown. It required going through several hatches and down four flights of mooncrete steps. That far down was warm, moist, and stank of generations of protein soups. The overhead lamps only partially lifted the gloom of the tubeways between the biovat tubes as Q-Bess made her way from chamber to chamber.

Turning a corner in the tubeway, she nearly bumped into the deputy who was standing there, his hands on his hips. He turned and tipped his cap. "Hello, lady."

"What are you doing down here?"

From below came Crescent carrying a capped bucket of chicken protein. She looked up, then lowered her eyes and scurried past Q-Bess and the deputy, her steps echoing as she climbed. The deputy's eyes followed her. "Deputy," Q-Bess said, "I asked you why you're down here."

The deputy smiled, though there was no warmth to it. "Sheriff say keep eye on that creature."

"Crescent is not a creature, Deputy. She's a member of the Dust Palace's staff. Please leave and tell the sheriff if I need somebody to watch over me and my people, I'll be certain to let him know. You would, of course, be my last choice."

The deputy seemed to go through a calculation, then said, "I will tell Sheriff what you say." He put his hand on Q-Bess's waist and she sucked in a breath. "You nice lady for old lady."

"If you enjoy having that hand, Deputy, you will take it off my person immediately."

The deputy withdrew his hand and placed it on the butt of his holstered pistol. "Too bad. Maybe I be your last chance for kissy-kissy."

"Get out!"

The deputy grinned, then shrugged and climbed up the steps. Q-Bess waited until his footsteps receded, then leaned against the wall and put her hand over her heart, which was pounding in her ears. After she'd regained control, she made her way to the kitchen where she found Crescent at the sink, washing carrots. "Crescent," she said, "did that deputy say or do anything to you?"

Crescent began washing the carrots with furious intensity. Q-Bess reached out and touched Crescent's arm. Crescent pulled her arm away, grabbed a knife from the sideboard, threw Q-Bess to the floor, and put the knife to her throat.

The kitchen, normally all rattling pots and pans, went deathly silent.

"Crescent," Q-Bess said. "Put the knife down."

Crescent, as if coming out of a trance, dropped the knife and turned away, then fell to her knees and scrabbled to a corner where she huddled, her hands to her face. Kurto helped Q-Bess up. "I'm all right," she said and walked to Crescent and knelt beside her.

"I am a monster," Crescent said. "Everyone says so. They think I don't hear but I do. My ears are very sensitive."

"What does Deputy Jones say?"

"He says evil things."

"What kind of evil things?"

"He says I'm pretty but I am not pretty. My kind are not bred to be handsome in any way. We are bred to kill. That is why I almost killed you just now. I wanted to. I'm not sure why I didn't. I have had many strange feelings since I've been with humans."

"That's because you're human too. Your Trainers, they taught you things that weren't true about who you really are. You're starting to figure that out."

"Deputy Jones said he wanted to make me happy. He said he wanted to touch me."

"Did you let him?"

"No. I heard you coming so I ran."

Q-Bess exhaled and realized she'd been holding her breath. "I'll have a chat with the sheriff. Deputy Jones won't bother you again."

Q-Bess rose and walked over to the cutlery table, selected a knife, its edge gleaming in the harsh kitchen lights, and handed it to Crescent. "You can go back to work now, Crescent."

The little crowhopper looked at the knife, then took it, got up and went back to the sink to cut up the carrots. All the cooks and kitchen staff seemed frozen in various positions of food preparation. Q-Bess waved a regal hand. "Get to work, people!"

The volume of kitchen noise jumped exponentially and Q-Bess headed for the sheriff's office. She didn't make it there, mainly because she found him in the cafeteria. He was at the coffee station, drawing a cup of Q-Bess's special blend which she called Moon Dust Special #17. One cup of MS17 and a heel-3 miner was set for the day and probably the night too. "Sheriff, I was just coming to see you."

"Thought I'd save you the trouble, not to mention getting a cup of this grand coffee. When I send a deputy to his duty, ma'am, to his duty he must go. Only the Colonel can countermand my orders."

Q-Bess raised a regal eyebrow. "Deputy Jones is entirely too interested in Crescent."

"That ugly creature? You are imagining things."

Q-Bess crossed her arms and tapped her toe on the mooncrete floor. "What sent you to prison on Earth, Sheriff? I've always wondered."

"Murder," the sheriff answered with no sign of discomfort or embarrassment.

"Who did you murder?"

"A wife who deserved it. It was her or me, whoever could get to the gun the quickest. Now that I've answered your question, ma'am, let me ask you one. You really the Queen of England? Or is that your scam?"

"Both," Q-Bess answered, also with no sign of discomfort or embarrassment. "I am indeed the wife of the last and late king. My fellow countrymen sent me and the Prince of Wales here to await a summons back to the throne."

"Ah, yes—Petro. The princely prince, not to mention the best cheat at cards I've ever observed. I've missed him around here. He always had a joke to tell or some scam I needed to break up. Have you heard from him lately?"

The way the sheriff asked so casually about Petro told Q-Bess he already knew the answer. "How did you intercept that envelope?" she asked.

The sheriff winked and lowered his voice. "I didn't. The Colonel told me about it. He sent that envelope. It was an act of kindness. He knew you were worried about the boy."

"Petro's working for the Colonel? What's he doing? Is he in danger?"

"A special assignment. As for danger, we who work for the Colonel are always in danger. You know that."

Q-Bess pondered the sheriff. "If the Colonel went to the trouble of sending me that envelope in such a secretive manner, why are you telling me this now?"

The sheriff finished his coffee and set the cup down. "Never get in the way of my deputies again, ma'am."

"Then tell Jones to leave Crescent alone."

"The Colonel is concerned about that creature," the sheriff said. "It bothers him that she's here. He told me he loses sleep, worrying she might hurt one of his employees. I suppose that means you."

"Tell the Colonel he needn't be concerned. Crescent is a good girl."

"Was she being good when she tossed Amos against the wall? Was she being good when she had that knife to your throat?" The sheriff tipped his hat and strolled toward the exit hatch where he stopped and looked over his shoulder. "You'd best figure out whose side you're on, your royalness.

The Colonel will make his decision on that creature. When he does, your job will be to get out of the way. Remember, he holds in his hands the life of someone close to you."

Q-Bess's hand went over her heart. "You threaten me with the life of my son?"

"Not me, ma'am. I'm just a lowly sheriff doing my job."

::: FIFTEEN

Crater truly loved being the Colonel's jumpcar pilot. He flew the Colonel and company officials across the moon and also saw to the maintenance, repair, refurbishment, and general health of the suborbital vehicle. Based on an original design by Tim Pickens, the famous rocket builder of the early twenty-first century, jumpcars were rocket ships with old-fashioned chemical engines that burned hydrogen and oxygen, byproducts of Helium-3 production. They came in various sizes for both private and commercial use, and were designed to carry passengers and small cargos. Although some were manufactured on Earth and exported to the moon, most jumpcars were built in Armstrong City, fabricated by the Medaris Jumpcar Company. They were sleek and had fins, although there was no requirement for aerodynamics in the near-vacuum of the moon. The design was for looks, to entice the interested buyer into purchasing something that looked fast and fun. Their exterior was whatever color the buyer wanted, the most popular being silver, gold, black, and copper. They were simply fabulous vehicles, and Crater was never happier than when he was in the pilot's seat, blowing the scrag out of the jumpcar's pipes.

The laboratory in the jumpcar hangar was also a source of enormous satisfaction. Crater mostly worked on his moon dust water extraction system, which didn't always work, and he wasn't certain why. Until he understood why, he wasn't going to let anyone go off into the dust and die because of an imperfect machine. The invention used a neutron emitter to find patches of water, then a microwave transmitter to excite the dispersed water molecules and turn them into clusters. The resulting vapor pressure caused them to rise and collect into pools below the regolith. After that, a pipe could be inserted into the pools and the water extracted without exposing it to the big suck. Crater was aware of the enormous implications of such a device. For one thing, the moon could hold a much larger population. He built a lunasteel safe with a special lock to keep his plans and equipment from prying eyes. Occasionally he'd put his equipment in his fastbug, one that he'd rebuilt for speed, and roar out to a desolate area to try his latest design. But no matter how he tweaked it, the extraction system sometimes worked and sometimes failed.

One of the three jumpcar techies who reported to Crater came over, wiping her hands on a rag, and said, "Good morning, sir. We've greased the gimbals and adjusted the servos. What do you want us to do next?"

It bothered Crater that the techie, who called herself Retro Roxy, had to ask him what to do. He always figured people at work should figure things out for themselves. Crater asked, "Have you checked the panels in the cockpit?"

"They're not due a maintenance check for another one hundred hours," Roxy replied.

"Maintenance intervals are suggestions, not absolutes."

"You think I should check them out?"

"If you have nothing better to do."

After Roxy went off to do the obvious, Crater looked out at the scrapes. The great shadow of two weeks duration had descended on Moontown and down the valley he could see the flashing helmet beams of the miners as they went about their business. A constellation of lights pinpointed the construction of a new solar tower. A flare off the cluster of sun towers to the north of town temporarily boiled away the darkness, then vanished. Twin headlights moved through the gloom, fastbugs laden with full heel-3 canisters departing from the furnaces, their destination the depot where the big convoy trucks waited.

Out of the corner of Crater's eye he saw Riley Bishop walking his way. She was a techie who never needed to be told what to do. "Pilot Trueblood, sir," she said in her distinct Irish brogue, "I've done the maintenance required and every block on the sheet has been checked. If ye have nothing else planned, I'll touch up the dings on the landing fins."

"A good idea, Techman Bishop," Crater said.

She blinked her big blues and said, "Forgive me, sir, but I heard ye once sung at the Earthrise and ye had a big hit called 'Moon Dust Girls.' I'll be there tonight, meaning the Earthrise. Would ye come, then, and sing your song?"

Crater had nearly forgotten his band. Two of the musicians had been killed in the war and his brother, Petro . . . well, who knew where he was? "I don't think so," he said. "That was another time."

"Oh, please, sir. It would mean so much to hear ye. I'm the lead singer of the Moontown Mollys and we're playing tonight. We could back ye up."

"Well . . ."

"Great! Around nine, then? Thank ye, sir. It'll be a great honor. I'll just take meself back to work now if that meets your approval."

"Yes, of course. Go ahead."

Riley walked toward the jumpcar while Crater pretended not to watch. She was a pretty girl, a hard worker, and very smart, which, of course, meant she was troublesome in Crater's mind.

That night Crater went to the Earthrise as promised and sang his old hit with the Moontown Mollys backing him up.

All I want is a moon dust girl,
Down in a crater waitin' for love.
All I want is a moon dust girl,
Kissin' me 'neath the world above.

All I need is a moon dust girl,
Makes workin' in the dust almost fun.
All I need is a moon dust girl,
Scrapes Heel-3 up by the megaton.

Now I have a moon dust girl,
Puts her helmet next to mine.
Now I have a moon dust girl,
She's one-sixth gravity fine.

The room went insane with applause and then Riley told him to sit down because she had a surprise. The Moontown Mollys proceeded to sing their new song, "Moon Dust Boy."

> *All I want is a moon dust boy,*
> *Arms so strong, holds me so tight.*
>
> *All I want is a moon dust boy,*
> *His lips on mine, ever'thing's right.*
> *All I need is a moon dust boy,*
> *Plays shovelball like a champ,*
> *All I need is a moon dust boy,*
> *He's my hero, I'm his scamp.*
>
> *Now I have a moon dust boy,*
> *Our helmets side by each.*
> *All I need is a moon dust boy,*
> *Crater's got lessons he can teach!*

On the last line, all the girls pointed at Crater and the audience of heel-3 miners erupted with cries for Crater to get back up there and kiss those pretty girls. Crater, blushing furiously, climbed up on stage. He kissed them one by one on the cheek, but when he started to peck Riley there, she turned her head and presented her lips. Crater didn't hesitate, Riley smiled coyly, and then the Moontown Mollys sang again. Crater sat down, dizzy with Riley's perfume and the memory of her soft lips on his.

After the set was finished and the applause died away, Riley sat down beside Crater. Their eyes met and Crater could feel the unasked questions. He looked away, then down at the table. "Riley, there's somebody . . . I can't . . . not until I figure it out."

Her hand touched his. He looked back into soft eyes now damp. "Aye, lad," she whispered. "But can't an Irishwoman dream?"

::: SIXTEEN

Crater, wake up!"

It was Q-Bess. "Crater, the sheriff has arrested Crescent! He's in the cafeteria with her now!"

Crater sat up in bed and waited until his mind caught up with Q-Bess's words. "Why has she been arrested?"

"The sheriff said she murdered Deputy Jones. They found him in one of the biovats."

"What's Crescent saying?"

"She's saying he deserved it."

Crater's mind raced. "Don't leave the sheriff alone with her. I'll be there as soon as I get dressed."

Q-Bess rushed off and Crater bound out of bed, got dressed, then made his way to the cafeteria where he saw Crescent, barefoot and in a plain white bed smock, sitting in a chair, her head bowed. The sheriff sat on a bench in front of her, holding a rope attached to a collar around her neck. A greenie was taking blood from her arm. When she pulled her arm away, the sheriff gave the rope a hard yank and Crescent squeezed her eyes shut. Q-Bess was being held back by a deputy.

"Sheriff," Crater said, "what's all this?"

The sheriff squinted at Crater. "It's pretty simple. Your creature here lured Deputy Jones down into the biovat tubes and there she drowned him in the chicken vat. My loyal deputy, done in by a monster."

The greenie pulled the needle out and bagged it. A trickle of dark blood flowed from the hole in her arm. The greenie placed a patch on it and left. Crescent's eyes were riveted on Crater. "Did you kill the deputy, Crescent?" Crater asked.

"He deserved to die," she answered.

The sheriff smiled. "You see? She's confessed."

"That was not a confession. She just said he got what he deserved."

"Lawyer talk," the sheriff dismissively replied. "Against the Colonel's rules, as you well know."

Crater tried again. "Crescent, did you kill the deputy? Tell me yes or no."

Crescent looked at him, then turned her face away.

"There," the sheriff said, "that's what a guilty man—or in this case, creature—does. It can't look you in the eye."

"Where's Deputy Jones?" Crater asked.

"Still in the chicken vat."

"Do you mind if I have a look?"

The sheriff shrugged. "Why not? Deputy Zageev, keep an eye on this thing. It isn't to move, do you understand?"

Q-Bess dragged a chair over and sat down beside Crescent and put her arm around her shoulders. Crescent leaned into her. "Go ahead, Crater, honey," Q-Bess said. "I've got her."

Crater followed the sheriff through the biovat hatch and down the winding stairs to the lower levels. There was a heavy mix of vegetation, meat, and dairy odors permeating the tubes that was almost enough to make Crater sick. At the tube marked BIOVAT #12, CHICKEN PROTEIN, the sheriff swung open the hatch. Inside was a cylindrical vat six feet high, twelve feet in diameter, with a platform above it to support the paddles that kept the pot stirred. Facedown in the bubbling stew bobbed Deputy Jones. The sheriff got a rake, ordinarily used to skim off grease, and hooked it over the back of the deputy and dragged him in, then flipped the body over. Chicken protein goop poured from the deputy's open mouth. "You see? Deader'n a hammer and drowned in this scrag stuff."

"Can we get him out of the vat?"

"I figured to do that later," the sheriff said.

"Can we do it now? There might be evidence."

"We don't need evidence. Your crowhopper murdered my deputy and you know it as well as I. Come on, Crater, don't look at me like that. She had plenty of motive—we all know Deputy Jones had a peculiar thing for her—and she works down in these biovats all the time. Who else would have done it?"

Crater ignored the sheriff and grasped the deputy by his collar. With a mighty heave, he dragged him out of the vat, a wave of chicken goop splashing out on the floor and running down the side. The man was heavy, and it took all of Crater's strength to lower him to the deck.

"Don't tamper with the evidence," the sheriff tut-tutted.

Crater knelt beside the deputy. The first thing he noticed was he wasn't wearing any leggings. "Did you find his leggings?" Crater asked.

"Tossed in a corner with his boots," the sheriff replied. "She enticed him down here to have her way with him, then pushed him into the vat."

"Since the vat is six feet above the deck, she couldn't have pushed him in unless he climbed up there." Crater pointed to the paddle platform.

"Then I guess she enticed him up there," the sheriff answered with a shrug.

Crater looked dubious, then went to a supply locker and got a towel. He wiped off the deputy's face with it, then his hands. "His nose is freshly broken."

"I'll add assault to the charge."

"His knuckles are skinned." Crater ran his hand over the deputy's head. "There are knots on his head. And a scab."

"Brave lad, fighting back like that. I hear your creature is monstrously strong."

"The scab would indicate after he was hit in the head, it had time to heal."

The sheriff shrugged.

"He's also covered with goop," Crater pointed out. "I'm covered with goop. I see some has splashed on you too."

"You'll be paying my laundry bill."

"But there's not a drop of goop on Crescent."

The sheriff's eyes narrowed. "She took a shower. She changed her smock. So what?"

"I didn't see any goop on the way down here. Wouldn't she have dripped going back up the steps?"

"The person committing the perfect crime is going to be one who knows how to clean up after themselves. Isn't your monster employed as a maid?"

"Kitchen staff."

"Same thing, maybe better. She knows how clean up goop."

"Then where's the goop-covered smock?" Crater asked. "And if she cleaned this room and the steps, where's the gooped-up mop? For all we know, this might have been a suicide."

"That's enough, Crater," the sheriff growled. "It was murder and that foul thing did it. If necessary, I'll find a goopy smock and a goopy mop."

"You'll manufacture evidence?"

"You said that, I didn't."

"Isn't it far more likely that it was the deputy who brought Crescent down here to have his way with her?"

The sheriff held up his hand for Crater to be silent, pressed his other hand into his do4u earpiece, then smiled. "Crater, you're talking more sense than you know. In fact, I believe that's exactly what happened. I just got back the report of the creature's blood. It's loaded with Phenolune. You know what that stuff does. You can walk, you can talk, but you don't have a clue what you're doing. Even though it's outlawed on the moon, it's available in Armstrong City if one knows where to ask. The greenie says the amount your creature has in it was enough to confuse an army. Deputy Jones probably sprayed the stuff in its face after sneaking into its room."

"Then she's innocent! Jones gave her a drug, then walked her down here. Whatever she did, if anything, was in self-defense."

The sheriff shrugged. "I'm sure an Earthside lawyer would argue it that way. Too bad for your monster the Colonel outlawed that profession in Moontown. One's motivation for doing evil is never weighed here, self-defense or not. It is always the evil itself that is judged."

Crater opened his mouth to debate, then closed it, recognizing the futility of arguing with a mind forever closed to anything other than the Colonel's rules and directives. "You still don't have any hard evidence Crescent did this."

The sheriff reached into his shirt pocket and drew out a pendant and a broken silver chain. "Got any idea who this belongs to?" He nodded toward the vat. "Found it right over there."

When the sheriff offered it to him, Crater took the pendant and the chain. Without question, the fiery eagle symbol—presumably a phoenix rising from the ashes—belonged to Crescent. "All right, she was here," he relented. "It still doesn't mean she killed him. What happens now?"

The sheriff put out his hand and Crater dropped the pendant and the chain into it. He put them back into his tunic pocket. "I will try your creature before the Colonel, he will find her guilty, then sentence her."

"Sentence her to what?"

"There's no death penalty in Moontown and we don't have a jail. What do you think?"

Crater didn't have to think. He knew. "Dust walk," he said.

"The very same," the sheriff agreed, then stepped out of the way as a squad of greenies arrived to pick up his dead deputy.

::: SEVENTEEN

hree Legionnaire *contubernium*—the term borrowed from the ancient Roman equivalent of a platoon—waited patiently and with no hope in the giant hangar. Their *decans*—a borrowed Roman term for noncommissioned officers—walked down the ranks, stopping only to tighten a strap or rearrange a piece of gear. The Trainers were there, strutting along the edges, watching over everything. The transports had landed and were already dropping their ramps, the dark caverns within beckoning. Spiderwalkers crabbed toward the transports, ridden by technicians.

The decans barked an order and forty-eight boot heels slammed together as the contubernium, called contus for short and each consisting of eight men, came to attention. The centurion, who would not be going on this mission, wheeled about and saluted. After a moment, as if considering whether the centurion was worthy, the Major Trainer returned the salute.

"Hear me, Legionnaires!" he said, his voice amplified by speakers throughout the hangar. "You have already been told your mission. Proceed now with all your skill and breeding. Kill anyone who dares stand in your way. Accomplish the bidding of those who rent you, according to the letter of our contract! This is my charge to you! Where does our spirit go after we die?"

Twenty-four Legionnaires and three decans responded in full throat:

It goes to glory.

"Where does the spirit of our enemy go after we kill them?"

To a place of darkness.

"When will we die?"

When we so choose.

"When will our enemy die?"

When we kill them.

"What is our secret?"

Life is death! Death is life!

The Major Trainer strutted away and the contus peeled off, jogging to the transport designated for infantry. Bucket seats lined each side. The Legionnaires sat and strapped in. A trio of Legionnaires—Absalom, Dion, and Lucien—sat together. They had been born together, grown through childhood together, trained together as spiderwalker troops, and were now sent forth on their first mission together. It was a desperate mission but they all were, one way or the other. Desperation made for motivation, according to the Trainers and their creed.

Absalom leaned forward and turned his face toward his two friends. "Are you frightened?" he whispered.

"Terrified," Dion said.

"Completely," Lucien said.

"Life is death," Absalom said.

"I hope not," Dion and Lucien replied in unison.

The three young Legionnaires smiled at the joke. They were well trained and prepared to die. To laugh in spite of doom, that was their strength.

"Silence in the ranks!" their decan roared. His name was Flaubert. Decan Flaubert stomped back to the three youths, who looked up at him with respectful, wide eyes. "Hear me, you three. You are the major foul-ups of my contu. If you fail me in any way, I will kill you with my bare hands. Do you understand?"

"Yes, Decan!" they shouted.

He slapped them on their helmets so hard their ears rang. "What is your one purpose in life?" he demanded.

"To kill for those who rent us, Decan!"

Decan Flaubert screwed his lips into the grimace that passed for a smile on his scarred mug. "Fine. Don't forget that and you will do well."

The ranking decan—a man named Mollet—opened a cylindrical container strapped to his waist and withdrew a photograph. He held it so every man could see it as he walked up and down the ranks. "You have seen the vids and pix of this woman many times. You should have her image embedded in your brain. She is our goal. She is the purpose of our contract. She is the reason you will kill. Do you understand?"

"Yes, Decan!" twenty-four men screamed.

"Her name is Maria Medaris. She is the spawn of the devil, the vilest of the vile. You will capture her if you can. If you can't, you will kill her upon my command or that of the other decans. Understood?"

"Yes, Decan!"

"Prepared and ready?"

"Yes, Decan!"

Decan Mollet nodded to Decan Flaubert of the spiderwalkers and Decan Nicolas of the light infantry. They nodded back and then all three sat down and strapped in. Absalom, Lucien, and Dion surreptitiously touched gloves.

The transports, their engines hot, lifted off, bound for space.

::: EIGHTEEN

The *Moontown Scrapes* told the news. The murdering crowhopper, tried and convicted, was sentenced to a dust walk. For the edification of newbies in town, the paper described what a dust walk for the crowhopper would be like. After a reading of the charges and the sentence, the felon would be shoved outside a dustlock wearing an old pressure suit and an hour's worth of air in its pack. All hatches would be locked for the next hour. The creature's choices would be few. It could strike out across the dust in an attempt to find shelter before its air ran out, or it could sit quietly until it died of asphyxiation. Of the two Moontown men and one woman, all three convicted murderers, who'd been sent on a dust walk, one of the men had gone wandering, his body later found in the dust less than a mile away. The other man, within minutes of being put outside, had pulled the latch loose on his helmet. The woman chose to sit outside the dustlock and keep breathing until she ran out of air. No one, in all the history of the moon, had ever survived a dust walk.

Crater read the article in the jumpcar hangar office. He

tossed his reader down and went out on the mooncrete floor where the jumpcar sat, held in a vertical hardstand. The jumpcar had been hauled into the pressurized hangar for a series of required tests. Riley had the engine hatch open and was monitoring the spark in the igniters. For a long second, he admired the jumpcar that he had come to love. Then he shook his head and allowed a sigh. "If anybody needs me," he said, "I'll be at the Colonel's office."

"Yes, sir," Riley said. "And when will ye be back now?"

"As soon as I can."

"Is it your creature, sir?"

"Her name is Crescent."

"Sorry, sir. Is it Crescent, then?"

"Yes."

"'Tis a terrible unfair thing. Just me opinion, of course."

"Well, you're right, Riley, but thank you."

"If I can do something to help, just tell me."

"I will, thank you," Crater said, then pushed through the hatch into the main tube and headed for the Colonel's suite of offices. He had no choice but to confront the Colonel. If anybody could relax his own rules, it was the dictator of Moontown.

The Colonel had a new receptionist, a doe-eyed brunette from Hong Kong. "Do you have an appointment, sir?" she asked, her voice sweet as biovat honey. Crater ignored her and threw open the Colonel's massive door. The Colonel looked up as Crater walked in. After a moment of confusion, he said, "I don't recall asking my pilot to appear in front of me. What do you want?"

"Mercy for Crescent."

"Your murdering creature?"

"She's a young woman, Colonel, and she's innocent."

"A crowhopper is not human," the Colonel said. "As for her innocence, she murdered one of my deputies."

"If she killed him, she had just cause."

"If she killed him, she must be punished no matter why she did it. That is my rule."

Crater glanced at the placard on the Colonel's desk that read "*De inimico non loquaris sed cogites,*" which meant "Do not wish ill for your enemy. Plan it." "There are extenuating circumstances in this case, Colonel. For one, there was Phenolune in Crescent's system. For another—"

The Colonel cut him off. "I stopped listening at 'extenuating circumstances.' Lawyerly talk is forbidden in Moontown, as you well know. Say what you mean, mean what you say. But let me say it for you. Deputy Jones was a vicious knave, worse than even you know, who deserved killing. Your creature accomplished a good thing in ridding Moontown of him. However, I can't let it wander my tubeways after it has killed. Think how frightened our tubewives and tubehusbands would be for their children."

"Sir, if you will spare her," Crater said, "I will go to every manjack and womanjill in Moontown and promise them Crescent will be under my personal control at all times."

The Colonel was unmoved. "I'm sure you're sincere, Crater, but no. It was tried, convicted, and sentenced, all properly done."

"I would be willing to make a trade for her life, sir."

The Colonel raised his eyebrows. "And what could you possibly have that would be worthy of such a trade?"

"My invention for gathering water from moon dust."

"Interesting. I thought it wasn't ready."

"It's not. But it's all I have."

The Colonel shook his head. "You don't have it. I do. Anything built in one of my labs belongs to me. Everyone who works in Moontown signs a contract. You did too, when you started working on the scrapes. What were you? Twelve? No matter. There's nothing you've done in that lab I don't know about. As for your safe, the sheriff picked its lock within a week of you building it. It pleases me to let you work on your invention, but if you stopped, I'd put my best engineers on it."

"You would steal my invention?"

"I just told you it's mine, not yours."

Crater tried a different tack. "What if I proved Crescent didn't kill the deputy? That somebody else did?"

"How do you propose to do that?"

"I will look for evidence."

"Evidence is lawyerly talk."

"Can't you bend just once in your life?"

The Colonel made a long ponder of Crater, then grunted and shook his head. "I can see you're not going to be happy until I give a little in this matter. Never it let be said that Colonel John H. E. Medaris lets his employees go around being unhappy. Go find your evidence, if it exists, and I will consider it. You have a week. Now, go away. I have work to do and so do you."

It was as good a deal as Crater was likely to get. Before the Colonel could change his mind, he left. The Colonel soon followed him, strolling out into the anteroom. "Abigail, that boy is going to drive me crazy someday."

"He seems like a nice boy, sir."

"That's his entire problem," the Colonel said. "And yours too. Before Crater ever got close to my door, you should have tackled him. I hope you enjoy your new job as a company store clerk."

::: NINETEEN

How to prove Crescent was innocent? Crater called Riley and told her he would be gone for the rest of the day, then headed for the kitchen to see Q-Bess. He found her making ice cream in an old-fashioned churn.

"I've just come from the Colonel. He's given me a week to prove Crescent innocent."

Q-Bess took her hand off the churn crank and extended it. "Oh, bless you, child!"

Crater took her hand. "I'm just getting started. I've never been a detective before."

"You are the smartest person in Moontown," Q-Bess said. "You will fix this. I know you will."

Crater wished he had the same confidence. "I need to ask you something," he said. "How did you find out the sheriff had arrested Crescent?"

Q-Bess took her hand back and rested it on the churn. "Well, let me see. It was Kurto who told me. He was up late, baking pies for the morning. He knocked on my door and told me the sheriff had Crescent in the cafeteria. I dressed, went to see about it, and then came after you."

"How did the sheriff know Jones was killed?"

Q-Bess looked thoughtful, then said, "I have no idea."

"Did Crescent say anything to you at all about this?"

"Well, she knew the deputy was stalking her. I know she was afraid of him. It took that Phenolune to get her down into the biovats. Otherwise, she'd have never gone willingly."

"Was there any evidence of anybody cleaning up biogoop on the steps or anywhere else?"

"Not a bit. It's really sticky. I went down there before they carried the deputy away. There was not a drop to be seen on the steps. It would have taken a dozen maids and lots of soap and water to get it that clean. There just wasn't time to do it."

Crater gave that some thought, then said, "I think the deputy was dumped into the biovat after he was unconscious, maybe even after he was dead. Crescent was under the influence of Phenolune. She's strong, but I don't think she could have picked up the deputy and slid him into that tank without causing at least a little goop slopping out."

Q-Bess shook her head. "Of course, there had to be more to it than what the sheriff said. But why didn't Crescent just tell us she didn't do it?"

"I don't know. I hope to be able to visit her and ask her that."

Q-Bess dabbed her eyes with her apron. "Oh, Crater, I've tried to see her but they've got her locked away."

Crater walked to the hatch. "Don't give up hope."

"Where are you going?"

"To interrogate the sheriff."

"Be careful. He's dangerous."

"So am I."

Crater went to see the sheriff. After checking at his office and finding it empty, Crater walked along the main tubeway until he spotted the sheriff coming out of the company dentist's office. He did not look happy. He was rubbing his jaw and carrying a small black bag. "Could I ask you a question, sheriff?"

The sheriff held up the bag. "You know what this is, Crater? It's a sonic machine. I'm losing bone in my jaw because of the moon's low gravity and I'm supposed to vibrate it an hour every day with this contraption. What a nuisance this low gravity is. What do you want?"

"How did you find out about Deputy Jones?"

"I heard your creature got a few extra days for you to play detective. I wouldn't waste my time. She's guilty and that's it." The sheriff moved his jaw a few times, then said, "Deputy Zageev told me about Deputy Jones."

"How did he know about Jones?"

The sheriff scratched up under his cap. "Now that you mention it, I never asked him. Perhaps he received an anonymous call. You should ask Zageev."

"Shouldn't you ask him?"

"I should if I cared but I don't. Look, Crater, what does it matter? Your monster's confessed."

"No, she didn't. She just said Jones deserved what he got."

"Isn't that the same thing?"

"You know it isn't."

The sheriff rubbed his jaw again, then shrugged. "I'm walking to my office now. Alone."

Crater didn't follow the sheriff but sought out Deputy Zageev. He found him on guard duty, sitting on a stool at the company bank. "How did you find out Jones was murdered?" Crater asked.

Zageev regarded Crater nonchalantly. "Do you have any concept how foolish it is to guard this bank?"

"How did you find out Deputy Jones was murdered?" Crater asked again.

"It's not as if anybody in this town would try to rob their own bank," Zageev said, shaking his head. "Did you ask how I found out Jones was murdered?"

"Yes, the sheriff said you told him. How did you know?"

Zageev looked up at the bank tube ceiling, apparently forming his thoughts or perhaps putting together his lie, then brought his eyes back to Crater and said, "Deputy Jones was supposed to work the overnight watch in the main tube. I had the evening watch. When he didn't come to replace me, I tried to call him but got no answer. So I went looking for him in his tube but he wasn't there. I kept looking, then I saw Chef Kurto at the company store. He has his own key so he can pick up supplies for late-night baking. I asked him if he'd seen Deputy Jones and he said he had passed him not far from the Dust Palace. I tried to call Jones again, still got no answer, so I went to the Dust Palace and saw the door to the biovats ajar. I went down and found Jones afloat in biovat number twelve. I called the sheriff straightaway."

Crater thought the deputy's story sounded plausible but a little too perfect. "Did you notice Jones had a broken nose and scrapes on his knuckles?"

"He was facedown, so no, I didn't. By the way, you know who Jones was, don't you?"

When Crater's frown provided the answer, Zageev smiled. "You're a pretty poor detective. Deputy Jones was Josef Warto, the former president of the Democratic Republic of Centropia."

A faint bell rang in Crater's mind. "Didn't he kill about half the people in his country?"

"Yes, the half that were the ethnic nationality known as Tovars. He nationalized all businesses and the economy completely collapsed. Then he nationalized the farms. The famines were extensive. He also sponsored gladiator games."

"Gladiators? Like in Rome?"

"Yes, except Warto had thousands of Tovars with rifles up against tanks, machine guns, and artillery. It was one massacre after another. He put the battles on live vid."

"How did he end up on the moon?"

"His own people tried to assassinate him, but he escaped and ran down here. The Colonel gave him a job as a scragline picker, but the sheriff apparently saw his potential and made him a deputy."

"His potential?"

"Likely his Franco-Swiss bank account."

"So the sheriff had a reason to see Jones dead."

"Barking up the wrong tree on that one," Zageev said. "If I know the sheriff, he squeezed Jones dry long ago."

"How about you, Deputy? How'd you get this job? Were you also the dictator of a small country?"

"Hardly!" Zageev chuckled. "I was just a lowly cop back on Earth. When I lost my job—the result of a small bribe from the wrong person at the wrong time—I came here. As a law enforcement officer who's done some investigating in my time, let me give you some advice. If I were you, I would track Jones's movements the evening of his death and I'd start with the Earthrise Bar & Grill. He was almost always there when he was off duty. But listen, Crater, why bother? Your monster's confessed."

"No, she hasn't. She only said Jones deserved killing. The Colonel said if I could prove she didn't do it, he would let her go."

"You are a trusting lad," Zageev said.

"Thank you."

"It wasn't a compliment."

Crater headed to the Earthrise. It was misnamed, of course, because the Earth never rose on the moon but stayed pretty much at the same point in the sky. The original owner of the bar, however, liked the name and didn't let the facts get in his way. The barkeep on duty, a retired miner who called himself Simply Will, remembered Deputy Jones very well from the evening prior to his death, mainly because he had broken a pool cue over the deputy's head. "He got in a fight with some fellow about something. Jones was a hothead. To slow him down, I smacked him with the pool cue. He was also a hardhead because the cue broke in two."

Crater recalled the deputy's wounds—skinned knuckles, a broken nose, bumps and a scab on his head. A cue stick certainly could have provided one of the bumps and probably some bleeding too. "Did you also bust his nose?" Crater asked.

"I don't know anything about a busted nose."

"Who was he fighting with?"

"Viking Val."

Viking Val was a sundancer, a miner who worked with the solar arrays, shakers, and furnaces that separated the Helium-3 from the dust. Crater thanked Simply Will and went outside to find Val. He found him monitoring the shaker pan on array number eighteen. He was a big fellow—jutting jaw, blue eyes, and blond hair pulled back in a ponytail. "Ya, we had a bit of a knockdown that evening," Viking Val acknowledged. "Deputy Jones, he was a very bad man. He said t'ings I could not abide. So I hit him and then he tried to hit me but

I ducked and he struck the wall with his fist instead. Then he tried to butt me and I stepped aside and he hit the bar with his head. The bar is made out of mooncrete, you know."

All this explains the scrapes on the deputy's knuckles, Crater thought, *and the head bumps and the scab on his scalp.* "What things did he say that you couldn't abide?" he asked.

"He say Viking men is stupid, Viking women is more stupid and also ugly. So I hit him hard."

"Did you break his nose?"

"No, I knock him side of his head, not nose. The barkeep, he broke a pool cue over the deputy's head and then we stopped fighting."

"Where did he go after that?"

"Go? He go nowhere. He sit down and we drink. We both get very drunk."

"Did you talk about anything?"

"Shovelball. He loved shovelball. He also went on about how much he wanted a wife. Said no woman in Moontown liked him and he didn't like them either, except for maybe one."

"Did he say which one?"

"Sure. That ugly little crowhopper what killed him."

"We don't know who killed him," Crater said. "Do you know who broke his nose?"

"I only know it wasn't me."

Crater got little else from Viking Val so he went looking for Deputy Zageev again, finding him this time loitering at the company store. He looked unhappy. "What's wrong?" Crater asked.

"Everybody's too honest around here. I haven't pinched anybody in ages."

"I'm sorry," Crater said, then told him what he'd discovered from Viking Val. "I still don't know how he got his nose broken," Crater added. "Wonder where he went after the Earthrise?"

"Probably to his tube," the deputy said.

"Could I visit it?"

"I don't see why not. I'll even take you there. Doesn't look like this crowd's going to do anything criminal."

Crater noticed Abigail, the Colonel's executive assistant, standing forlornly behind a counter that contained work gloves. "Why are you here?" he asked.

Her eyes went hard. "Because of you."

"Because I barged in? You couldn't have stopped me. Ten scrag pickers couldn't have stopped me."

"That was not the opinion of the Colonel. But you know what? I'm glad I got fired. It was going to happen eventually anyway. The lifespan of his executive assistants is only about six weeks. I calculated it. Here at the store, I have much nicer people to talk to."

"Well, I'm sorry for what happened. I sincerely apologize."

"That's nice of you. The Colonel said that was your entire problem, that you were too nice."

Crater frowned. "I'm not all that nice."

She shrugged. "Let me know if you need a new pair of work gloves."

"What was that all about?" Zageev asked as he and Crater walked out of the store into the main tube.

"I got that woman fired."

"Let's see. One girl—and I use that term loosely—you brought here is going to be executed. Another, you got fired. You're not exactly good with women, are you?"

"No," Crater confessed.

"Well, most men aren't," Zageev said. "Including me and every manjack you see walking these tubes."

Deputy Jones's tube was not far from the edge of the commercial sector so it was a short walk from the company store. Zageev opened the hatch, stepped in, and turned on the lights. Crater followed. The sink was piled high with dirty dishes. Clothing was strewn everywhere. The furniture was grimy. "This place is a mess," Crater said.

"Yeah, looks like somebody turned it over, don't it? But this is just the way Jones lived. With five million people as his personal servants, I guess he wasn't used to picking up after himself."

"Puter, turn on the wall vid," Crater said to the tube computer and the shovelball channel came up.

"Jones loved his shovelball," Zageev said.

"That's what Viking Val said too." Crater spotted the corner of a reader protruding from beneath a pile of dirty clothes on the couch. "Is this his reader?"

"See if his name's on it," Zageev said.

Crater drew the reader from beneath the laundry. It had *Deputy C. L. Jones* lettered on its cover. Crater checked its history, finding several disreputable sites Jones had recently visited. He'd also looked up the Moontown Scrapers shovelball practice schedule. Crater showed it to Zageev. "Guess you should visit the shovelball practice field," Zageev said.

"You're not going with me?"

Zageev was into Jones's refrigerator, loading a plaston bag with beers. "This is your investigation, not mine," he said over his shoulder. "But have fun, Detective Trueblood."

The Moontown shovelball practice field was in an abandoned maintenance facility on the south side of town. When Crater walked on the field, the coach was overjoyed. "You come to join the team? We'll win the trophy if you do."

Crater hated to disappoint the coach but he did anyway. "Sorry, no. Wish I had time but I don't. I'm investigating something for, um, the Colonel. Did you know the late Deputy Jones?"

"President-for-life Warto? Yeah, I knew him. He was always trying to get my guys to throw games or shave points."

"Did he succeed?"

"Probably. That's why when he stuck his big nose in the huddle night before last, I hit him with a shovel. Oh, I made it look like an accident, but I got him good and down he went."

"Did you break his nose?"

"Naw. I walloped him on the back of the head. That old man was tough, I'll give him that. He walked off on his own power."

Crater was beginning to wonder how the deputy had lived long enough to be murdered. "Anything else you remember?"

"I remember what a good shovelball player you are. Sure you won't join the team?"

"Not now, but thanks, Coach."

"How about giving these clodhoppers a demonstration?"

Crater didn't have time for it but he couldn't resist. "Give me a shovel and serve it up," he said.

"I'll pick four of my scrubs to be on your team."

"I don't need them. Put your best five out there and I'll take them all on."

The rules for shovelball were simple. The shovels were replicas of normal scrape shovels except made stronger around the neck. The ball was four inches in diameter. Goals were nets six feet in diameter halfway up the end walls. Full pipe ramps led to the roof. The ball could be advanced by either hitting the ball with the shovel or bounced on the shovel while running. The coach served up the ball and Crater leaped high, caught the ball on his shovel, then looped it toward the roof. While the team reacted to the ball, jumping for it, Crater ran up a pipe and emerged upside down on the roof, his momentum carrying him forward. He caught the ball before any other player could reach it and swatted it. In a blur, the ball zoomed to the goal. When the goalie tipped it with his shovel, Crater barged through the other players and knocked it in for the score.

He handed the coach the borrowed shovel. "Thanks. That was fun."

The coach and the Moontown team, their jaws slack, watched him as he walked from the field.

"Coach?" one of the players asked. "Who is that?"

"Crater Trueblood."

"Really? He's like a legend."

The coach nodded. "Yes, he is. Now I know why."

Crater ducked out through the hatch.

::: TWENTY

rater visited his mother in her room. She sat on her throne. "They are not men of good will," Q-Bess said. "No matter what you do, the Colonel and his sheriff intend to see Crescent dead."

"Have you thought of talking to the Colonel?" Crater asked.

Q-Bess looked ashamed, then told him about Petro and the threat the sheriff had made in behalf of the Colonel. "I don't really think the Colonel would deliberately hurt Petro," Q-Bess said, "but he might subconsciously put him in harm's way. I can't risk that. I have thought of something you might do." She told him what it was.

Crater was a bit shocked. "If anyone found out," he said, "I would be fired. Perhaps even exiled."

"I know," Q-Bess said. "It's a lot to ask of you. I know you love what you do and you love Moontown. It is a hard choice, Crater. Do what you think is best."

"How will I know what is best, Mother?"

"By what seems right to you."

"Is it ever right to steal?"

"Never," said Q-Bess.

"And yet . . ."

She nodded gravely. "And yet to not steal in this case . . ."

"Let me think about it."

Q-Bess nodded. "As always, Crater. Now, go. The creation of this plan has left me much fatigued. I must rest from it."

Crater bowed, then left. His thinking was complete by the time he was through the Dust Palace hatch. He headed for his dustlock. It was between scrape shifts so no dusties were on duty. He selected a convoy backpack, then slapped a red maintenance tag on it. If anyone saw him with it, they would assume he was carrying it to the repair shop. Carrying the pack along with a bag containing his outside gear, he headed for the east maintenance shed where his fastbug was stored in a mooncrete truck shelter. After registering with the dispatcher, he exited through the shed's dustlock, opened the shelter, then drove his fastbug onto the dust. After loading it, he drove to the Copperhead Bridge that spanned the rille of the same name and then drove back again. He garaged the fastbug in the shelter, then went inside to log out. He keyed in the necessary information, then asked the dispatcher, "Do you have a pencil?"

The dispatcher, a little man with old-fashioned wire spectacles, raised his eyebrows. "A what?"

"A pencil. You know, to write with? Most dispatchers have at least one around."

His moustache twitched. "Maybe the previous dispatcher, but not me. Let me look in the junk drawer." He leaned over and dug into a cluttered drawer. "What do you know?" he said after stirring the contents around. He held aloft a stubby yellow pencil. "The old fellow left one behind."

"Perfect. How about a scrap of paper?"

"You don't ask for much," the dispatcher grumbled. He scratched his head, then brightened. "How about a paper bag? I got a couple of those. Company on Earth still uses them to ship peanuts in."

"That will do fine."

The dispatcher got off his chair and opened a locker, then carried back a grease-stained brown paper bag. "You gonna write something? Kind of a lost art, isn't it?"

"It is," Crater said, then tore a scrap off the bag, went to an empty counter and wrote on it, tucked the scrap in his pocket, then returned the pencil to the dispatcher. "Thanks a lot."

"You're welcome. People used to do that, didn't they? Write notes by hand?"

"They did. They'd write them, put them in an envelope, and send them to people anywhere in the world. Sometimes it took weeks before an answer came back, but according to the history books, it worked pretty well."

The dispatcher tossed the pencil back into the cluttered drawer. "Well, I was never much for history. I'll stick to the puters."

"If your puter ever goes down, you can use that pencil to keep track of things on your paper bags."

"I never thought of that. Problem is I can type but I never learned to write by hand."

"Never too late to learn," Crater advised, then headed for the sheriff's office. At the entrance hatch was a dozing deputy, a skinny fellow named Campos. He was leaned back in a chair, his cap over his eyes. Crater ignored him and pushed through the hatch where he found the sheriff also dozing, his boots up on his desk and his hands clasped over his ample belly. Crater eased around him and opened one by one the drawers in the desk until he found what he was looking for. He then touched him on his shoulder, which had the happy result of the sheriff jerking awake, swinging his boots to the floor with a crash, and crying out, "Don't kill me! I wasn't the snitch! T'was someone else!"

"It's just me, Sheriff," Crater said. "Nothing to fear."

The sheriff blinked at Crater, then moved his shoulders around as if rearranging his body to a different place. "Of course it's you. Fear? I'm not fearful of anything. I'm the sheriff. People fear me." He gulped. "Don't they?"

"Yes, sir, they do. I'm heartily sorry to interrupt your busy day, but Q-Bess sent me to remind you of your bill."

The sheriff's eyes narrowed. "What bill?"

"Check your puter. It's all there. Under company debt."

The sheriff eyed Crater suspiciously, then clicked the necessary keys. "A large number," he concluded. "There must be a mistake."

"No mistake, Sheriff. Q-Bess has kept track of what food and drink you and your deputies have taken from the cafeteria since your appointment as sheriff. By the Colonel's rules, all expenditures at the Dust Palace must be accounted for. She has vids of all these unpaid transactions, of course."

The sheriff leaned back in his chair. "There is more to this. What does Q-Bess want?"

Crater shrugged. "She just wants to be paid. When will you send the funds over?"

"Never. I'll go to the Colonel about this."

"Are you sure you want to do that? Even if the Colonel wipes the slate clean, he will probably tell you to pay for your food and drink in the Dust Palace from now on. Do you want that to happen?"

The sheriff rocked in his chair. "Despite your denial, I think you and Q-Bess want something else."

Crater shrugged. "Well . . ."

The sheriff sighed. "Let's hear it."

"I want to see Crescent."

The sheriff processed Crater's request. "For what purpose?"

"I need to apologize. After all, she wouldn't be in this mess if I hadn't brought her back to Moontown." He dug into a pocket on his tunic and drew out the phoenix pendant with a new chain. "And I want to give her this."

"How did you get that?"

"I took it from your desk while you were asleep. It's important to Crescent. If she's going to die, she ought to have it."

The sheriff frowned. "Frankly, I think this is a ruse. I suspect you mean to help her escape."

"How could I help her escape? I'm certain you have recorders all over her tube, not to mention vidcams. You'll hear and see everything I say and do."

"True," the sheriff conceded. He drummed his fingers on his desk, then shrugged. "All right. When do you want to do it?"

"Now."

"The charges on the puter?"

"Wiped out the moment I complete my visit."

The sheriff's eyes never left Crater. "Deputy Campos!"

There were scrambling noises followed by the sound of a chair turning over. Finally, the deputy appeared, his cap sitting askew. "You bellowed, Sheriff?"

"Careful, Deputy. You might find what it's like to work as a scragline picker. Wake up and take Crater along to see the creature. Stay with him the entire time."

"It'll be awkward with Deputy Campos hanging over my

shoulder," Crater said. "You can watch the vids later. There's no way I can get away with anything."

The sheriff studied Crater's innocent face for a long second, then said, "Deputy, pat Crater down before he goes inside. He is not to carry anything with him save that chain and pendant he's holding. Then stay outside the door until he leaves." The sheriff glanced at Crater. "Ten minutes. No more."

"That's all I need. Thank you, Sheriff."

"Nothing nefarious, hear?"

"It is well known that I am an honest man," Crater replied.

"You just rifled my desk."

"But I told you about it."

The sheriff pointed a finger at him. "If you do anything to help your monster escape, you will regret it for the rest of your life."

"I'm certain of that. Nobody can do your job better than you."

"Thank you."

"It wasn't a compliment," Crater muttered under his breath as he turned and walked out of the office and past the deputy. Campos hurried to catch up. "I'm supposed to take you there."

"I know my way, Deputy. I grew up in these tubes."

"Really? I've been here six months and this place is about to drive me nuts. Same tubes, same people, day after day."

"It grows on you," Crater said and kept walking, the deputy sheepishly following.

At the tube where Crescent was housed, the deputy patted Crater down, then waited at the hatch while Crater went inside. He found Crescent watching a black-and-white movie on the vidputer. "I thought never to see you again," she said, looking up.

"Q-Bess misses you and so do I. She sends her love. What are you watching?"

"*Citizen Kane.* The best movie ever according to the reviewers. It's okay, I guess."

"Well, you're almost at the end. Go ahead and watch it. I'll fix us some tea. You like tea, don't you?"

"Yes, very much."

While Crescent watched the end of her movie, Crater glanced around before going to the kitchen. The tube that was her prison was a pleasantly furnished one, painted a cheerful, sunny yellow, the plaston furniture cushioned and comfortable. It also had four security vidcams that were exactly where they were supposed to be, that knowledge gained by an easy hack into Moontown's security system using the passwords the gillie had provided him years ago. At the time, Crater had condemned the gillie for being a bad gillie but had kept the passwords just the same. He silently thanked the gillie for being bad and the sheriff for being too lazy to change the passwords.

The kitchen was modest but functional. He noted the location of the vidcam there, then got to work and soon had the tea pot whistling. He stooped down to a low cabinet for a tray, then placed the teapot, two cups, a bowl of sugar, and a container of milk on it. He carried the tray to a small table. The movie over, Crescent joined him there. "Is this all you do every day, Crescent? Watch movies?"

"There isn't much else to do," she said, "except when men come to ask me things."

"What kind of things do they ask?"

"They ask me how I was created, what my childhood was like, what kind of training I was given, and to name any names I might recall."

"What do you tell them?"

"I tell them what I remember although, like every Legionnaire, I was given a drug that makes me forget much of my early life."

"And what do they say about what you tell them?"

"Not much. They just smile and nod. I don't always know what humans are thinking because I can't read their expressions very well. You are the exception. Worry is written all over your face. What is it?"

"Crescent, I want you to know something. I've tried everything I can think of to find proof that you're innocent but I've come up short. Is there anything you can tell me about that night that might help?"

"The deputy deserved to die," she said.

"He deserved to be punished but did you kill him?"

Crescent said nothing, just looked at him with a fixed expression.

"I'm sorry I brought you here," Crater said. "If I had just left you where I found you, it would not have come to this."

"That is true."

He pulled the pendant and chain from his pocket and handed it to her. She took it and draped it around her neck. "Thank you. I missed it."

"Do you still consider me your enemy?"

"What difference does it make? You are you. I am me. I will die soon. You will live a little longer. We'll end up at the same place."

The deputy swung open the hatch. "Your ten minutes are up."

"We're not quite done with our tea," Crescent said. "Could he stay a little longer?"

The deputy shrugged and closed the hatch.

They had their tea quietly, until Crater said, "I've been rebuilding a fastbug. I drove it over to the Copperhead Bridge the other day."

"Was it fun?"

"It was very fun. I caught vacuum a few times by launching off crater rims."

"I wish I could do that."

The deputy swung the hatch open again. "All right. That's it or the sheriff will have my rear end."

Crater started to pick up the tray but Crescent stopped him. "It's okay. I'll clean up."

She walked with Crater to the hatch. "Don't give up hope," he said, then put out his hand.

Crescent looked at his hand, then grasped it. Her hand was rough and very strong. "Good-bye," she said. Crater was astonished when she leaned in and hugged him, her arms like steel bands. "I found you pleasant," she said, then turned away.

Outside, the deputy scratched up under his cap. "I thought that creature was going to crush you. You're braver than I am."

"She's just a girl."

"She's a monster."

Crater heard the deputy lock the hatch as he walked away.

::: **TWENTY-ONE**

For two weeks, the transport was forced to loiter in orbit until finally the warpod arrived. The transport docked to it and the Legionnaires, sticky boots on, filed off, entering a bay with a deck of aluminum plate. "Get used to it, gents," the ranking decan said. "It's your home for at least a month."

Lucien, Dion, and Absalom found a space near a spaghetti of conduit and humming electronics, doffed their packs, slapped them sticky side down, and hooked their boots through the straps to keep from floating away. "A month in this hole," Lucien moaned. "We shall all go mad."

Absalom produced a pack of sticky cards designed for weightless conditions from a pocket on the tunic that covered his armor. "We can while the time away with these."

"And play for what?" Lucien demanded. "We have no money."

"I will remember the amount you owe me and collect later."

"That will be in Hades." Dion laughed. "We won't live long enough to collect."

A veteran came over and slapped Dion on his helmet. "That kind of talk is forbidden," he growled.

Dion was not intimidated. "If that is so, Carillon," he said, "why did I hear you whimpering to the decan about needing more armor?"

"The armor I was issued is defective, sprout. Not that I should explain anything to you."

Absalom held up the deck of cards. "Could you explain how to play a game with these?"

Carillon squinted at the raw recruit. "Are you telling me you do not know how to play cards?"

"I know you're supposed to match them in some way with these odd symbols."

The veteran squatted and held out his hand. "Then I will demonstrate a game I just happen to know. It is called five-card stud poker. But to play it correctly, bets must be made. What do you have?"

Lucien, Absalom, and Dion all traded amused glances. They knew the game very well, of course. They had played it many times after being taught by their decan. Carillon, transferred in from a different contu, did not know that. "We have this," Absalom said, producing a small reader from his pocket. "We will keep track of these things you call bets."

"Put me down for one hundred johncredits to begin," Carillon said. "Each of you must put down the same."

Lucien pressed the reader, which had a sticky cover, to the aluminum deck. Carillon shuffled the cards and dealt them, one by one. An hour later all their johncredits were gone according to the marks on the reader. Carillon scratched up under his armor. "You will pay me as soon as we get back. If you don't, I will kill you."

Absalom studied Carillon. "What are you looking at, sprout?" he demanded.

"I am trying to figure out how you cheated."

"Who says I cheated?"

"I do. Lucien and Dion do too. We say you cheated because we also cheated and did not win. What is your trick?"

Carillon formed his lips into a misshapen smile. He reached in his pocket and produced a deck of cards. "We have been playing with my cards, not yours. I swapped them within seconds of you handing your deck to me. This does not change anything. You will still pay me."

"We will not pay," Lucien said, grabbing the cards from Carillon and throwing them across the room where they hung in the air like the fluttering wings of birds.

Carillon drew a huge elk sticker from a holster strapped to his leg. "I should kill you," he growled.

Decan Flaubert flew over and touched down on deck. "You know the rule, Carillon," he said. "If you draw a knife in anger, it must taste blood."

"That was my intention," Carillon said. "Which of you is to supply the blood for my elk sticker?"

Lucien, Dion, and Absalom drew back. Flaubert grabbed them by their armor and shoved them forward. "You will fight," he growled.

Reluctantly, the trio drew their knives. Carillon laughed and attacked. He kicked Lucien's knife away, elbowed Dion in the stomach, wrenched his knife away, then nicked Absalom's cheek. It all happened so fast, Absalom dropped his knife, which hung in the air, while he grabbed the bloody notch in his cheek. Decan Flaubert laughed. "Let that be a lesson to you sprouts. Don't fight Carillon. He is a poor excuse for a soldier at times, but he knows his moves."

Carillon held up the elk sticker, which had a drop of blood on its tip. "Does this satisfy the rule, Decan?"

"It does, Carillon." He studied Dion, Absalom, and Lucien who had drawn together. "You are to keep away from these three scragheads for the remainder of this mission. Do you hear?"

Carillon knuckled his forehead. "I will comply, Decan."

Flaubert shook his head. "If so, it will be the first time."

After Decan Flaubert had gone back to huddle with the other two decans, Carillon waved the three young Legionnaires to a corner where they couldn't be seen. "Now, boys, bygones will be bygones, right? We're all in this together. You are well trained on spiderwalkers, yes? And I think you know how the walkers work much better than poor Carillon. Right?"

Lucien said, "Of course. We grew up playing spiderwalker games on the vids. We know the software and hardware as if we designed it ourselves."

"Good, good. I think you are also survivors. Is it not true?"

"We want to survive," Dion cautiously answered.

Carillon looked over his shoulder. The decans were involved in some deep conversation. He turned back to the trio. "This is a cheap-charlie mission," he said. "Scuttlebutt says the Trainers are being paid next to nothing for it. That means our cut will be very small. I prefer to save myself for another operation, one where the cut will be larger."

"We don't know anything about that," Lucien said.

"Well, you do now." Carillon leaned forward. "Do you know when most Legionnaires die?"

They shook their heads and Carillon said, "At the beginning of an operation and at the end. We must therefore be especially careful and intelligent during those times." He grinned, showing a gap in his teeth. "You will do what I tell you and we will live to fight not only for this cheap-charlie pay but for a bigger wad of johncredits in the future. Agreed?"

Lucien, Absalom, and Dion nodded eagerly.

rater's do4u buzzed him awake. "Sorry to bother ye, sir," Riley said, "but we have a high priority mission alert. The Colonel wants the jumpcar to lift off in thirty minutes."

Crater climbed out of bed and reached for his tunic. "What's up?"

"You're headed to Cleomedes. Your passenger is Doctor Laura Wilson. She's a cardio expert."

Cleomedes was located southeastward across the Caucasus Mountains and the Sea of Serenity, a distance of around six hundred miles. From liftoff to landing, it would take approximately twenty minutes. It would take a truck four days to make the same distance and that was on a fast convoy down the Helium-3 dustway. There was no established track to Cleomedes from Moontown.

Crater met the doctor in the hangar so no pressure suit was required. "What's the emergency, Doctor?" he asked.

"I'm not sure," she said. "My boss said they needed a consult in Cleomedes. I'm to see a Doctor Vankineni at their hospital. That's all I know."

"Sounds like you need to get there in a hurry."

"I heard you were into acrobatics." She patted her stomach. "Unless you want to clean up my breakfast, I suggest you keep the flight smooth."

"Got it, Doc. No acrobatics," Crater said, taking her bag. "Riley, see the doctor to her chair, would you? And stow her bag away too."

Riley took the bag and escorted the doctor up the ramp to the passenger compartment. Crater followed, climbing into the cockpit. Riley stuck her head through the cockpit hatch. "She's strapped in, sir, and her luggage is all set. Ye best keep an eye on that port vernier. Should be all right, but it came out marginal on the tests. I was going to replace it today."

"Will do," Crater said, turning to look at her over his shoulder. She had tucked her bountiful red hair beneath a work cap. It made her look all the more fetching. "You know, you can call me Crater when the other techies aren't around."

"T'wouldn't be right, sir. You being me boss and all." Her eyes were bright. "Maybe someday?"

Before Crater could answer, Riley disappeared below. He waited until he got a light that the outer hatch was closed and the ramp retracted, then called, "Ready for pad transport."

"Ready for pad transport, aye, sir," Riley responded. The huge hangar doors ponderously slid open and the jumpcar and its launch pad rolled into the airlock. The inner doors closed and the outer ones opened to the vacuum. The pad rolled outside, then stabilized itself with four legs that pushed out until they made contact with the dust.

"Pad ready for launch, sir," a techie, not Riley, said.

"Pad ready for launch," Crater said, then went through the checklist with the puter. He called up the tower, "Jumpcar one ready for launch."

"You're number one on the runway, Pilot Trueblood."

"Thank you. On my mark. Mark. Ten-nine-eight . . ."

Crater firewalled the throttles and the jumpcar lifted off as if it were on greased rails. He rotated the ship, watched the port vernier, and saw it was green ball all the way. At thirty miles altitude, he lowered the nose and saw the peaks of the Caucasus and the crater Calippas.

"Puter, turn off the auto navigator," Crater said.

Autonav off.

Crater preferred to navigate using landmarks. He flew down the northern edge of the Serenity dustbowl and lined up on the astonishing delta of drainage rilles called Rimii Daniell, a system that aimed like an arrow toward Cleomedes. Past the delta was the *Lacus Somniorium* or Lake of Dreams, a plain that had the deepest dust on the moon. Farther on was the remnant of the crater named Williams. Off to the north, he could make out the big well-formed twin craters, Atlas and Hercules. Within minutes, he was soaring over the battered Taurus Mountains and then *Lacus Bonitatis*, the Lake of Goodness, covered with huge boulders tossed there by asteroids smashing into the Tauruses. He pulled up a few miles and saw the domed city of Cleomedes right where it was supposed to be.

Prior to setting up his approach, Crater flew the jumpcar over the town to give the doctor a look at it, so different from Moontown's severe industrial design. Cleomedes's transparent geodesic domes covered parks and ponds, and there were many buildings above the surface, all painted bright colors, one of them a casino. Cleomedes was known as the "Lunar Las Vegas."

Crater called up Cleomedes control and requested permission to land. "Doctor on board," he added.

"Roger that, Moontown One," came the reply. "Do you want a hangar?"

"Roger. The doctor needs to get to the surgery in a hurry."

"Go to mobile pad eight, west field. Welcome to Cleomedes. Casino tokens may be purchased at the landing field."

Crater backed the jumpcar to a precision landing onto the designated mobile pad, then shut the engines down. He looked over his shoulder and saw Doctor Wilson on the couch, studying her reader. She looked up. "Thank you for the smooth flight," she said.

"You're welcome. We've landed on a mobile pad so no pressure suit is required after they've ported us into the hangar." He felt the jumpcar move. "There we go now. Just be a couple of minutes."

Crater watched the giant double doors of the hangar airlock slide open as the mobile pad crept ahead on its tracks. Once inside, the outer doors closed, the airlock was pressurized, and the inner doors opened and the mobile pad completed its journey. Crater climbed down from the cockpit, opened the hatch, and waited for the hangar ramp to arrive. "All ready, Doctor Wilson," Crater said.

"Thank you, Pilot Trueblood," she answered, tucking away the reader in a holding net.

Crater followed her down and saw the Cleomedes crew had already removed her bags. "I'll give you a call when I'm ready to go," she said.

"Okay, Doctor. Just let me know."

Doctor Wilson was met by a Cleomedes greenie and led to a hatch while Crater sought out the jumpcar ground crew. "Check the oil and top her off, please."

"High test or regular?" a techie asked, a standard old joke for ground crews.

"Pure liquid oxygen and hydrogen," Crater replied after pretending to chuckle. Then he asked, "Where's the best place to hang out while I'm waiting?"

"Depends on what you like to do," the techie answered. "Food and drink, there's the Retro Restaurant over on Augustus Street. Something a little stronger, there's the Upper Atmosphere Bar. Of course, there's the Casino. We got a lot of parks too. You like to fish? They keep the Paddlewheel Pond well stocked with lunabass. For a hotel, try the Roman. You have any johncredits? Cleomedes's expensive."

"I have a Moontown chit," Crater said.

"Lucky you."

Crater thanked the techie and, after an inspection walk-around of the jumpcar, entered the main tubeway, which was brightly lit and lined with shops. Unlike the Spartan tubes of Moontown, there were fountains that played water across modernistic sculptures of lunasteel. The aroma of the day was apparently chocolate, much stronger than the aromas of the day back home. Before long, he found himself in a small ice-cream shop where he purchased a chocolate and vanilla cone, then went outside to sit on a bench and watch people walk by. They appeared prosperous.

Afterward, he wandered into one of the park domes and sat down on a bench and enjoyed the beauty of the place, the delightful smell of the enriched soil, and the flowers and trees that sprouted from it. The solar lamps were warm on the back of his neck. He wanted to stretch out in the grass and take a nap, and before long, he gave into it. He dozed until his do4u chirped.

It was Doctor Wilson. "Sorry, Crater," she said. "Looks like you'd better find a place to overnight."

Crater thanked the doctor for letting him know, then hung up and asked one of the gardeners to give him directions to the Roman Hotel. This was done, and after a pleasant stroll through the clean and bustling streets, Crater came to a hatch with a sign that announced that he was at the entrance of Cleomedes's best and only hotel. He went inside, checked himself in, and dropped his bag at the tube assigned. Except for a brief foray for dinner at one of the tubeway hamburger stands and a visit to the jumpcar to make certain it was ready for flight, he spent the remainder of the evening there, watching a shovelball game on the vidputer. When he woke the next morning, there was no message from the doctor on his do4u. Breakfast was served in the hotel restaurant so that's where he went, then checked out. He walked around the shopping area, then had a seat on a bench. He called the doctor but got no response. He left a message and prepared to be bored for a little while.

Before long, the man who owned everything in Cleomedes, General Caesar Augustus Nero, dressed in a silver tunic, black leggings, and silver boots, walked by with an entourage of a dozen men and women following him. He was expounding on some topic, his arms waving as he talked, and a woman, cloaked in a maroon robe, walked beside him. Everyone was intently listening until they began to bump into one another because the general had stopped dead in his tracks to stare at Crater. "Is this the fastbug driver who beat my entry in the

Founder's Day race before the war? I am certain it is. Name and purpose, boy."

Crater stood out of respect. "Crater Trueblood, sir. I am the pilot of the Colonel's jumpcar, here to deliver Doctor Wilson to assist one of your surgeons."

"Bloody nice of the Colonel to send her too. Are you driving in the race this year?"

"I sincerely doubt it, sir," Crater said.

"Good. Maybe we'll have a chance. Now, join us. There is something I wish you to see." And with that General Nero walked on, the entourage picking up behind him.

The destination proved to be a casino being constructed beneath a huge dome. Crater was astonished at the size of it. He'd seen it as he'd flown in and noted it was twice the size of the other domes, but it wasn't until he was inside that its sheer grandeur was obvious.

While General Nero conversed with the construction foreman who'd come running, the woman in the maroon cloak approached Crater. When she let the hood of the cloak slide from her head, Crater was surprised to discover she was an Umlap. Her long arms and robust chest had all been masked by the cloak. She was a beautiful woman whose hair, long and lustrous, was as maroon as her robe. "The General would like a word," she said. "So, if you don't mind, will you wait here until he is ready?"

"Yes, ma'am," Crater said.

Her lips were also painted maroon and they turned down into a frown, which Crater knew meant she was pleased. She delicately proffered her hand. "I am Perpetually Hopeful, the General's wife."

Crater didn't know if he should bow or what he should do

so he simply nodded deferentially. "Wonderful to meet you, ma'am. I'm Crater Trueblood."

She frowned a little deeper, then nodded toward a mooncrete bench. "Sit. Rest. The General will be with you soon. Do you mind if I sit with you?"

Crater didn't mind at all. They sat and Crater gazed upward at the great dome. "I've never seen anything like this," he said.

"The General is a man of vision. Much as your Colonel Medaris, I'd say."

"The Colonel has his ways," Crater replied. "Are you from Baikal? I hope you don't mind me asking."

Baikal was the main Umlap settlement, or had been until a recent battle between its inhabitants had killed off its men. Umlaps were biologically designed to be hard workers, but the men could also be stubborn, crafty, and a little murderous. The women, by contrast, were generally intelligent and gentle.

Perpetually Hopeful nodded. "Yes, I am the sister of Queen No Nonsense Talker, whom you very nicely saved at Aristillus several years ago." She smiled, which meant she was about to say something unhappy. "I was once the wife of Hit Your Face."

This information caught Crater by surprise. Hit Your Face was a brute, having come by his name by performing the act often and well. He had been murdered by another Umlap by the name of Bad Haircut as Crater watched.

"Bad Haircut was my brother," Perpetually Hopeful went on to say. "Did you know him?"

"I knew him. He was a pretty fair mechanic."

She chuckled, the Umlap version of sobbing. "I miss him every day!"

Crater thought it best not to say anything else, mainly because Perpetually Hopeful was smiling and therefore sad.

She wiped her tears with the sleeve of her robe and brushed her hair back to reveal the hole she had for an ear. She touched it and the General abruptly finished his discussion with the construction foreman and came over. Crater stood. "This is an amazing place, sir," he said.

"Yes, it is," he answered. "Nothing like it in old Moontown, eh?" The General held out his hand. "Well, Crater, good to see you. If you ever want a job, I could use a boy—I should say man—like you. I have aspirations as great as the Colonel's, although in different ways. I would hire you in a second and you could name your own salary. For instance, I've heard you know quite a lot about hydraulics. Pumping water through Cleomedes is a great challenge, and I've yet to find an engineer who can get a grasp of it."

"I suppose I do know a bit about water," Crater said.

"You are being modest. We are very aware of your invention to retrieve water from moon dust. We hope it might go to market soon."

"It has a way to go," Crater said. "But I'm working on it."

"Good boy."

The General talked on for a little more, and then Perpetually Hopeful reminded him of an appointment. After some pleasant fare-thee-wells, he walked rapidly away, his entourage scurrying to catch up. Perpetually Hopeful remained behind. She studied him. "I sense there is something worrying you, Mr. Trueblood. Is it something I or the General has said or done?"

Umlap women were renowned for their near-telepathic ability to discern what others were thinking. "No, ma'am. Not at all. Especially you. There's nothing you could ever do to upset me."

Her face clouded over, which meant she was pleased. "Tell me what it is, then."

Crater told her about Crescent and her sentence of death and how he had investigated the situation but was having trouble proving her innocence. Perpetually Hopeful inclined her head, taking in the story, then said, "Murder and hate go hand in hand. If not the girl, who would have hated this bloody dictator enough to kill him?"

Crater gave that some thought. "I suppose anyone who was a Tovar. He murdered almost all of them."

"Well then, what of the Tovars in Moontown?"

Crater stared at her. "I never thought of that!"

"Sometimes a mystery requires an outsider to see clearly the path toward a solution."

"Is there a way to call a Moontown do4u?"

"Of course, but not with yours." She withdrew a do4u from her robes. "This one will call anywhere on the moon."

Crater gratefully took it from her, walked out of hearing distance from Perpetually Hopeful, and asked it to call Riley in Moontown. Riley answered. "Riley, this is Crater. Do something for me, will you? Go to the hangar puter and use the following code to access the personnel files from the main puter." He gave the number the gillie had stolen years before. "See if there are any Moontown citizens with the nationality of Tovar. I'll call you back in ten minutes."

"Aye, will do, sir," Riley said.

Crater waited with Perpetually Hopeful for ten minutes, which seemed an age to pass, then called Riley back. "It was most easy," she said. "There is only one Tovar in town. Kurto, the chef at the Dust Palace."

Crater thanked Riley, clicked off, then stood up. He handed

Perpetually Hopeful her do4u. "I must take my leave, ma'am," he said. "But I will never be able to thank you enough."

She rose, frowning in pleasure. "A promise to visit us in the future will be thanks enough."

Crater made the promise, then called the jumpcar techies to prepare the jumpcar and took off running for the hangar. He didn't wait for the ramp but clambered up the jumpcar ladder. Dropping into his chair, he called up the techies. "Prepare for launch, please," he said. "I'm in a bit of a hurry."

"Aren't you waiting for the doctor?" a techie asked.

"If she shows up, tell her to wait until I get back or look for another ride!"

As the mobile pad crawled out of the hangar, Crater went through his checklist. As soon as the pad stopped, he called for clearance. "You're number one on the runway, sir," came the reply.

Crater fired up the engines and jetted aloft, turned toward Moontown, and firewalled the throttles.

TWENTY-THREE

Crater rotated the jumpcar and backed down onto the Moontown mobile pad. He did a post flight while being transported into the hangar, then climbed down the ladder where Riley waited for him. "Thanks for everything, Riley," he said and tossed his helmet to her. "If I'm not back in a few hours, how about flying the jumpcar over to Cleomedes and picking up the doc?"

"Roger, wilco, sir, but do ye have a second now?" Riley asked.

"Later, okay?" Crater said and ducked through the hangar hatch, leaving her frowning after him. Crater loped through the tubeways, saying, "Sorry, ma'am," and "Excuse me, sir," to the tubewives and tubehusbands as he ran by. He arrived at the Colonel's office, surprising the new executive assistant, a young olive-skinned woman from Greater Israel. She rose to stop him. "See here, sir, you can't go in there!"

"Don't worry. He'll want to see me," Crater said and flung open the great door, only to find the office empty. He turned around as the assistant came up behind him. "Where is he?"

Her eyes were wide. "On the scrapes."

"Where on the scrapes?"

She took a step back. "I don't know."

Crater thought she was lying but he didn't have time to worm the truth out of her. "Thank you," he said, his inherent politeness asserting itself, then ran past her and headed for the sheriff's office only to find it empty too. He next headed for his assigned dustlock, climbed into his biolastic sheath, pulled on his suit and helmet, and went outside. He jumped aboard a fastbug and headed for the scrapes. There were eight of them being worked. It was on the fifth one that he found the Colonel.

The Colonel was dressed in the white coveralls of a supervisor as were the two men accompanying him. "Sir, a word, if you don't mind."

"I am inspecting this scrape at the moment, Crater," the Colonel said. "Make an appointment."

"This is very important, sir."

"So are the scrapes," he said. "I'm doing my job. Now, go away and do yours."

"Colonel, you said that if I could produce evidence showing Crescent innocent, you'd let her go. I want to tell you what I've found out."

The Colonel sighed. "Go to my private channel." When that was done, the Colonel said, "I should have known it was about that barbaric creature."

"Colonel, do you know who Deputy Jones was back on Earth?"

The Colonel's eyes turned frosty. "President Warto of Centropia. I didn't know that until after I'd hired him. He covered his tracks very well."

"Even though you knew he killed millions of people, you kept him on your payroll?"

"Actually, at the time of his murder, I was considering how to rid myself of him."

"Do you know who else in Moontown is from Centropia?"

"No, I don't," the Colonel replied with a sigh, "but I suppose you do."

"Kurto, the chef at the Dust Palace. He's also a Tovar, the people Warto all but wiped out. According to Deputy Zageev, the night Warto died, Kurto told him that Warto was seen near the Dust Palace. When Zageev went looking for him, he found him in the chicken goop. I think what actually happened was Kurto spotted the dictator at the Dust Palace, saw what he was doing with Crescent, and took the opportunity to kill him. Then Zageev came over and helped him clean up the mess."

"Why would he do that?"

"He and Kurto are friends."

"So you're saying these two fine men, both of whom work hard at their jobs, therefore supporting my production schedule in their own way, are so craven they would let your creature take the blame?"

Crater hadn't thought about that although he supposed it was so.

The Colonel allowed a long sigh. "Not that it matters now, of course."

"Of course it matters, sir. This is about Crescent's life."

The Colonel shook his head. "I believe I have mentioned to you before that you have this soft side about you that severely needs toughening up. Oh, you've performed admirably in combat but I'm talking about mental toughness, that which allows you to see past the sentimentality of any particular situation to the sometimes cruel realities of life. Now, listen to me carefully, Crater, because I'm going to say this but once. That little crowhopper was a lot of trouble and I think it would have eventually killed somebody. That you brought it to Moontown was a mistake, so all this is your fault, not mine. You placed the people of Moontown in jeopardy, which therefore put my production schedule into jeopardy. That had to be addressed and so it has. It's all done now, so you need no longer concern yourself."

"What's done now?"

"Your creature has gone into the dust."

Crater's heart thumped. "When?"

"Yesterday morning."

"Yesterday morning? You sent me away deliberately!"

"Not at all. It was a real emergency, but it was a coincidence I took advantage of, knowing that you might make a scene. But never mind that, Crater. It's amazing how you go off in tangents. What's done is done. It's time we both got back to work."

Crater wanted to pound the Colonel until his face was a bloody pulp but he knew he wasn't going to, partly because he knew it wouldn't do any good. "What time did you put her out?" he asked.

"Around ten in the morning, I believe."

"Where did she go?"

"Where? I have no idea. Wherever the air in its pack could take it, I suppose. We'll find it out there sooner or later. The important thing is it was let out into the dust with dignity. I even quoted to the thing from Romans, as if it deserved to hear holy scriptures. One of my favorites. 'If you do wrong, be afraid, for rulers do not bear the sword for no reason. They are God's servants, agents of wrath to bring punishment on the wrongdoer.' Yes, a great verse, that one. By the way, go this instant to pick up the doctor. Afterward, I will need you to fly me to Armstrong City this afternoon."

Crater ignored the Colonel and focused on a quick calculation. Crescent had been outside for twenty-seven hours and therefore, based on the limited duration pack she'd been given, had been dead for twenty-six. Crater ran to the fastbug, jumped in and floored the accelerator, its wheels spinning twin rooster tails.

The Colonel was showered by dust. "Crater!" the Colonel yelled. "Come back here!"

Crater had the hammer down. He drove up the side of a crater and vaulted nearly a hundred feet into the vacuum, landing hard. At the dustlock, he jammed on the brakes and skidded to a shuddering, dust-spraying stop, jumped out, pulled open the hatch, pressurized the airlock, then threw open the hatch leading to the showers and lockers. He stripped off his gear while shouting for the dustie, who came running. "You yelled, sir?"

"I need you to get two long-endurance convoy packs ready. I'll be back in thirty minutes to get them."

"But, sir—"

"Thirty minutes!"

Crater threw on his tunic and leggings and burst through the final hatch into the main tubeway. When he reached the Dust Palace, he went straight to the kitchen, finding Kurto there. "I need to talk to you privately," he said and nodded toward the pantry.

With the pantry hatch closed behind them, Crater said, "I know where you're from. You killed Warto and let Crescent take the blame!"

"Not so," Kurto replied calmly. "I find Warto in chicken goop and call Zageev. He come, happy for me at the death of this awful man, then he call sheriff."

Crater studied the cook's face. "Did he have a broken nose when you found him?"

"Zageev and me, we think Crescent, she hit him hard on the face. That made me happy."

Crater kept studying the cook, but all he saw was sincerity. "If you're lying to me, I can't tell."

"If I lie, what difference? Warto is dead. Crescent, she confess. Now she dead."

"She didn't confess!"

Kurto made a helpless gesture, then went back to work while Crater sought out Q-Bess in her tube. He rang the bell, then went inside, finding her sitting on the mooncrete throne that someone had constructed for her. It had lions and unicorns carved in its back and had purple cushions. Her face was clouded, her makeup smeared, her eyes red from crying. She gasped at the sight of him. "My darling boy. How awful the news! I tried to call you but the comm people said you were in Cleomedes."

"I was sent there deliberately."

"As I suspected." She waved him to a gilded chair. "Come, sit with me, Crater. Let us mourn Crescent."

"There's no time," Crater said. "I have to go look for her."

"Her body will be found in due time."

"There may not be a body."

Q-Bess's swollen eyes widened. "Ah, you did it, then."

"I did. Whether it worked or not, I don't know."

"You're an awful sneak, Crater Trueblood."

"I'm sorry."

"Don't be. It was a compliment."

Q-Bess rose from her throne and gathered Crater into her arms. "No mother ever had a better child. You did what you had to do. I will defend you to the death. Be safe, my son."

Being safe was the last thing on Crater's mind as he ran all the way back to the dustlock. There, he clambered inside, calling for the dustie who reappeared. "Are my convoy packs ready?"

"No, sir. I tried to tell you before you ran out of here. We had one stolen and, since then, no convoy packs are to be issued without a chit from the company. Do you have one?"

Crater grabbed the dustie and threw him to the deck. "Don't move," he said, then took away the dustie's do4u, tossed it into a corner, threw open a random locker, and grabbed a pair of leggings which he used to tie the dustie's hands behind his back. He rifled another locker for another pair of leggings which he used to tie the dustie's feet together at the ankles.

During all this, the dustie submitted meekly, although the expression on his face was incredulous. "Mr. Trueblood," he said, "what are you doing? There's no big deal on the convoy packs. Just get approval and a chit. What's so difficult?"

Crater locked the entrance hatch, then came back inside the locker room, threw open the backpack storage locker, and removed two convoy backpacks. "If you take those without permission, you'll be a thief," the dustie said.

"It's for a good cause."

"The wages of sin are death, Mr. Trueblood."

Crater decided to stop talking to the philosophical dustie.

He climbed into his dust gear and strapped on one of the packs. Carrying the extra pack, he crossed into the airlock, closed the hatch behind him, drained out the air, opened the hatch into the big suck, and went outside, climbing into the fastbug he'd left there. He drove it around to his garaged fastbug, switched to it, and drove through the convoy staging area. Then, with the lights of Moontown to his back, he turned east and floored the accelerator.

From the observation tower overlooking the maintenance shed, the sheriff and Deputy Campos watched as Crater's fastbug threw up twin rooster tails and streaked away. The sheriff chuckled. "Go find your creature, Crater," he said. "Or what's left of it."

"Why'd you let him go, Sheriff?" the deputy asked.

"Colonel's orders. We figured he'd do something stupid. Well, all he'll find is a corpse. When he comes back, he'll be charged with theft and assault. After that, the Colonel will be pulling his strings for the rest of his pathetic life."

The deputy scratched up under his cap. "I dunno, Sheriff. That boy strikes me as being pretty slick."

"Slick as moon dust," the sheriff retorted, "and thick as mooncrete. We've got him now, the Colonel and me, right where we want him."

::: TWENTY-FOUR

rater drove to the Copperhead Bridge that crossed the Copperhead Rille that wound down the length of the Alpine Valley. He stopped at the entrance to the bridge and climbed out to have a look beneath its ramparts on the near side. It was a hundred feet to the bottom of the rille so Crater took his time. Beneath the bridge, he saw that the convoy pack he'd left there was gone. Crescent had read the note he'd left her on the tray beneath the sugar pot. In a world of electronics, do4u's, and puters, he'd sent her a message the old-fashioned, and least expected, way. On a scrap of a paper bag, he'd written "Go to the bridge. Look under." The deputy had patted him down, not ever expecting a paper note. What was written on it was succinct but apparently it was enough.

Crater got back in his fastbug and drove across the high bridge, a gossamer design of spaghetti-thin cables. The sinuous gorge below, the result of a river of collapsed melted rock, was in partial shadow and ranged from a deep chocolate color to a bright yellow. After he'd crossed the bridge, he struck out along the dustway—the main overland road—until he reached the site of the crowhopper ambush where Crescent had been captured. He turned and went off-road until he reached the crowhopper jumpcar.

Crater got out and saw an obvious trail from the fin. Something had been dragged away. It occurred to him that perhaps the dead crowhopper he'd left sitting against the fin hadn't been picked up by the greenies. He followed the trail, and not far away, in a small crater, the drag marks ended with a shallow grave and a marker of stacked rocks. There also sat Crescent on the rim of the crater, her helmet down, her knees pulled up under her chin, her arms wrapped around her legs. She was not moving. Crater activated his do4u. "Crescent, are you all right?"

"I am alive," she said, although she did not lift her head to look at him.

"I was afraid you'd be out of air."

"Legionnaires don't use as much air as humans," she replied. "But thank you for the extra pack. I would be dead without it."

"It was Q-Bess's idea."

"But you placed it there. I thank you both."

"You have given this man a fine grave," Crater said.

"He watched out for me during my training. He also saved me during the battle that brought you here. He took my weapon away and ordered me to live. He gave me his pendant because I lost mine. Then you gave it to me again."

"I knew it was important to you."

"The mythology of the phoenix is it dies, yet it lives, rising from its former self. It is the symbol of my military unit. Life is death. Death is life. You've heard that before. Why Trabonnet wanted me to live, I do not know."

"He cared about you," Crater said. "And you cared about him."

"If those things are so, they are of no consequence."

"Yet you came here to honor him."

"I prayed for him as you taught me. Dust to dust. I even said amen."

"That's good, Crescent."

Crescent turned her face to Crater. "Why are you here?"

"To make certain you are okay. And I have brought more air."

"I wish you hadn't. You must go back. My fate is my fate and you have no part of it."

"Tell me if you killed Deputy Jones."

"I didn't kill him."

"Then who did?"

"What difference does it make?"

"To me, it makes a great deal of difference. My life has changed because of that murder."

Her big, dark eyes were riveting. "The sheriff killed him."

"The sheriff?"

"He punched him in the face and he fell down. Then he straddled the deputy and broke his neck. It was excellently done. The Trainers could not have done it better."

"Why was the sheriff there?"

"I'm not sure. That drug put me in something like a dream. I knew I was with the deputy in the biovat room and then the sheriff was there. He yelled at the deputy about a lot of things I didn't understand and then killed him. The sheriff told me to help him carry the deputy up to the platform. We got him on the platform and the sheriff said to lower him in, which I did. I am very strong, so it was no problem."

"That's why there was no mess. Why didn't you tell me what really happened?"

"The sheriff said it was my fault the deputy died. If I hadn't come to Moontown, the deputy would have stayed within the law. He also said they were going to punish you for not killing me and they were going to fire Q-Bess for taking me in. But then he said if I would confess, they'd leave you and the queen alone. So I did."

"No, you didn't. You just said he deserved to die."

Crescent shrugged. "A fine point. It makes no difference. I have performed this service and now I will die. Go back to Moontown and I will take care of myself."

Crater made a helpless gesture. "I can't go back. I'm a thief and I roughed up a dustie. I'm on the run, Crescent, and so are you. We're going to Armstrong City."

She frowned. "Why Armstrong City?"

"It's big. We can hide there until we figure out what to do."

"Armstrong City is almost a thousand miles away. We don't have enough air."

Crater inclined his head toward the jumpcar. "If that ship is flyable and has enough fuel, it'll get us there."

Crescent shook her head. "No, go back. The Colonel will forgive you."

"I don't care about the Colonel."

"You love your job. Q-Bess told me."

"Your life is worth more than any job."

Crescent looked away. "My life is worth nothing."

Crater walked to the jumpcar, climbed the ladder, and opened the hatch. In the cockpit, he fired up the controls, ran through the checks, then climbed back down. "There's enough fuel to reach Armstrong City. Let's go."

When Crescent didn't move, Crater sat down on the lip of the crater. "All right. I'll stay and breathe my air down too."

She looked at him. "You wouldn't."

"Let's see who dies first. You say Legionnaires don't use much air. We'll find out."

A minute passed, then another. Then Crescent stood up and walked to the jumpcar. "All right. I will go."

"You first," Crater said, nodding toward the ladder.

"You don't trust me."

"Trust but verify, a wise man once said."

Crescent shrugged, then climbed the ladder and crawled through the hatch. Crater followed her. "Take the copilot's seat."

"I don't know how to fly a jumpcar."

"That's okay. I do."

Crater closed the hatch, then ran through the checklist with the puter. "Hang on," he said, then punched the engines.

Crescent closed her eyes and gripped the armrests while Crater kept the nose pointed straight up until they'd reached an altitude of eighty miles. He nudged the nose to the southeast and allowed the jumpcar to fly in a ballistic arc toward the shimmering vertical rainbow of the lunar elevator and the bright glow of Armstrong City. On the down side of the arc, Crater spotted a heel-3 convoy trundling down the dustway. He swerved the nose toward it, flipped the jumpcar over, and backed it down.

"Spacecraft eight point nine miles east and descending, identify yourself."

It was Armstrong City Flight Control. Crater ignored their call and landed the jumpcar, then keyed in a command. He unbuckled his seat belt. When Crescent didn't move, he unbuckled her seat belt for her. Her eyes were wide and she had a tight grip on the armrests. "What's wrong?" Crater demanded.

"I'm afraid of heights," she squeaked.

"Are you afraid of being blown up? I programmed the jumpcar to take off and crash. We have about thirty seconds."

Crescent blinked, then released the armrests and clambered out of the cockpit, Crater right behind her. Once on the ground, they ran. A few seconds later the jumpcar spurted its jets and took off. It roared south, then rotated until its nose was aimed straight down. When it struck the dust, it exploded in a fiery ball.

"We've got to catch that convoy," Crater said.

Crescent stared at him. "Sometimes you act crazy."

"It's my secret weapon. Come on."

The convoy was stopped, its drivers watching the flames from the crash. Crater and Crescent sneaked aboard the last truck, hiding themselves within a load of Helium-3 canisters.

TWENTY-FIVE

Message for you, Miss Medaris," Jarvis said, handing her a puter memplug.

Maria flipped her reader open and touched the memplug to it. It contained a message from the Colonel who came on screen and explained the situation to her, ending with, "Crater is likely heading to Armstrong City, to either escape up the elevator to a Cycler or just disappear. If you see him, don't let him near you. He's dangerous. Just let me know where you saw him and I will take care of everything. Be safe, my dear. Your grandfather loves you."

Maria closed the reader and sat back. After a while, she discovered she was smiling, and not a little thrilled. She had always hoped Crater would come to Armstrong City and make something of himself. But then her smile faded. Crater's new occupation of outlaw was not what she had in mind.

I will find him, she said to herself. But . . . *what will I do then?*

She didn't know. She rose from her desk. "I'll be back in an hour," she told Jarvis.

The secretary looked stricken. "You have a meeting with your CBO in twenty minutes."

"Reschedule it," Maria said and kept going. She needed to think and there was one place she thought best. She went outside and headed east. Streetlights lined the mooncrete sidewalk. It was the middle of the two-week dark phase, the so-called great shadow. Maria wasn't afraid. She could handle any pickpocket or lowlife lout. She walked until she reached the factory entrance. A big sign proclaimed Medaris Jumpcar Plant #1. She went through the hatch. Inside, the assembly line was hopping, her employees and machines synchronized. Four jumpcars were in the line, each in various stages of assembly. A foreman came running. "Miss Medaris. Good to see you."

Her practiced eye had already taken in the progress since her last visit. "Number three hasn't moved much," she observed.

"No, ma'am. We're waiting for a batch of extruded aluminum. I was told it will be here tomorrow."

"Coming from Australia, right? Let me know if it doesn't arrive."

"Yes, ma'am. Of course."

Maria walked to where a welder was working, his spot flashing, a wisp of smoke rising from the weld. She waited until he'd finished and raised his helmet, then tapped him on the shoulder. "Let me take over, Jack. Do you mind?"

The welder stepped aside and handed Maria his helmet. She put it on with its visor up, tied on a leather apron, then checked the plans. She fired up the spot, flipped the helmet visor down, then got busy. Working with her hands always helped her think. She needed to figure out a way to keep Crater safe even while all the rest of the moon tried to kill him. Then she remembered what had always kept Crater safe. But was it possible? She stopped welding and raised the helmet visor. There was only one way to find out.

::: Part Two

ENDLESS DUST

Happiness is like a crystal,
Fair and exquisite and clear,
Broken in a million pieces,
Shattered, scattered far and near.
Now and then along life's pathway,
Lo! Some shining fragments fall;
But there are so many pieces
No one ever finds them all.

—Priscilla Leonard

::: TWENTY-SIX

heck them out, gents," Decan Flaubert said, flicking on the lights in the hangar deck to reveal eight spiderwalkers. "Clean out the packing grease and limber them up. We're going into action soon."

Absalom, Lucien, and Dion, carrying their boots in their arms, floated to their beasts along with the other five drivers. They'd been in space for so long, being weightless now seemed second nature, but to work on the walkers, they'd need their sticky boots. The feet of the walkers were already outfitted with sticky pads. Walking them around in zero-G conditions wouldn't be perfect, but the pads would at least allow the drivers to test their machines.

The first job was to get the walkers out of their packing skeletons of aluminum and plywood. It was hot work, and soon the bodies of the drivers were steaming. It wasn't long before they requested permission to strip off their armor and tunics. Flaubert nodded his approval.

"Check Carillon out," Lucien said. "Not much room for another tat on that one."

Carillon was a veteran of many battles and his tattoos reflected each one of them. There were rows of tombstones across his back, each representing an enemy he'd killed. Names of battles—New Bombay, Nashville, Brasilia—ran up and down his arms. Mottos—"My holy water is blood;" "Enemy, don't run away, you'll just die tired."—crossed his chest. "What are you looking at, sprouts?" he demanded. "Ah, I see. You're jealous of my war ink." He walked over to Lucien, then waved Absalom and Dion in. He tapped on the hatch that held the spiderwalker's puter. "You can modify this?"

"Of course," Absalom said. "And I only need access to mine. I will tell it to feed its data to all the walkers. No one will be able to discover what I've done."

"There will be a breakdown as soon as we land?"

"It will be intermittent. Very difficult to troubleshoot. I will come up with the fix after the battle is nearly over."

Carillon looked over his shoulder. "If we're found out, we'll go before a firing squad."

"We won't be found out. Decan Flaubert is ignorant of walker software. Just like you."

Carillon made the gap-toothed grimace that passed for his smile. "Then he must be truly ignorant!"

"You four!"

Decan Flaubert floated over to the four plotters, then swung his sticky boots to the deck. "Carillon, there is no reason for you to be anywhere other than with your walker."

"I am giving these novices the benefit of my experience," Carillon replied.

Flaubert balled up his fist and struck Carillon in the side

of his head with such force it caused the veteran's boots to come unstuck. He tumbled away. Flaubert turned on the trio of youthful Legionnaires. "Didn't I tell you to stay away from Carillon?"

"Y-Yes, sir," the three warbled.

"He is always plotting something. What is it this time? Tell me now and it will go easy on you. Keep it from me and when I find out—and I will find out—I will skin you alive, then toss you into space to let your blood boil."

"He is asking us to loan him money, Decan," Lucien said.

Absalom backed him up. "That is all, Decan."

Dion added, "It's the truth. I swear!"

Flaubert frowned. "All three of you, come to attention."

When they did, Flaubert struck each of them in turn. Blood ran from Dion's nose, from Lucien's ears, and from Absalom's mouth, forming scarlet droplets that drifted away. The other spiderwalker drivers pretended not to notice, their heads down.

"I have my eyes on you," Flaubert said. "Carillon!"

Carillon was back on his feet. He came to attention. "Yes, Decan! Would you like to crush my face with your fist again?"

"The only thing that keeps me from chucking you into space," Flaubert growled, "is I would be short a walker driver."

"Yes, Decan. For you and the glory of the Legion, I would gladly chuck myself into space!"

Flaubert looked doubtful but waved them back to work.

When he was sure he wasn't being watched, Lucien swung open the hatch to his walker's puter and tapped in the necessary commands. Afterward, when he caught their eye, he winked to his partners in crime and survival that everything was going according to plan.

In the control room beside the hangar, Flaubert, monitoring a hidden surveillance camera, took note of the winks. The three lads and Carillon were up to something, but what it was, he wasn't certain. He only knew if they spoiled the upcoming fight, they were not likely to survive, mainly because he would kill them himself.

::: TWENTY-SEVEN

eep in the utilities tubes, Crater plugged into the city power grid puter and called up his announcement on the Armstrong City do4u book under Guide Services:

> Guide Across the Wayback to Anywhere You Want to Go.
> Price Negotiable.
> Serious Inquiries Only.
> Contact do4u #9532

The do4u number belonged to an Umlap woman, a tailor by trade, named Mends Your Britches. For her trouble, and because she'd also agreed to take a certain party on as an apprentice tailor, the guide provided Mends Your Britches five percent of any income he made as a result of the ad.

It was a fair trade.

The Umlap woman was an excellent judge of callers and could sense if they were serious or not. During Crater's short career as a guide, he had guided three groups: prisoners to the Australian mining town of New Woomera in the far eastern

Smythe's Sea, a collection of rowdy Russian miners north to New St. Petersburg (they had yet to pay him), and the representatives of a Japanese mining company sent to inspect the crowhopper-destroyed town of Nekko. What they found— bodies heaped in a mound, the mining equipment destroyed, the tubes desecrated—had so nauseated and disgusted them, they had decided to leave Nekko permanently closed.

There was only one message on the server. *Come see me.* It was from Mends Your Britches. Crater slipped through the tubes to an outside hatch beneath the Buzz Aldrin Dome. After checking to make sure he wasn't observed, he pulled his scarf over his nose and, cap pulled down, made his way along the dark, tree-lined street lit by dim street lamps. People passed by, all of whom seemed busy and purposeful. Armstrong City was home to nearly four thousand people. New tubes were being buried every day, and small and medium-sized domes containing parks, farms, and vineyards were being constructed at an astonishing pace. Peace seemed to be in the air. The UCW and the allied countries against it were talking. Scramjet ferries up to the Lunar Cyclers were booked for months. Four new Cyclers were being constructed. War followed by peace was always good for business.

A man approached. He was accompanied by a young woman pulling a cart laden high with boxes. Crater studied them. The man looked healthy, yet the woman was doing all the work. When the wheel of the cart caught the corner of a building, one of the boxes was knocked off. "Mouse!" the man yelled. "If anything is broken in that box, you'll find your ration cut."

"My strident apologies, sir," the woman answered, bobbing her head obediently as she placed the box back, then took up the yoke of the cart. "I mean only to help, sir."

"Come along, then," he said and walked ahead while she strained to keep up, leaving the guide to wonder what he'd just seen.

Crater reached the shop of the Umlap tailor. It was in a basement that led to an old-fashioned tube. He descended down the steps and entered the hatch. Although buildings beneath the domes had no need of airlocks, they were still built into most buildings as safety devices. In the Umlap's shop, the hatch was original equipment.

The Umlap woman was at her sewing machine. The "certain party," a crowhopper girl, was busy in the kitchen. The Umlap looked up. "Well, Crater," she said with a smile that meant she was unhappy. "It is about time you visited us."

Crescent turned from the stove and worked her lips into a smile. "I am most glad to see your face," she said.

"And I your face, Crescent," Crater said. "Hello, Ike."

Ike was the Umlap's dog. He thumped his tail against the deck.

"Sit down," Mends Your Britches directed, pointing at a hard mooncrete chair. "I have work for you. His name is Jake Barrows and says he will pay in cash if you will be his guide."

"Cash is always good," Crater said.

The Umlap looked around sharply when Crescent began whacking joyfully with a big knife on the cutting board. "Crescent, you're supposed to be slicing those carrots, not destroying them!"

"Sorry, Missus!" Crescent brayed, though she didn't appear to be sorry at all and kept merrily chopping.

Mends Your Britches rolled her eyes and lowered her voice. "She gets it in her head to do a thing a particular way, it's hard to turn her around. Crescent! For goodness' sake. Slice, not chop!"

"Yes, Missus!" The chopping slowed.

"Is she doing okay otherwise?"

The tailor shrugged. "Well enough. She's smart and she's got very good mechanical ability. She can take a sewing machine apart and put it back together in ten minutes. Her biggest drawbacks are her fingers. They're thick and not made for fine handwork. Still, I wouldn't trade her for a brace of thin-fingered Earth girls. She's honest to a fault. And she adores Ike, who equally adores her. She brushes him faithfully and takes him for walks in the park and cleans up after him. Sometimes I find his head on her feet sound asleep. Dogs are a good judge of character. Of course, I had to tell her to kindly stop choking a customer the other day who complained about a pair of leggings I'd mended. True, he was obnoxious and was refusing to pay, but Crescent still shouldn't have jumped over the counter and grabbed his throat."

"He paid, didn't he?" Crescent declared from the kitchen.

The Umlap smiled unhappily. "Yes, he did, dear, but I fear he will not be a repeat customer." She turned to Crater. "You'll find Jake Barrows in the northern maintenance shed. He said there are four in his party."

"Even better. Small parties are the easiest. What else do you know about them?"

"Not much, but I can guess. Chased off Earth by people who didn't like their religion or their beliefs or just the way they look."

"Where do they want to go?"

"He wouldn't say, only that he would discuss that with you when you came by."

"A group that won't say where they're going sounds like trouble."

Mends Your Britches smiled again. "Did you know, perchance, that your fee for Crescent's rent is overdue?"

Crater got the message. "I will talk to Barrows. I'm sure we can work something out."

Mends Your Britches frowned deeply. "Splendid! Crescent, dear, set another plate for Crater, won't you?"

"I will, Missus!"

"And go into the pantry. Fetch me the special hot sauce I made last weekend."

"Yes, Missus!"

Mends Your Britches waited until Crescent was out of the room and then inclined her head toward Crater. "I fear for her," she said. "Sometimes I notice she is in pain. It's subtle, but I can see it in the way her eyes narrow and her lips go tight. She should visit a doctor."

"She's a crowhopper," Crater said. "Any doctor in Armstrong City would turn her in."

"Yet she needs help. Of this, I am certain."

"She hasn't complained?"

"She never complains about anything. She is a special girl."

Crescent returned to the kitchen. "I have the hot sauce, Missus!"

"Thank you, dear," Mends Your Britches said, then gave Crater a significant look that included a raised eyebrow.

Crater sat back and watched Crescent bustle around the kitchen. She didn't look sick at all. He thought probably the old woman was imagining things and, before long, had put the entire conversation out of his head. It was the new clients he needed to worry about. He would visit them on the morrow, then get an advance payment and head out on the dust.

::: **TWENTY-EIGHT**

rater moved through the underground service tubes that housed the utilities of Armstrong City. It had taken a little time, but he'd mapped them all and could slip just about anywhere without detection. He popped out near the northern maintenance shed, kept his scarf up and his head down, and pushed open the hatch.

The shed was a cavernous bay filled with trucks, fastbugs, and mining machines under the care of dozens of mechanics and various other techies. Crater took a moment to savor the marvelous sound of busy machinery, the shouts of working men and women, and the sweet fragrance of grease and bio-fuel. He wished he could work there, only it was too visible. The guide business was perfect for someone on the run. The authorities didn't pay much attention to guides, and Crater's hideout in the maintenance tubes kept him mostly out of sight except when he needed to visit a client. After a quick look around to make certain no one was watching him, he walked to the appointed meeting place near the generator room. Two men and two women, the men in blue coveralls, the women in long gray skirts and white blouses, were waiting for him. Crater thought they looked like pictures he'd seen of the old American western pioneers of the nineteenth century—sturdy, strong, and plain. One of the men extended his hand. "I'm thinking you're our guide. I'm Jake Barrows."

"Crater Trueblood," Crater said, taking Jake's hand, which was calloused and strong.

"This is my wife, Trudelle," Jake said, gesturing toward a young, plump woman with braided blond hair. Trudelle provided a cautious smile. "And here is Clarence Tolliver and his wife, Eliza."

Clarence was a big fellow with a round, friendly face and mischievous gray eyes. "Pleased to meetcha!" he boomed.

Eliza was thin as a crack in a stone and her auburn hair was pulled back into an old-fashioned ponytail. "Been an age, seems like, since we left Earth," she said. "It'll be good to get to our new place."

"You're younger than the other guides," Clarence observed.

"I began working on the scrapes when I was twelve," Crater replied. "And I scouted a heel-3 convoy across the moon when I was sixteen. I am now nearly twenty. You will find me a competent guide."

"How soon can we leave?" Jake asked.

"That depends. Where do you want to go?"

"The town of Endless Dust. Do you know it?"

"I've heard of it. It's out west about three hundred miles from here. As I recall, it's abandoned. I think General Nero owns it."

"Right on all counts. We leased the place through General Nero's holding company. He said the Helium-3 scrapes had a low yield but that don't bother us. We're after Thorium. A lot of folks on Earth are getting off the grid. Thorium packs in their garage are the big new thing."

This bit of Earthly news surprised Crater. "What are Thorium packs?"

"Small reactors. Not much bigger than a refrigerator and safe as a turtle in its shell. According to the geological charts, there should be lots of Thorium around Endless Dust."

"Do you know anything about moon mining?"

"Strip mining's strip mining," Clarence said. "Doze off the top, load the dust, shake it out, and ship it off. We mined coal before we got run off our land so we know what we're doing."

Jake explained, "We're Appalachians, Crater. Maybe you've heard us called Apps. We're descendants of the people who settled the Appalachian Mountains of North America. Our ancestors were farmers and miners and so are we. We've worked hard and dug in the dirt for generations, one way or the other."

Crater searched his memory. "Wasn't your land turned into a park or something?"

"They call it a park," Eliza scoffed, "but what they turned it into is a playground for the elites!"

"The government passed a law," Jake said, "then came in, rounded us up, and forced us into cities. Then they razed our towns, covered up our mines, and destroyed our farms, all in the name of putting the land back the way it was four hundred years ago. Only instead of letting it go entirely wild, they built resorts for government leaders and their families. Some of us sneaked back into our hills, but we were tracked down and either killed or put into internment camps. That's when a lot of the Apps got together and decided to come here and build a new life. We saved up, borrowed from relatives, did whatever we could, and leased Endless Dust with an option to buy. There's a hundred more waiting to come after we've made sure it has enough Thorium."

"What kind of equipment do you have?" Crater asked.

"We were told there's abandoned scrapers and loaders left over from the previous mining operations."

"A seller will often tell a buyer what he wants to hear."

"Well, we got ourselves a truck and a crusher," Jake said, pointing at a dented truck and a rock crusher mounted on tracks.

"Why the crusher?" Crater asked.

"Thorium ain't a gas like Helium-3," Clarence said. "It's in the rock. A crusher will let us get at it. Byproduct is Titanium, which is at its highest price ever."

Trudelle spoke up. "Look, Mr. Trueblood, we're 250,000 miles from home and don't know anything about what we're doing except we got this dream to start a new life. We've left our kids to come down here and see what's what in Endless Dust. Will you help us do that?"

"That's my job," Crater said. "Three thousand johncredits is my standard price, one thousand up front, the rest payable upon arrival at Endless Dust."

"Oh, bless you!" Trudelle cried, and both women moved in for a hug. Crater accepted it. The men settled for slapping him on the back. He accepted that too, along with the thousand johncredits, laboriously counted out from a money belt around Jake's waist.

After saying good-bye and promising to get with them the first thing the next day, Crater headed for the exit. He did his best to keep to the back alleys, but there were plazas he couldn't avoid crossing. At one of those, he was drawn to a store with a crowd in front of it. Signs were being held aloft and there was chanting. The name of the store was Helpers. He slipped into the crowd and found himself alongside a woman carrying a sign that read: No Helpers on Luna!

Curious, Crater asked, "What are Helpers?"

The woman looked at him through old-fashioned spectacles. "Are you completely ignorant? Helpers are enslaved humans."

"Slavery! Slavery! Slavery!" a woman chanted. Others picked up the cry.

There was a rumbling sound and Crater turned to see the doors being lifted in front of the store. Some people went inside while others continued to march back and forth with their signs. Crater went inside to see what all the fuss was about.

The store was bright and painted in cheerful colors. On a stage stood three men and three women. They were dressed in blue tunics with white leggings and matching boots. Around their necks were signs with numbers on them. Crater was shocked to see the signs were price tags. Two hundred and fifty thousand johncredits was the cheapest, and that was for a stout, balding young man with pleasant features. A clerk came over. "Are you interested in this Helper, young sir?"

"I'm not sure what a Helper is," Crater confessed.

"From the wayback, are you? Well, a Helper is just what the name implies. Whatever you want them to do for you, they will cheerfully do. That is to say, as long as it is within certain cognitive limitations. They are not for, ahem, any, ah, personal—shall we say?—needs. You see, they have no ability to enjoy, ahem, personal, um, relationships of, ahem, the flesh, so to speak."

Crater thought about that for a second, then said, "Oh."

"But"—the salesman brightened—"if you have need of help in your home or shop or perhaps doing simple chores in your place of business, a Helper is for you! Would you like to talk to one? Go ahead. They won't bite."

"May I help you, sir? Ask me anything," the stout young man said.

"Where are you from?" Crater asked, not able to think of anything else.

"I am from this store," the man said. "Helpers of Armstrong City."

"But where did you come from before being here?"

The man's smile faded, then returned. "I don't know. May I help you, sir?"

The salesman slithered up beside Crater. "What do you think?"

"I guess I don't need a Helper," Crater said. "Do you sell many of them?"

"We've sold but one so far," the salesman confessed, "but we only opened last week. I anticipate we will sell quite a few more after people understand their value. Helpers are very popular on Earth. Say you have kids. A Helper can drive them to school, then pick them up at the appointed hour. Or perhaps you have an infirm parent. A Helper will happily cook and clean and generally nurse the sick or anyone unable to care for themselves."

A man and a woman entered the store, and Crater recognized them as the man he'd seen with the woman pulling a cart. "This helper is too weak," the man said to the clerk. "I need a stronger one."

"Of course, sir. We are only too glad to exchange Helpers.

You," he said to the woman, "go in the back and report yourself to the exchange manager."

"I did my best to help, sir," the young woman said, her eyes downcast.

"Well, help me by going to the back."

The clerk and the man went away, leaving the woman standing alone and staring at her feet. Before long, a man emerged from the rear of the store and roughly took her by the arm and led her off.

Crater exited the shop. Outside, the woman with the sign stopped him. "Well?" she demanded. "Doesn't it make you sick?"

The woman didn't wait for Crater to form an answer. She lowered her sign with a heavy sigh and said, "For centuries, scientists tried to create robots to do menial chores, but they never could build one that really worked. Who would have thought the best way to build a robot would be to turn a human into one?" She shook her head. "Call them what you will, explain them how you want, but they are still nothing but slaves. And when you are done with one—it gets too old or injured or whatever—then what do you do with it?"

When she raised her eyebrows in a questioning manner, Crater said, "I don't know," mainly because he didn't know. He was still feeling sorry for the young woman.

"Exactly," she replied, then raised her sign and went back to waving it around and Crater left, feeling troubled. Was the woman with the sign right or were the others right? He could certainly see why some people needed a Helper and the Helpers didn't seem to mind. On the other hand, when he'd first encountered Crescent, she didn't seem to mind being a bloodthirsty warrior, but now that she'd seen something of human kindness, she'd changed. At least, Crater thought she had. Crescent was hard to read, and it really wasn't fair to compare her to a Helper.

Or was it? That was when he was reminded that Mends Your Britches thought Crescent was sick. What could be done with a sick crowhopper? Crater didn't want to think about it. He instead thought of Endless Dust and wondered why it had really been abandoned. There had to be more to the story and he decided to find out what it was.

::: TWENTY-NINE

Armstrong City was still cloaked in the great shadow, and the weak streetlights of the Buzz Aldrin Dome provided only a blue-green phosphorescence to dispel the gloom. Crater, grateful for the dim light since that meant he could lower the scarf from his face, strolled along the street to the tailor's shop. Before he could descend the stairs, a familiar voice—although one not heard for years—called out his name.

Crater turned in disbelief. There standing before him was Maria Medaris. She wore a hooded cloak but he knew it was her, not just by her voice, but by the way she stood and moved. It was as if everything about her had been permanently welded into his brain. She pushed back the hood of the cloak. Her eyes, blue and bright as the Earth even in the wan light, were steady and strong, just as he remembered them, and her lips, which he had kissed almost as if in a dream when she'd allowed it, were a lovely pink. Everything about her, including her cloak and her silver-threaded leggings, was exquisite. In contrast, Crater was dressed in a shabby brown tunic, threadbare leggings, and scuffed boots.

"You are a sight, Crater," Maria said. "Have you considered visiting a clothing shop?"

"It's difficult when you're an outlaw to visit any shop," he said. He looked around. "I hope the sheriff is not in the shadows."

"I am alone," she said.

"How did you find me?"

"You led some Russians to New St. Pete and a dustie saw you there. My detectives got wind of it. They've been looking for you."

"Lots of people have been looking for me," Crater answered. "But I never expected one of them was you."

Maria held out a small, carved box. "Only because I wanted to give you something. Take it, please."

Crater took the box and moved to where the light was better. He ran his fingers over the silver design on its lid. "I've never seen anything like it."

"That's because it's made of wood from a real tree grown on Earth. It is mahogany—quite rare, Crater—and inlaid with platinum and silver. The design is my family crest, a shield with the Greek god Atlas carrying the world on his shoulders, only it isn't the Earth, it's the moon."

Crater pondered the crest, then opened the lid of the box. Within it, on a soft purple cloth, was a clump of slime mold cells. "Is this my gillie?" he croaked.

"Yes. It was found near the wreckage of the crowhopper jumpcar it destroyed."

"I was certain it was also destroyed."

"Gillies can regenerate if enough cells remain," she explained. "I was told this by a gillie expert on Earth and that caused me to spare no expense to find yours. I had four teams out there looking. It was a miracle they found it because it was under the dust. When they did, I flew out there to see it. It was amazing, Crater. I'm glad I could find it for you."

"I don't know what else to say except thank you. Otherwise, I'm a little stunned."

She smiled. "Good. I like both reactions."

Crater gently touched the gillie. It didn't move.

"It's alive," Maria said. "I flew in the gillie expert from Earth to make certain of that. Give it time, he said. It's still regenerating."

He looked at her. "Why did you do this?"

Maria bit her lip hesitantly, then said, "I thought you would like it."

"I love it! But your letter..."

"I was sick when I wrote that. I'm healthy now and can see things more clearly. My injury was not your fault, Crater, although I blamed you for it at first. As to why you never came to see me, or made any attempt to communicate with me, I'm sure you had your reasons. But let me be clear. I am pleased to return your gillie to you as an act of past friendship, nothing more. Let me also add this warning. If I found out where you are, my grandfather will too. For all I know, he already has. You must leave Armstrong City."

"What about Crescent?"

"Your creature? Leave her. What is she to you?"

"She's my friend."

Maria inclined her head, a gesture of profundity. "Crater, if you had shown half the loyalty to me as you have to that creature, who knows what might have happened?" She sighed. "But if she means that much to you, I suppose I could arrange to smuggle her back to Earth."

"Would you really do that?"

"You don't trust me? Well, whether you do or not doesn't matter. Grandfather is extremely angry with you because of your various crimes."

"My crimes are light compared to his," Crater replied, "and Crescent has committed no crime at all. The sheriff killed the dictator Warto and I'm certain the Colonel ordered it."

"I won't argue with you. Nobody will believe you, in any case. Grandfather hates that little crowhopper and will have her dead—and you with it, if necessary."

"I just don't understand why he hates her so much."

Maria shook her head. "You really don't know? Crowhoppers killed my Uncle Willy. He was the Colonel's youngest son. They flayed off his skin. The Colonel found him screaming and begging to die. It's not just your crowhopper, Crater. He detests them all."

Crater searched for something to say but nothing came. He understood now, but the situation remained the same.

"He also knew about the pack you placed at the bridge," she said. "The sheriff read your note while you were writing it. There are security cams in the dispatcher's office, Crater! They didn't care. They were sure your creature would die before you could get to it."

"But then . . ." Crater raised his eyebrows.

"But then it lived longer than they thought and you hit upon the idea of flying the jumpcar over here. Now I think the Colonel means to truly hurt you. You must run."

Crater closed the box with the dormant gillie inside and placed it on the ground. He took Maria by her hands, then kissed her lips. Surprised, she pushed him away. "Crater," she gasped, "what are you doing?"

Crater took her in his arms and kissed her again. This time they both allowed the kiss to linger. When they broke apart, Maria's eyes were wide, her lips parted, a tendril of hair loose and dangling across her forehead. Crater picked up the box. "Thank you for the gillie," he said. "And don't worry. I have a place to go where I can hide for a while."

"Will I ever see you again?"

"Well," he said, "we'll always have Armstrong City."

"*Casablanca*," she said, understanding the reference. "But this is hardly Paris. Look. I've got another idea. Come to my office. I will protect you. Together, we'll fight the Colonel."

"Not unless I can bring Crescent and you fight for her too."

Maria shook her head. "I can't do that. I can fight him for you, but he'll never change his mind about that crowhopper."

"Then I guess I need to get going."

"You're choosing that . . . *thing* over me?"

"It's not that simple."

"Yes, it is! It is really that simple! Good-bye, Crater!"

He reached for her, but she had already turned and was walking away. He didn't follow. She was, after all, a Medaris and he was an outlaw. This did not keep his heart from feeling like it was in a vise, or keep him from watching her as she receded, streetlight by streetlight, until she had disappeared.

::: THIRTY

During his visit with Mends Your Britches and Crescent, Crater was quiet while he tried to decide what to do. He agreed with Maria about one thing. If she'd found him, the Colonel was probably close behind. He needed to take Crescent with him, but he wasn't certain how she would take the news that they were going to have to run again. His greatest fear was that she'd turn herself in, to save him from himself.

Neither of the women intruded on his thoughts as he stirred his food around, not even remotely hungry. They seemed to sense he was deep inside a nameless worry so they left him alone. He returned to the nook he'd fashioned in the utility tubes and was grateful when sleep finally came. He might have slept longer but was brought awake by the sound of himself singing at the top of his lungs.

> *All I want is a moon dust girl,*
> *Down in a crater waitin' for love.*
> *All I want is a moon dust girl,*
> *Kissin' me 'neath the world above.*

Only it wasn't him singing the song but instead the gillie, which mimicked his voice perfectly. It stood, though it had no legs, and sang, though it had no mouth, and looked at Crater, though it had no eyes. "Are you truly alive, Gillie?" Crater asked.

The gillie continued to look at him, then lapsed into silence.

To see if the gillie was functioning, he thought of something to ask. "Gillie? Tell me about Endless Dust."

The gillie did not answer. Crater picked it up. It was a colorless color and felt neutral to the touch. He lightly shook it. "Gillie? What's wrong with you?"

The gillie continued to say and do nothing. Crater put it down and went back to sleep. He had no time to waste with gillies that were sometimes dead and sometimes alive.

The next morning, after eating stale bread smeared with biovat peanut butter and washing it down with biovat orange juice, Crater wrapped the gillie in a bandana, stuffed it in his coveralls pocket, and headed through the underground tubes to the north maintenance shed. Along the way, he felt the gillie move, then go still. "Keep regenerating, little buddy," he said.

To prepare for the coming journey that had now turned into an escape, the first thing Crater did was work on the old truck the Apps had bought from a used truck lot. He welded cracks, replaced wiring, changed the biogoop in its fuel cell, beefed up its chassis, replaced the pressure seals in its cabin, charged up its oxygen tanks, put in new scrubbers, and replaced its worn-out tires. All of this he did by digging into the pile of tossed junk in the maintenance shed, saving the Apps the expense of buying new parts. Happily, the crusher they'd purchased was in good condition so not much was required to get it ready except some strengthening of the suspension with welded lunasteel beams. When he discovered the Apps only had one do4u, he scrounged up three more from the dumpsters behind an Armstrong City electronics store, then tinkered with them until they worked. He also topped off the water tank by tapping into the reservoir that fed the fountains in the park beneath the Michael Collins Dome. As for food, he inspected their stores, then gave the Apps a list of what was needed. Jake looked it over. "We don't have enough money for all this," he confessed.

"But you will owe me two thousand johncredits when we get to Endless Dust."

When Jake did not reply, just looked at the floor, Crater knew the truth. "You don't have any money."

"We figured to pay you after we sell our Thorium."

He had already paid Mends Your Britches for Crescent's room and board so Crater said, "I'll cover it. You can add it to what you owe me."

"You know full well it'll be a long time before we make any money," Jake said.

"If it makes you feel better, I'll charge you interest," Crater said. "How about two and half percent annually?"

"Guess we can do that," Jake said and they shook hands.

Later Crater went over the map with Jake. Opening a reader, he traced his finger along the proposed route. "There's no track out to Endless Dust so we're going to have to bust one. First, we'll go north to Arago Crater, then west between the Ariadaeus and Hyginus Rilles. This will take us into the Mare Vaporum—the Sea of Vapors. At the entrance to the Sinus Aestuum—the Seething Bay—we'll turn south and go along the Flammarion peaks. As long as we keep the peaks to our left, we should come along to Alphonsus, which we'll recognize by its irregular rim, and after that, Endless Dust. If all goes well, we'll beat the return of the great shadow."

"All will go well," Jake said.

"If it does, it will be the first time for a trek across the moon."

Jake grinned. "Stop worrying, Crater. You've done all you can."

"There's always more to be done," Crater said. "But usually you don't know it until it's too late."

Jake gripped Crater's shoulder, then went off to help load lunasteel tubes on the trailer attached to the truck. The tubes were for a washing system needed for Thorium separation. Crater thought it would be a good idea to weld a crack on the trailer so he headed for the tricetylene and oxygen refill area. There were always tanks there that had a little left in them. Before he got there, a woman stepped out in front of him. "Hey, sailor!"

It was Riley, and she was wearing a jumpcar pilot's uniform, the Medaris Mining Company logo on its breast. She moved in for a hug and her auburn hair was soft on his cheek. Her perfume was pure, sweet rocket fuel. Crater couldn't hold back his grin. "You're the Colonel's new pilot. Nice work!"

"Took advantage of an opening. Seems his previous pilot decided to head off into the wild beyond. The rumor is he went to Earth but here ye are." When Crater looked around, she said, "Don't worry. I'm the only one here from Moontown, but let's get ye out of sight. Medaris Mining's got a chuckwagon being outfitted in this shed. We can hang there for a bit."

Riley led Crater to a large motorized van. It was a chrome and glass beauty, and Crater took a moment to admire it, whistling. Riley grinned. "The Colonel spared no expense. There are bunks, a kitchen that can feed a convoy, and a full machine shop in the rear."

Inside, she gave him a tour of the machine shop, the living quarters, and the kitchen with a dining parlor that included table booths. Everything was puter driven, including a full outfit of navigational units and ground radar. "What's your pleasure?" she asked, opening a kitchen cabinet. "Coffee or chai?"

"Chai," Crater said, and Riley drew them both cups of chai tea from a gleaming dispenser.

They sat down in one of the booths. "What's the news from Moontown?" Crater asked.

"The heel-3 cylinders are piling up waiting for the next convoy, but nobody knows when that'll be."

"Why's that?"

Riley shrugged. "No drivers. Most of them are hanging around town waiting for the war to be over. Did you know a warpod tried to kidnap the Colonel's granddaughter? What's her name?"

"Maria. Yes, I heard that."

"So it's more than a rumor. What a mess. By the way, I saw Q-Bess just yesterday. She's fine. Same for Asteroid Al."

"How about you, Riley?" Crater asked.

Riley's smile was tinged with regret. "Something ye should know. I've met someone. A pretty special fella."

Crater wasn't surprised. Riley was too sensible to keep earthing over the likes of him. "Good for you," he said, almost meaning it.

"So what are ye doing, m'boy, besides hiding out? Don't worry. Me lips are sealed."

"I'm a guide." Without thinking, he added, "Next stop Endless Dust. Nobody's been out there for a decade. Abandoned but why, I don't know."

"Oh, I know the reason," she said lightly. "Ghosts."

Crater lifted his eyebrows. "Ghosts?"

"Sure. Ghosts, spirits, whatever you want to call them. I used to work for the Neros before I came to Moontown. The miners at Endless Dust said they saw apparitions and heard them too. After a while, it scared them so much they sent their families away, then finally all of them quit and left."

Crater was astonished. "I never heard of ghosts on the moon."

"Are you afraid?"

"No, but I wonder what's really out there."

A maintenance tech knocked on the chuckwagon door. "Pilot Bishop? We've finished installing the new fuel impellor on your jumpcar. Want to test it?"

"Give me a minute."

Riley stood and Crater stood with her. "Keep watch on your jets, especially the portside one," he said. "It tends to run rough."

"Not anymore. I fixed it."

"Listen, Riley . . . I told you something I shouldn't have. About me going to Endless Dust."

She hugged Crater and kissed him on the cheek. "You needn't worry, Crater. Me lips are sealed."

After Riley had gone, Crater sat back down to finish his tea. He felt the gillie move in his pocket so he plucked it out, unwrapped the bandana, and sat it on the table whereupon it raised up.

Hello, the gillie said. *I am a gillie biocomputer. I was designed by the Macingillie Corporation in the Republic of Calimexica and manufactured in New Shanghai, Third Republic of East China. I am designed to assist you with communications, administration, scheduling, research, and advice. Whenever you are ready, I would be glad to assist you in any of these endeavors. Do you have any questions for me?*

Crater sighed. "I just wish you'd stay awake."

That is not a question. I believe your last question to me had to do with the town of Endless Dust.

Crater recalled he had indeed asked the gillie about Endless Dust when it had come awake briefly in the night. "Yes. Tell me about it," he said.

Endless Dust is a town founded by the Nero Corporation to mine Helium-3. It was abandoned in 2125 after the quality of the isotope was found to be inferior.

"What about ghosts?"

Gillie has no information on ghosts relating to Endless Dust. Would you like to know about Alphonsus Crater?

"What about Alphonsus Crater?"

Alphonsus is 5.8 miles from Endless Dust and is located on the eastern edge of Mare Nubium. It is seventy-three miles in diameter. It has been associated with transient lunar phenomena, also known as TLP.

Crater perked up. "Why is it associated with TLP?"

On November 3, 1958, the Soviet astronomer Nikolai A. Kozyrev observed what he called "strange red clouds" over Alphonsus Crater. Such clouds have since been observed many times. Kozyrev also observed a bright light in the center of Alphonsus Crater.

When the gillie fell silent, Crater asked, "Anything else?"

Nothing else.

"Thank you. You've been very helpful."

The gillie looked pleased even though it could look no way at all. Crater, in any case, wasn't paying attention. He was deep in thought, wondering why red clouds and strange lights had been observed in an obscure crater on the moon.

::: THIRTY-ONE

rater was awakened by tremors that he thought were a moonquake, but then the gillie came alert and said, *The city is under attack.*

"Who's attacking?" Crater asked.

A warpod. It intends to blast a hole in the Buzz Aldrin Dome, then land Legionnaire troops.

Gillies were notorious puter hackers, and Crater realized it must have already hacked its way into the warpod. "What is their mission?"

Unknown at this time.

"Call Mends Your Britches."

Done. There is no answer.

"Call Crescent."

Done. There is no answer.

If a dome was breached, a pressure suit was required. Crater pulled on his biolastic sheath, his coveralls—putting the gillie in one of its pockets—and a backpack. Then he plopped on his helmet and sealed it, strapped on a nine millimeter moontype pistol, and headed uptube to the Buzz Aldrin

Dome, which covered the neighborhood where Mends Your Britches had her shop. Popping out of a tube hatch, he emerged into chaos. The dome had been breached and air was rushing from it. People, dressed only in their tube clothes, were grasping their throats and writhing in pain as the air in their blood boiled. There was nothing Crater could do except hold on to the hatch and wait it out.

When the wind diminished, he ran through the streets and the rubble, dodging big chunks of the dome as it fell. He reached the tailor shop and pushed inside, relieved to find Crescent alive and in her pressure suit. She was holding Mends Your Britches in her arms and Ike was draped across her legs. "They're dead," she said in a flat tone. "When we heard a big noise, she went up to see and something fell on her. Then the air began to escape. Poor Ike died instantly. I slammed the hatch shut and got into my suit."

"We're being attacked by the Legion."

Crescent nodded. "I can feel them."

"We've got to leave," Crater said, but when Crescent didn't move, he added, "They mean to kill everyone."

The gillie spoke from within Crater's coverall breast pocket. *Update. Secure voice transmissions indicate this is a capture mission.*

"What is that?" Crescent demanded.

Crater opened his pocket and the gillie stuck out its head even though it had no head. "It's a gillie."

"Gillies are illegal."

"It knows that."

The target's code name is Eaglet, the gillie said.

"How does it know that?" Crescent asked.

"It's an expert hacker," Crater explained.

More just in. Their target is the Medaris Building.

Crater waited for the gillie to tell him more. When it didn't, he prodded it but it remained silent.

"Did its batteries run down?" Crescent asked.

"It doesn't have batteries. It's regenerating. I'll explain later." Crater turned over the gillie's report in his mind. "Maria Medaris must be Eaglet. They've tried to kidnap her before. I have to stop them."

"The Legion is probably already there," Crescent said.

"The Medaris Building is well defended."

"They will slaughter them, and you too if you go there."

"I've fought your Legion before," Crater reminded her.

"Yes, and you were lucky."

"I'm going anyway."

"Wait." Crescent gently moved Mends Your Britches and Ike, then stood, gazed fondly down at them for a moment and walked to a wall chest and swung it open, taking from it a long, curved sword. Its blade gleamed in the flickering, failing lights. "I had it made at the local foundry with my earnings from the missus. It is called a *talwar*. Legionnaires are trained in its art."

Crater had never seen such a vicious-looking blade. "Are you going with me?"

"Of course I am."

"You'll fight against Legionnaires?"

"I will fight alongside you," she said, adding, "It is not unknown for Legionnaires to be on opposing sides. It is all according to the contracts."

Outside, they emerged into a devastated neighborhood where the soft, warm air trapped beneath the dome had been flushed into the coldness of space. Bodies littered the streets. Crescent said, "This is a diversion. Note there are no Legionnaires here. Security forces will be heading in this direction while their goal is elsewhere. Very clever."

"Scrag crowhoppers!" Crater seethed, then said, "I didn't mean you, Crescent."

"It doesn't matter."

"Yes, it does."

Crescent looked at him. "That you believe it is enough. Now, let us blood our enemy and crush him beneath our boot. That is a Legionnaire saying meant to stir the spirit."

Crater's spirit was not stirred. He dreaded what came next, surely more fighting and more dying, both of which never seemed to solve anything. He hoped they might at least be in time to save Maria. He plunged through the utility tubes, Crescent on his heels.

THIRTY-TWO

C rescent had been told by the Trainers that she had been born into a beautiful life where death had no victory. Yet she was feeling sad about two deaths, neither of whom mattered anything to the world or the moon or the glory of the Legion. Tears kept appearing in her eyes, nuisance things causing her vision to blur, all because the kindly tailor and her silly little dog were gone, taken forever from her life. She missed them already.

As she followed Crater through the passageways and hatches of underground Armstrong City, Crescent also felt another emotion that was like a monster inside her. Crater seemed desperate to save Maria Medaris, but as far as Crescent knew, she had only hurt Crater. She recalled Q-Bess saying Maria was a rich, spoiled girl, but she'd also added, "Crater loves her more than life. I don't know if there will ever be room in his heart for anyone else."

Crescent was jealous. It was an emotion no Legionnaire was ever supposed to have and, for that reason, no Trainer had ever mentioned it, or instructed her what to do about it. Yet she knew it was unproductive. What difference did it make to her who Crater loved? She certainly had no ambition—or possibility—to be more than what she was in his eyes, whatever that was. Still, it was an emotion that had been there for some time, just waiting to burst out of her heart like some terrible worm in a spoiled apple. That other woman—Riley something or other—the red-headed mechanic who had been after Crater, Crescent had disliked her so much she wished sometimes the jumpcar she was working on would fall over and burst into flames. Crescent had voiced that wish once to one of the cooks and she'd put down her spatula and replied, "My, Crescent, are you jealous?"

Crescent had pushed the cook down and had been instantly sorry, mainly because she knew Q-Bess and Crater would find out about it. But they hadn't. The cook kept her mouth shut and that made Crescent feel even more regretful for what she'd done. Living among standard-issue humans was difficult. Crescent never knew if they were going to be kind or cruel.

But maybe none of it would matter. Perhaps death awaited her outside and she would go to the dark world where neither sadness or jealousy would cause her pain. She gripped the talwar in anticipation. The hatch for the Michael Collins Dome loomed. Crater pushed it open and climbed outside, moving out of the way for her. She expertly dived through, rolled as she'd been taught, and came up with the sword at the ready. A glance upward and she knew the dome was still intact. This confirmed to her that the attack was a kidnap operation. Otherwise, they would have busted down all three domes to kill everyone inside.

"Keep your helmet latched," Crater said.

Crescent did not reply. The Trainers said to always keep the chatter small. Of course, she would keep her helmet latched! Did he think she was stupid? Just because the dome hadn't been breached didn't mean it would stay that way.

They made their way to the Medaris Building, coming out in an alley that gave them a good view of a Legionnaire squad at the front door. Three Medaris guards lay dead in the street. Two more fought on, only to be cut down by flechettes. The Legionnaires paused and reloaded before advancing. Crescent was not impressed by their timid approach. In her opinion, they should have sprinted to the building, burst inside, and captured their target instead of acting like school children afraid to cross the road. That was when she noticed the stripe on their helmets and everything became clear. She started to remark on it but then Crater pointed at a fastbug and said, "Follow me."

He sprinted to the fastbug and climbed behind the wheel. Crescent, understanding his intention, stood up in the passenger seat, braced herself with one hand on the roll bar, and readied the talwar in the other. Crater pressed the accelerator and aimed the fastbug down the street. He was still accelerating when he plowed into the Legionnaires, running over three, the others scattering except for two who were minus their heads, thanks to Crescent's terrible, swift sword. As their bodies collapsed, blood spurted from their necks like scarlet volcanoes. Crescent smiled. She had exacted a small measure of vengeance for Mends Your Britches and Ike against these enemy troops.

Crater stopped the fastbug in front of the building, then jumped out and headed for the door, only to be driven back by a hail of flechettes. A flechette ricocheted off Crescent's helmet and then two crowhoppers attacked, their rifles sparkling.

Crescent boldly charged, and one of their heads went flying and the other lost an arm. Holding the bloody stump and looking up at her, the Legionnaire wailed, "Betrayer! Treasonous dog!"

Unimpressed, Crescent swung her wet sword, silencing her accuser forever. She picked up his rifle, then looked over her shoulder and saw Crater shoot another trooper with his pistol.

"Get your woman!" she yelled, ducking behind the fastbug as a volley of flechettes came after her. She dropped the sword in the fastbug and fired the railgun from her hip as she backed through the building's front door. Inside, she saw that Crater had found Maria Medaris, who was clinging to him. "It's all right," Crater said, holding her. "Stay close. I don't intend to lose you again."

Maria, Crescent noted with irritation, did not reply with an equal declaration of faithfulness nor even a little gratitude. Instead, she looked at Crescent and said, "Is that the creature?"

"Her name is Crescent," Crater said.

And then, as if there was nothing better to talk about in the midst of a deadly firefight, Maria said, "Yes, of course it is."

It. At that moment, Crescent wanted to cut off the woman's head. She contented herself with, "I know who you are too." Then to Crater she said, "Did you notice the white stripe on the helmets of some of these legionnaires? That means they're chokras. Chokras have basic skills that allow them to perform adequately in the field but likely this is their first real mission. That's why we're still alive."

"What's your advice?" Crater asked.

"Take to the underground. You know it better than anyone. We can hide down there until help comes."

"There's somebody else we need to save. My clients."

"They're probably already dead."

"I have to try."

Crescent shrugged. "Try is out that door," she said.

Outside was chaos. Armstrong City security guards had arrived and a battle had begun. A man, balding and stout and dressed in a blue tunic, ran up to Crater. "What's happening, sir? I don't understand, sir."

Crater apparently knew him. "I'll explain it later," he said. "Get in the fastbug."

"Do I belong to you now, sir?"

"Yes. Do what I say."

"Yes, sir. I will help in any way I can."

After the man climbed in beside Crescent, Crater yelled, "Hang on!" and stomped on the accelerator, steering the fastbug out of the square and into one of the side streets. As they gained speed, Crescent glanced at the man. He had no expression on his face and did not appear to care what was happening. The fastbug shot out into a square, then dodged down another side street. Crescent turned to the man. "Who are you?" she asked.

The man blinked. "I am a Helper. May I help you?"

Crescent turned away. He was apparently simple. Why Crater had brought him along didn't make sense, but she didn't have time to think about it because just then Maria was jerked aloft, snatched into the arms of a Legionnaire dangling by one leg from a flypod above, its jets pulsing, its pilot bent over its controls. Crescent stood up and swung her sword, which whacked off the crowhopper's leg. The flypod, released from its load, went out of control, then slammed into a building and erupted into a fireball. Maria and the dying black-suited warrior fell back into the fastbug. Crescent pushed the crowhopper out while Maria, soaked in blood, crawled back into the passenger seat.

"I do not understand this," the Helper said, looking with some dismay at the blood on his tunic.

"It is war," Crescent said.

"I am not allowed to fight," he said.

"Are you allowed to die?"

"Yes, if it would help."

Crescent did not think if this man lived or died would make any difference so she picked up a rifle and scanned the street ahead and behind and above, ready to fire the instant she saw a threat. She recalled the training she'd received dangling by one leg on a cable while being carried aloft by a flypod. It was a technique used primarily to recover Legionnaires cut off on the battlefield, but she admired the way it had just been used. The dangler had been brave and so had the flypod pilot, but Crescent recalled a Trainer saying courage was never enough, that skill in battle made all the difference.

Crescent murmured, "Life is death. Death is life," in salute to the pair of brave, skilled Legionnaires who had just died. Then she saw Maria reach out and touch Crater's shoulder. Crescent's face flushed hot. She put down the rifle and gripped the handle of her talwar and felt the sinews and muscles in her arms tighten in anticipation but then she forced them to relax. Killing Maria Medaris, as pleasurable as that might be, was wrong. Q-Bess had taught her that, and so had Mends Your Britches. Yet even proper instruction could not stop the jealousy that coursed through Crescent's nervous system like liquid fire.

::: THIRTY-THREE

rater turned a corner and saw the maintenance shed ahead. The big rollup door was wide open so he drove through it, jumped out, and hit the emergency door closer and watched as it trundled down. "Crescent, stand guard," he said, then went looking for the Apps, finding them huddled amongst their vehicles.

"What happened?" Jake asked. "All of a sudden the techies ran out of here. We heard explosions."

"We've been attacked by crowhoppers. Get into your suits and into your vehicles. Button up and prepare to go outside. We're getting out of here."

Crater ran back to the fastbug and pointed out the chuckwagon to Maria. "We'll take it with us."

The order astonished Maria. "My grandfather spent a hundred thousand johncredits for that machine. We can't just drive off in it."

"Maria, for scrag's sake, just this once, do what I say." There was a furious pounding on the rollup door. "Hear that? The crowhoppers will break in soon. Crescent, you go with Maria to the chuckwagon. Take the Helper and get him into a suit too."

"Where are you going?" Maria demanded.

"I've got four clients. They're going with us. Now go!"

The Helper did not move until Crescent grabbed his hand and pulled him along. Maria hesitated, then followed. Crater withdrew the gillie from his pocket. "Gillie, wake up. I want to blow up the maintenance shed. How can I do that?"

The gillie remained silent even though Crater pinched and prodded it. "Scrag thing," Crater muttered. "I should throw you away." He looked around. "All right, I'll figure it out for myself."

Crater noticed a welder's rig, which gave him an idea. He ran to a mooncrete igloo that held a stack of oxygen and tricetylene welding tanks. Mixed together in the air, the two chemicals would explode. He came back outside and saw Maria, now dressed in a pressure suit, drive the shiny new chuckwagon toward the exit doors. The truck and the crusher of the Apps pulled up alongside her. Crater pushed the big red button that opened the inside door of the vehicle dustlock and waved the vehicles inside. Then he closed it and opened the outer one. "Go to the top of that first hill out there, then stop unless something's after you. One way or the other, I'll catch up!"

Crater watched as Maria drove the chuckwagon into the dust, the truck and crusher following. He left the outer door open, then went back to the igloo and went from tank to tank, cracking their valves open. He placed a do4u on the deck, then pulled the hatch shut behind him. As he emerged from the igloo, the door of the shed crashed open and inside poured crowhoppers. Dodging flechettes, Crater ran to the fastbug and ducked behind it, then again withdrew the gillie from his pocket. "Gillie," he begged. "Wake up. I need you. I *really* need you!"

The gillie stirred. *I am a gillie biocomputer. I was designed by the Macingillie Corporation in the Republic of Calimexica and manufactured in—*

"Yes, yes, I know all that. Listen, Gillie. When I tell you to do it, I need you to call my do4u and tell it to short its circuits."

My diagnostic of your do4u indicates that it is in sound working condition and does not require its circuits to be shorted.

"Don't argue with me! When I tell you, I want you to short it out."

Gillie senses your do4u is in an explosive atmosphere. To short its circuits may cause a detonation.

"I know. I'm trying to cause one."

It will be a small explosion.

"I know that. I'm doing the best I can with what I've got."

Would you like a large explosion?

"I would like a *very* large explosion, yes."

It will take approximately twelve minutes to make that happen.

"We don't have time for that. Blow up the igloo first."

I will blow up the igloo and then I will make the larger explosion if you wish. I have calculated you are much too close. I am therefore opening the maintenance shed doors. Go through them and get as far away as possible.

"Open both the inner and outer doors."

The air inside will escape.

"That's all right. I'm in a pressure suit and there's no one else in here that matters."

The igloo will not explode in a vacuum. I am sealing the igloo and opening the doors.

The inner and outer doors began to rumble open. Crater,

staying as low as he could, leaped into the fastbug, then drove through the doors into the dust. Flechettes swarmed after him. "Blow up the igloo, Gillie!"

You are still too close.

"Do it anyway!"

The gillie shrugged, though it had no shoulders, and said, *Gillie will detonate the igloo.*

Crater looked over his shoulder and saw the flash caused by the mixture of oxygen and tricetylene ignited by the spark from the do4u. Smoke and flame burst out of the igloo, killing a crowhopper and causing the rest to dive for cover or draw back. The delay didn't last long. Within minutes, a contingent of crowhoppers emerged from the shed. "Gillie," Crater said, "if you're going to cause a very big explosion, now would be a good time."

You are far too close.

"I don't care. Now, Gillie. Now!"

Very well, the gillie said with something akin to a sigh. *Now it is.*

The maintenance shed erupted into a mighty fireball, its massive roof torn off and hurled into the sky. Though no sound reached Crater because of the vacuum, the ground shook as if a giant moonquake had struck and debris flew his way. He turned the fastbug around and ran for his life. At the top of the next hill, he braked and looked back. The maintenance shed was a black, broken shambles and a vast dust cloud hovered over the city. Crater knew the cloud was held up by a peculiarity of moon dust, its magnetic properties causing it to be repelled by the surface. The chuckwagon drove up and Maria, at the wheel with Crescent in the passenger seat, gaped at the sight. "You did that?" she asked.

"It was the gillie."

"How?"

The gillie spoke up. *Explosives storage was in the north quadrant of the shed. The puter told me that automated conveyor belts were used to bring up boxes of explosives bound for Helium-3 towns. Gillie ordered one point five tons of high performance glyco gel to the receiving station in the maintenance shed.*

Glyco gel was the main ingredient of the detpaks that mining operations used to blast the scrapes. Crater whistled. "That's a lot of glyco gel. How did you detonate it?"

Gillie also sent along ignition caps, then sent message for them to detonate.

"I'm glad it's on our side," Maria said.

"It's illegal, you know," Crater said, grinning.

"It knows that," Maria answered with a grin of her own.

Crescent pointed skyward. "The warpods are under attack and they're leaving."

Crater looked to see the jets of the warpods blinking out one by one. Darting amongst them was a silvery torpedo-shaped craft, the same kind he and Crescent had observed months ago engaging the Earthian warpods.

Crater used his helmet scope to scan the bodies of the crowhoppers around the destroyed maintenance shed. All seemed dead. But then he saw eight spiderwalkers, the agile eight-legged land machines that could walk, run, and hop, creeping around the edges of the town.

Out of the corner of his eye he glimpsed someone running past him. It was Jake, with Clarence close behind. They were not used to moon gravity, and a few steps down the hill they lost their balance and tumbled down the dusty slope. "What are you doing?" Crater yelled.

The App men got to their feet and ran on, adjusting for the light gravity. Crater now understood what they were up to. They were picking up railgun rifles and stripping the dead crowhoppers of bandoleers of flechettes. It was a good idea, but the spiderwalkers had seen them and turned their way. "Come on, boys," Crater said. "Get in your vehicles. We've got to go or they're going to catch us."

"I don't think so," Crescent said and pointed skyward once more.

Crater looked up. This time it wasn't warpods he saw but mooncrete and lunasteel. Tons of it.

What goes up must come down, the gillie said.

::: THIRTY-FOUR

Maria was simmering. She detested the enemy nations that sent the crowhoppers to ravage Armstrong City and murder innocent people, done only to kidnap her. What sense did that make? War was so stupid! And how many billions of johncredits was it going to take to rebuild the Buzz Aldrin Dome and repair all the other damage? The only thing that made her feel any better was she was certain that her grandfather would go after those dictators and exact a bloody vengeance. It might take weeks, months, or years, but the Colonel was patient. He'd figure out how to do it, then do it.

She was also angry at Crater. True, he had saved her, but other than that, she didn't much like the decisions he'd made. For one thing, he'd blown up the maintenance shed! That was going to cost a pretty penny to rebuild and who was going to pay for it? She also didn't like that Crater had ordered her to take the chuckwagon. It belonged to the company and it was meant to accompany Helium-3 convoys, not taken on a desperate lurch across the moon. And where were they going, anyway? They were off any track she knew and heading west-ward. It made no sense at all.

Maria had doubts about this new resolute Crater who had suddenly appeared when he'd kissed her after she'd given him the gillie. Maria liked the old Crater, soft around the edges and easily wrapped around her little finger. Then she recalled that kiss. Her hand touched her lips in remembrance. Maybe the new Crater wasn't so bad after all.

She became aware of the creature in the passenger seat watching her and she quickly dropped her fingers from her mouth. It was a pug-ugly thing, this girl crowhopper. When this strange odyssey to somewhere had begun, the creature had taken off her helmet and the pressurized cabin filled with her body odor. "There are showers in the back," Maria said.

"Do I stink?" Crescent asked. She didn't sound angry, just curious.

Maria never shied from a truth. "You are not fresh," she replied.

"Would you prefer me to be fresh or dead? The Legion is following. We do not know when they might catch up and I need to be prepared to defend us."

"Let's risk it," Maria answered in her crisp fashion.

"I think not," Crescent answered, just as crisply. "However, I will drive if you wish a shower. You have also sweated inside your pressure suit."

Maria's pride would not let her accept the offer. "I will wait," she answered, and then both lapsed into silence.

Ahead, all Maria could see were gray, rolling hills, sparse craters, and no tracks. Wherever they were going, no one else had gone before. Still, the driving was easy. The chuckwagon was a state-of-the-art moon vehicle, its articulated axles and studded wheels and power steering making it a snap to drive. Maria checked the nav system and saw that they were still heading generally west. She called up Crater's private number. "Where are we going?"

"Endless Dust," he answered before adding, "We need to keep comm down to a minimum."

"Why? This is a secure channel."

"We could always be intercepted. Besides, I need to focus," Crater replied.

In other words, Maria fumed, he didn't want to talk to her. Well, scrag that. She was Maria Medaris and she didn't follow any man around. It took a moment before Maria placed Endless Dust, but when she did, she didn't like it at all. "That's at least three hundred miles away," she said. "Why are we going there?"

Several seconds passed before Crater replied. "The people in the truck and the crusher are my clients. They hired me to take them there."

"The situation has changed. We should turn north to Aristillus. There's a security force there."

"My clients want to go to Endless Dust."

"If we get caught by those spiderwalkers, it won't matter where they want to go."

"We're going to Endless Dust," Crater said.

"Maybe I'll go to Aristillus by myself," Maria replied.

"Maria," Crater said with a sigh, "just drive, okay? I know you're tired. So am I. But we're going to Endless Dust and that's it. If you don't want to drive, let Crescent take over."

"She doesn't know how to drive this vehicle."

"I am perfectly capable of driving this vehicle," Crescent said.

"Excuse me, but this is between Crater and me," Maria snapped.

Crescent leaned back and cradled her rifle in her lap. "You're right," she said.

"Right about what?" Maria demanded.

"You're right that we should go to Aristillus. We could be there in two days. We might even be able to call ahead and get a security force out to us. Out here, it's just us against the Legion and they will catch us. Crater is wrong."

Surprised, Maria glanced at the crowhopper, then back to the terrain ahead. On second thought, maybe this humanoid or whatever she was wasn't all that ugly. And the odor that had come from her hadn't been all that bad, just natural perspiration for what had been, after all, hot work. "Thank you for saving my life," Maria said.

"Crater saved your life, not me," Crescent replied.

"When I was plucked out of the fastbug, you cut that creature's leg off."

"I am trained to react quickly and violently. But you're welcome."

Maria glanced at Crescent again. The girl looked strong, but Maria was strong too. Since her return to Armstrong City, she'd worked out every day in the company gym with a professional trainer. She was toned and fit, her energy tireless. She'd learned a variety of fighting skills—tai chi, kung fu, karate, and the new style of hand-to-hand combat called bergerhauster where hands, feet, elbows, and knees were used as lethal weapons. "I could turn the chuckwagon north," Maria said. "Crater would have to follow us."

"I'm not so certain," Crescent replied. "It is a matter of honor for him to take those people to Endless Dust."

"You said the Legion will catch us."

"Yes. And then they will probably kill us all except for you. You, they will take for ransom."

Maria absorbed the girl's declaration. "You say that so matter-of-factly. How can you be so calm about it?"

"I was born to die in battle. It is no great surprise that it will occur. But perhaps I am wrong. If nothing else, Crater is lucky. I was taught to never discount luck, especially in war. A plan does not last long in a fight. In this case, Crater has no plan, other than to do what he promised his clients, but he will come up with something. I trust him to do that."

Maria drove on, following the fastbug until she couldn't keep her eyes open any longer. The girl crowhopper didn't seem to be tired at all. "Would you like to drive?" Maria asked.

Crescent nodded. "You would trust me?"

"Just don't wreck my grandfather's chuckwagon," Maria said, slipping out of the seat while holding on to the steering wheel.

Crescent handed Maria the railgun rifle, then grasped the steering wheel and sat down. "Do you know how to use it?" she asked, meaning the rifle.

"Better than you, honey," Maria replied, subsiding in the passenger's seat.

Crescent made no reply, which surprised Maria. She'd expected an argument and was a little disappointed she hadn't gotten one. The crowhopper girl was interesting. Maria might have thought about that a little longer and tried to figure out how to turn it to her advantage, but she soon fell into a deep sleep. A few hours later she received a call from Crater. "Would you like to drive the fastbug?" he asked. "I recall you were a pretty good scout. I'd also like to get to know the chuckwagon."

"Sure thing!" Maria chirped. She looked over at Crescent. "You've done well."

"It is a fine machine," Crescent said with a shrug, then stopped the chuckwagon to let Maria get out and Crater climb in.

Outside, Maria settled into the fastbug. "This feels good," she said and meant it. For far too long she'd allowed herself to be cooped up inside an office. It was exhilarating to once more be in the wayback even if the situation was a desperate one.

"Remember you're breaking a new trail," Crater said. "Don't go too fast. If you do, even a small crater can do a lot of damage."

Maria wanted to growl that she knew very well how to drive a fastbug but she held herself back. "Look, Crater," she said, "we really should head for Aristillus. Even Crescent agrees."

"We're going to Endless Dust."

"The spiderwalkers will catch us," Crescent said.

Crater looked back toward the horizon. All he could see were gray hills and black sky. "The crusher is slowing us down," he said.

"Why don't we abandon it?"

"My clients need it."

"Crater, do you hear yourself?" Maria demanded. "This is no longer about your clients."

"We'll get through," Crater said.

"Do you really believe that?"

"I wouldn't say it if I didn't believe it. Now, get going but don't get too far ahead. Just stay generally westward."

Maria got going. At first she went fast but then, remembering Crater's words, slowed down so that she could keep the others in sight. It was strange the way she felt. She was excited to be driving a fastbug but she was also frightened to the marrow of her bones.

::: THIRTY-FIVE

Doing his best to avoid any of the deeper holes, Crater drove the chuckwagon through a ravaged field of eroded craters surrounded by steep blue-gray hills, equally torn to pieces by ancient meteors. Everything looked as if it had been blasted by pellets from giant shotguns. There were also huge boulders sparkling in the sunlight, fragments of asteroids soaring out of the primordial solar system to skim past the Earth to strike instead the near side of the moon.

Crescent sat beside him with a rifle on her lap. Behind them, the Helper, strapped in a chair, dozed. Close behind, Jake and Trudelle were driving the truck and trailer, and Clarence and Eliza were driving the crusher. Maria scouted ahead.

They had gone two days without stopping. Everyone in the little convoy, with the possible exception of the Helper, was exhausted. The biofuel cells that drove the vehicles had need of rest. Crater kept glancing at the radar. Though it covered twenty miles in any direction, there was a great deal of static from the pocked terrain. Pursuing spiderwalkers might easily be lost in the radar's ground clutter.

Crater looked over at Crescent and noticed her face was wet. "What's wrong?" he asked.

"Nothing."

"You're crying."

"Am I?"

"If you're not, it's raining and the roof is leaking."

Crater's answer made Crescent smile. She wiped her eyes with the back of her hand and said, "That is funny. I know for a fact you have never seen it rain."

"But I have a good imagination," Crater replied, glad for the conversation that he hoped would keep him awake. "My brother, Petro, was forever going on about what it would be like to see and feel rain. He claimed he remembered it from his childhood, but I don't think he did. He was just remembering what he'd read in books."

"I have been in the rain many times," Crescent said. "Rain is not always pleasant the way you moon people talk about it. Sometimes it is cold and sometimes it turns to ice and snow. It also causes the dirt to turn into mud, which clings to the feet and tires and tracks and makes a great mess. If it rained here, it would be the worst mud ever known. Everything on this little planet is the worst."

"It's still home," Crater said, then remembered what had started the conversation. "Why are you crying?"

Crescent looked out the window at the tortured landscape, then said, "I miss Mend Your Britches and Ike. They were good to me and did not deserve to die. I think of them and the tear ducts in my eyes start working. I don't wish it to happen but it does."

"I miss them too," Crater said. "If I started thinking about them, I'd probably cry too. It's nothing to be ashamed of."

Crescent was quiet for a while, then said, "This girl Maria.

I familiarized myself with her while we drove together. She is smart and she speaks her mind. I admire this but I also know she has treated you badly. Why do you love her?"

Crater shrugged. "I'm not sure I do. I thought I did but now I don't know." Crater felt a need to change the subject. "You told her you thought the spiderwalkers would catch us. I'm not even sure they're following."

"They are. It is their duty."

"What is their weakness?"

Crescent gave that some thought, then said, "As long as they have good leaders, they will be good fighters. If their leadership is poor, they will be poor fighters. It is the way of all fighting forces."

"Then let's hope for poor leadership. And we have an advantage they don't know about," Crater said.

"What's that?"

"You."

Crescent didn't think that her presence would make any difference at all but she didn't say it, not seeing the point of puncturing Crater's hopes. When the walkers caught them, they would attack viciously. To change the topic, she looked over her shoulder at the Helper who had come awake, although he was not moving and just staring blankly ahead. She asked, "What is this Helper?"

"They're humans used for menial chores."

"Genetically modified like me?"

"Yes."

"Why is he with us?"

"I felt sorry for him."

"Like you did me?" When Crater didn't answer, Crescent said, "I don't like that he doesn't have a name."

"Would you like to give him one?"

Crescent looked uncertain, then climbed out of her seat and went back to sit on a couch across from the Helper. He took note of her. "Hello. I am a Helper. May I help you?"

Crescent reached across and lifted the tag that was hanging from his neck. "What is this?"

"That is my price. I will help you."

"You are expensive."

"I am young. When old, I can be traded for a new Helper."

Crescent dropped the tag. "I am not going to buy you. You don't need to be bought. You are free."

The Helper looked distressed. "I do not understand."

Crescent turned toward Crater. "What should I do?"

"He thinks he has to be owned by someone. Take his tag off if you want him."

Crescent took the tag off. "You belong to me. Do you have a name?"

"No, but you may give me one if it will help."

"I will call you Ike. You remind me of . . . someone I used to know. Do you like your new name?"

"My name is Ike."

"Very good, Ike."

"How may I help you?"

"Just sit here for now."

Crater checked the radar again. There was still nothing moving behind them that he could see. By his calculations, they had traveled two hundred tough miles. They'd gone west, then turned north before turning west again into the tortured land of the Cayleys. In his rearview mirror, he could see their tracks glowing in the sunlight almost as if they were on fire. The walkers, if they were coming, would easily be able to track them.

He took the gillie from his pocket. "Have you heard the crowhoppers?" he asked.

No local transmissions.

"Have you heard anything else?"

Many military communications. The battle is in space.

"Who's winning?"

It is not clear who is fighting.

Before the gillie could continue, if it meant to, Crater slammed on the brakes to keep from running over Maria, who had stopped her fastbug. She was looking at a gleaming strip of dust set between a narrow passage. "I'm not sure we should cross this," she said. "It looks slippery."

Crater grabbed his helmet, then looked over his shoulder. "Ike?"

Ike stood up. "Yes, sir? May I help?"

"No. Stay where you are. I'm going to seal off your compartment. Crescent and I are getting out."

"Yes, sir. I am prepared to help when you need me." Ike sat down, put his hands on his knees, and stared straight ahead.

"Can we cross?" Jake called from the truck.

"Let me check," Crater replied, pulling a scragbar out of the chuckwagon. He walked up beside Maria and pondered the glistening material.

"What do you think it is?" Maria asked.

"Let's find out," Crater said, then drove the scragbar's point into the material and pried out a lump. Studying it with his helmet magnifier, he saw it had threads inside that gave it a yellowish tint.

"Odd," Maria said when Crater handed it to her.

Crater dug into his pocket and brought out the gillie. "Gillie," he said. "What is this mineral?"

The gillie said nothing and Crater realized it had gone to sleep again. Shaking his head, he tucked it back in his pocket as Jake and Clarence walked up. "May I?" Clarence asked, plucking the lump from Maria's hand. He studied it, then said, "Nickel. Based on its color, it is also suffused with a high gold content."

"Gold?" Crater and Maria asked in unison.

Clarence nodded. "Nickel and gold are commonly found together in nature."

"This is likely the remains of an asteroid," Jake added. He had walked out on the glittering surface, kicking the dust away. He skated back. "No atmosphere on the moon to burn it up, just crashed here in all its glory. Worth more johncredits than probably exist."

"How do you know?" Crater demanded.

"I have a degree in geology," Jake said. "Clarence has one in mining engineering. What? Did you think we were just ignorant Apps?" He put his hand to his chin, or tried to before being stymied by his helmet. "Do we have time for a core sample? We have a diamond core drill. It wouldn't take but a few minutes."

Maria stared at the two immigrants. "Forget going to Endless Dust. Claim this asteroid, dig it up, and be trillionaires."

Jake looked at Clarence who looked back, then both smiled. "We're going to Endless Dust. I guess you could say we are a hardheaded people."

"Something's moving on the radar," Crescent said. She had been standing on the running board of the chuckwagon so she could see through the window and keep her eye on the screen.

Crater stepped up beside her and watched the screen for a few seconds. "I don't see anything," he said.

"I saw movement at the far edge of the scope. A series of blips. I'm sure they were spiderwalkers."

"How many?"

"I think eight. A standard contubernium. And based on this terrain, I think they'll be at this spot in three hours or less."

Crater stepped off the running board and took Jake by the arm and walked him a little way off, making sure their do4u's were on private. "We're going to have to fight. Do the women know how to shoot?"

"We're Apps, Crater. We all grew up with guns."

"Good. I'll have Crescent run you through some quick rifle training."

Seeing the worry on Crater's face, Jake said, "We'll stop them."

"To stop a contu of spiderwalkers will take more than rifles. We've got to disable them."

"We have detpaks," Jake suggested.

"They would do the trick, but we can't just heave them over," Crater said. "Spiderwalkers are fast. What we need is some kind of artillery."

That was when Crater's eyes landed on the stack of pipe on the trailer. "What diameter core sample can you take?" he asked. "For instance, could you make a core the diameter of your water pipe?"

"Sure. The interior diameter of the small-sized pipe is three inches and that's one of the standard core sizes."

"How long are the cores?"

"Two or three inches."

"Make it three inches," Crater said. "And get started right away. As many of them as you can cut out of the nickel."

"You have a plan?"

"A desperate one."

"Best kind," Jake said, then went off to core sample the asteroid.

::: THIRTY-SIX

The rubble-covered hills formed a natural funnel. For Crater's plan to work, he hoped the spiderwalkers would take the easy route and follow the tracks of the convoy right up to the edge of the asteroid.

The surface of the asteroid was like a lake of ice. It wasn't easy, and there was a great deal of slipping and sliding, but they managed to get all the vehicles across. Crater parked the convoy aiming away, first the fastbug, then the chuckwagon, then the truck and trailer. The crusher was turned sideways at the edge of the metallic lake. Atop it, Crater mounted his cannon, a lunar version of a potato gun.

Potato guns built on Earth were simple. Usually made of polyvinyl tubes to form a combustion chamber and a barrel, the guns used hairspray or ether as a fuel to propel a potato at high velocity. They were just toys and Crater had never built one, there being a serious lack of oxygen in the lunar vacuum to cause the hairspray/ether to combust, but he knew about them and now had built one of his own, only deadlier than any on Earth.

Crater's version had two lunasteel water pipes welded

together to form a combustion chamber and a barrel. Piercing the combustion chamber was a valve to receive a puff of welding tricetylene and another valve to receive a puff of welding oxygen. The spark in the chamber was provided by two wires leading from a do4u battery pack into the chamber. The artillery round was a dense core sample of nickel suffused with gold drawn from the asteroid. Though the slug felt light in the lunar gravity, it still had considerable mass. It would be enough, Crater hoped, to cause damage to a spiderwalker.

His cannon was set up inside the hopper of the crusher. Aiming was simple. Using the well-equipped machine shop in the chuckwagon, Crater had welded a stand for the cannon so that it could be raised or lowered by turning a hand crank. He provided the muscle to aim it. Crescent's job was to load the cannon and feed the mixture of gases into the chamber. Maria served as a sniper, armed with a rifle. The Apps set up around the parked vehicles in case a walker broke through. Ike was in the chuckwagon, still sitting in his chair, his hands on his knees and looking straight ahead.

While waiting for the arrival of the walkers, Crater charged up the crusher's fuel cells. He and Maria were just finishing the folding and stacking of the solar panels when the first walker appeared, creeping around a hill that led into the funnel. A black-armored crowhopper rode atop, reining in his walker and waiting until several more of his fellows came up alongside him.

The sight of them gave Crater serious doubts about his plan. Although partially controlled by their riders, spiderwalkers were also automatons, able to make decisions on their own. They had sharp steel fangs and, when in battle mode, snapped their jaws and lunged toward anything they sensed was organic.

Tales of battle against spiderwalkers were rife with the amputated arms, legs, and heads of infantry trying to fight them.

Eight spiderwalkers crept up and stopped at the lake's edge, their riders sitting astride them and apparently studying the situation. They were talking amongst themselves—Crater could see that by the way they turned their helmeted heads toward one another. One of them had three white stripes on its helmet. He called Crescent's attention to it.

"Their ranking decan," Crescent explained. "Much like a sergeant in a human army. I see no evidence of officers. They were either killed at Armstrong City or, more likely, weren't sent on this raid. Officers are expensive."

The gillie, which was in one of Crater's breast pockets, climbed out. Crater, glad to see it, said, "Gillie, hack into the communicators on those spiderwalkers and link Crescent, Maria, and me in."

Gillie will comply, the gillie said.

Crater, Crescent, and Maria next heard the harsh, guttural voices peculiar to the Legion speaking in their Siberian-based language. "We should turn back," one of them was saying. "They must have a secret weapon or they wouldn't have stopped."

"Shut up, Carillon," another said.

"That is the decan who just spoke," Crescent advised.

"Carillon," the decan said. "Advance."

"By myself? This is not wise."

"Is it wise to die? I will kill you within five seconds if you do not follow my orders."

Carillon apparently believed the threat because a spiderwalker left the others and approached the nickel-gold lake. The cannon was loaded, but Crater decided to wait until the walker started across. On its first step, the walker's leg slipped out from under it, lurching to one side. When it struggled to stand, another leg slipped until it was splayed out on the slippery surface. Its rider, presumably Carillon, was thrown off.

The crowhopper decan laughed. "What's wrong, Carillon? Did you feel a need to kiss the moon?"

"Shoot it, Crater," Maria urged. "Now, while it can't move."

"Let's watch and see what happens," Crater replied. "Maybe the walkers won't be able to get across and they'll retreat. Anyway, I'm not certain of my aim. I'm not even certain if this cannon is going to work!"

Maria fell silent. Once more she sensed how doomed they were.

::: THIRTY-SEVEN

arillon tried to get to his feet. His spiderwalker was also trying, but every time it put a foot down, it slipped again. Carillon felt as if his back had a bull's-eye on it. He could see the tube on the crusher. It was some sort of heavy artillery. He started to crawl back to shore.

"Another step, Carillon, and I will shoot you down," Decan Flaubert said. "Get back to your walker and change to friction pads. All of you do the same. Now!"

Absalom, Lucien, and Dion dismounted and opened utility lockers on the sides of their robotic beasts and took out square-shaped foot pads that snapped onto the pointy feet of the walkers. The other three riders were veterans, eager to get into battle, and soon had the pads on. The three youths were slower. They were literally shaking in their boots.

Carillon, crawling to his walker, opened up the locker and took out the friction pads. As soon as he'd attached one of them to a foot on his walker, it stomped down and rose up on that side. Another pad on the other side and it lurched upright.

That was when the cannon on the crusher fired. The round

fell short but ricocheted into the thorax of Carillon's walker. Trying to get purchase, it threw its legs around and one of them struck Carillon in his helmet. He screamed a silent scream, then fell limp.

"Is Carillon dead?" Lucien asked, his eyes wide.

"What is that weapon?" Absalom cried. "It will kill us all!"

"Be silent!" Flaubert commanded. He leaned forward, squinting at the big machine and the tube that projected from it. "It can only fire one projectile at a time," he concluded. "No tactics required. Just straight ahead should do." He waved his hand forward. "You know the drill. Deploy and destroy."

The three youths looked at each other, waited until the veterans walked their walkers forward, then followed. They stamped onto the nickel lake, crept around the wounded walker and poor Carillon, then skittered ahead. Another round was punched out of the strange cannon. It hit one of the veterans in his chest, stripping him out of his saddle and flinging him away. The riderless walker lurched away from the group, then stopped when the cannon fired again and struck it in its head. The cannon fired yet again, the slug ripping headlong through the pincers and head of another spiderwalker. It fell forward, its rider flung to the hard surface and then crushed when the walker rolled onto its back, its legs wriggling toward the black sky.

The third veteran ran in from the flank and rose up in front of the crusher, its feet catching the edge of the hopper. A hail of flechettes at close range dispatched its rider. The spiderwalker, its front legs dangling into the hopper, stopped and waved its head around, its fangs snapping. Then one of the humans jumped on its back. He knew something of spiderwalkers, that much was certain. He opened a utility hatch and turned the walker off, then dismounted and slid and slithered back to the crusher. The cannon fired again, its round tearing out the guts of the disabled walker.

Lucien turned around first, then Absalom, then Dion. They urged their walkers off the lake past Flaubert, who hurled curses after them. When they got to shore, they sped up, not slowing until they'd turned the corner of the hill, out of sight of the deadly cannon.

Flaubert caught up with them. "Cowards!"

The three looked back at him. "We had no chance," Lucien said.

"We are Legionnaires. We always have a chance!" Flaubert rocked back and forth in his saddle. "I will show you how to fight. Follow me and watch a warrior at work."

They crept behind their decan, then stopped at the edge of the lake.

"Life is death! Death is life!" Flaubert yelled, then sent his walker at full tilt along the edge of the lake and up the side of the hill that formed part of the funnel. Midway, the walker leaped and fell on top of the crusher. The humans manning the cannon fled but Flaubert didn't follow. The legs of his walker were entangled in the cannon mount. He shook his fist at the humans as they got in their vehicles and sped away.

Absalom, Dion, and Lucien carefully crept across the lake, reaching the crusher just as Flaubert's walker pulled its last leg free. The decan looked at them. "You three are the sorriest excuses for Legionnaires in the history of the Legion." He let that sink in, then said, "It was no coincidence that you and Carillon had mechanical difficulties with your walkers at the start of this operation, was it? No, of course not. I should have killed you and put an infantry troop on your walkers. They couldn't have been any worse."

He drew his rifle from its holster and swung it in their direction. "One more act of cowardice from one of you and I will kill all three. Do you believe me?"

"Yes, Decan!" they chorused.

Flaubert started to laugh, then pointed behind them. They turned around in their saddles to see what was so funny. It was Carillon—alive. He staggered up to Lucien's walker and hung onto its leg. "I did my duty, Decan!" he yelled.

Flaubert nodded. "Yes, you did, you cur." He pointed at the crusher. "Get in that thing and drive. We will catch these humans and crush them under its tracks."

"One of them isn't human," Carillon said. "It is a Legionnaire. I could see it clearly. Only smaller."

"You are hallucinating, idiot," Flaubert said. "Get in the crusher, I said. Do it now!"

Carillon hesitated until Flaubert aimed the rifle at his head. "On my way, Decan!" he shouted, saluting and clicking his heels.

::: THIRTY-EIGHT

They're coming after us!" Clarence yelled. "And they've got the crusher!"

Crater, driving the chuckwagon, looked in the rearview screen and saw Clarence was right. Maria in the fastbug was in the lead, then the chuckwagon and the truck and trailer. They rolled down a valley pocked with large craters toward a low hill. Crater was thinking in terms of making a stand and for that, he needed high ground. Then he saw a whitish streak several miles away. "Maria, do you see that white dust off to the north? Turn toward it."

"What is it?" she asked.

"Maybe salvation. Don't drive across it. Go up ahead of it."

"Roger, wilco," Maria said and put the hammer down on the fastbug, catching vacuum across craters and rilles. She skirted the streak, then stopped on the other side. Crater followed her tracks. "May I help in any way?" Ike called from his chair.

"Not now, Ike," Crescent answered.

"I am here to help."

"I know. Take it easy."

The gillie suddenly spoke up. *I am sick*, it said.

"I'm a little busy right now, Gillie," Crater said.

I am very sick.

"Hush, Gillie," Crater said.

Crater stopped the chuckwagon beside Maria. He and Crescent got out and stood beside her. The truck soon roared up and the Apps got out too.

Gillie is really, really sick.

"Hush, Gillie." Crater turned to Crescent. "Will they attack us head-on?"

Crescent considered the terrain, then said, "Yes. I think so."

"They'd better," Crater said.

The crusher came first, the spiderwalkers using it for cover.

"Is this the end?" Jake asked. "If it is, my people would like to pray."

"Pray like it's the end," Crater said.

The Apps bowed their heads. "Our Father, Who art in heaven..."

The crusher clanked onto the white dust and rolled toward them. Then there was a puff of dust and the crusher disappeared, dropped into a yawning abyss.

The Apps rushed up to see. "The white dust was a skim over a collapsed lavatube," Crater explained. "I've seen them before. Almost fell into a few."

Maria looked across the chasm and said, "This isn't over. There are still four walkers left."

"They're withdrawing," Crescent observed. "Or at least three of them are. Now the other one is too."

Crater felt the gillie move in his pocket. "Are you still sick, Gillie?"

The gillie crawled out. *Not sick but busy.*

"Busy doing what?" Then Crater felt something else move in his pocket. He reached inside and plucked out the thing that was moving, but what he held between his thumb and finger was confusing. It looked like the gillie, only smaller. "Gillie, what is this?"

The gillie said nothing.

Maria laughed and said, "Congratulations, Crater."

"What for?"

"Your gillie just had a baby."

Crater stared at the two gillies. "Gillie? Is this true?"

The gillie on his shoulder said nothing although it looked proud, even though it could look no way at all.

::: THIRTY-NINE

The convoy continued westward through the squat hills and piles of primordial rubble between the Ariadaeus and Hyginus Rilles. The land was riddled with collapsed lavatubes, some no bigger than a truck wheel, others miles long and thousands of feet deep. Maria took the fastbug and zipped ahead to scout out a safe route. Before she climbed aboard the fastbug, she asked Crater for the baby gillie, but Crater suggested maybe it needed some raising by its mother or father or whatever the gillie was. Besides, both gillies seemed the same. When one spoke, so did the other, saying the same thing. They were literally on the same wavelength. To give them both time to recuperate, he put them in the chuckwagon refrigerator. Neither heat nor cold seemed to bother gillies so he figured they'd be safe in there and whatever was supposed to happen would happen without interference.

"I still want first dibs on the new gillie," Maria said. "When do you think it will be ready?"

"I have no idea," Crater confessed.

"It's mine," she said. "Don't forget that."

The way she said it reminded Crater that Maria was, after all, a member of the Medaris family and used to getting her way.

On the third day after the lavatube had swallowed the crusher, the convoy rolled up to where Maria stood beside her fastbug, its wheel stuck in the dust. "Looks like you found a miniature lavatube," Crater said, trying not to laugh.

Maria's scowl quickly shut him up. Salvaging the moment, Crescent said, "I think I've finally found a job for Ike."

Some minutes later Crescent and Ike, whom she had dressed in a pressure suit, exited the chuckwagon. "I have never been outside, Missus," Ike said. "Will I be able to breathe?"

"You're breathing now, aren't you? Don't be afraid."

"I want to help."

"Good." Crescent retrieved a shovel from the exterior toolbox of the chuckwagon and led Ike to the fastbug. She handed him the shovel. "Dig it out."

Ike stared at the shovel, then looked at the sunk fastbug wheel, then started digging with enthusiasm. "Take it easy, Ike," Crater said. "You don't have to wear yourself out."

"I am helping," he said.

"Yes, you are, but don't kill yourself doing it."

Ike slowed down. "Like this?"

"Like that. Very good."

While Ike helped, Crater asked Jake what he was going to do without the crusher. "If we have to, we will crush the rock by hand," Jake replied.

"You Apps are stubborn," Crater said, which made Jake grin and nod in agreement.

After the fastbug was freed, Crater inspected it and, as he feared, found its axle broken, which was, he supposed, at least better than it being bent. A busted axle he could weld but a bent one he doubted he could straighten. With Clarence's assistance, he used the mobile welder from the chuckwagon to weld the axle back together. After a test drive, he brought the fastbug back to Maria. "It should hold," he said wearily. "But I think you should slow down."

"If we don't hurry, we're going to be in the dark," she pointed out.

"The shadow's going to catch us anyway," Crater replied, looking aloft and shielding his eyes from the sun.

For the next two days, they journeyed in the sunlight, reaching the plain called Seething Bay. Then a fuel cell on one of the trucks began to overheat. Deciding it was about to die, Crater disconnected it, leaving one cell to push the truck along. The Seething Bay surface, which was white and fine grained, was especially hot. Crater could even feel it soaking into his boots, the biolastic sheath unable to fully compensate.

The shadow caught them just as they passed the Flammarion peaks. It wasn't completely dark as the blue glow of the Earth lit up the plains and hills but it was decidedly colder, which was a relief from the heat. Crater was starting to feel good about their chances. The radar remained clear.

Near the crater Palisa, which was within sight of the walled rim of the polygonal-shaped crater Ptolemaeus, the biofuel cells in all the vehicles started to show signs of distress. Crater called Maria and told her it was time to halt the convoy. They would stop for twelve hours so the cells could rest.

Maria turned around to rejoin the convoy. When she arrived, she saw Crater and the two App men working on the vehicles. The App women were posted as guards, one on a small rounded hill, one along the track they'd made. She studied the situation, then sought out Crescent. "Did you organize the defense?"

"I did."

"If you look over toward that hill," Maria said, pointing at a tall peak, "you will see it is a better place to put a guard than that low hill."

"I considered it," Crescent said, "but I decided it was too far away."

"I think it best if you put one of the women there," Maria insisted. "Please see to it."

"You're giving me an order?"

"As second in command, yes, I am."

Crescent came rigidly to attention and saluted smartly. "*Oui*, Madame Commandant!"

"Oh, don't be like that, Crescent," Maria said.

"Do you have any other orders, *mein fuhrer*?"

"Now you're going too far," Maria said, although it was to Crescent's back as she stalked away.

After dinner, Maria asked Crater to walk with her in the ghostly blue Earthlight. Crater was tired but agreed. There was a series of pointy little hills that he was curious about and he wanted to give them a closer look. He called Crescent. "Maria and I are going to walk to those hills to the east."

"You mean the commander and the second in command are leaving me without benefit of their leadership?"

"Crater and I have things we need to discuss," Maria said.

"I shall try my very best to manage without your supervision," Crescent replied.

"What's wrong with you?" Crater demanded. "We won't be gone long."

The click in both their ears told them Crescent had signed

off. "She is in love with you, you know," Maria said after they'd strolled a way toward the hills.

This was an obvious shock to Crater, who stopped and stared at Maria. "That's not true. She's just grateful I look after her."

"You know it's true. So what are you going to do about it?"

"I'm not going to do anything because I still don't believe it," Crater said, turning to walk again.

"All right, fine. So what are you going to do about us?"

Crater stopped again. "All I want to do is look at those little pointy hills."

"You can't look at little pointy hills or whatever and change the subject forever," Maria said. "Is it Riley? Has she stolen your heart?"

Crater's expression changed to one of astonishment. "There was never anything between Riley and me! How do you know about her, anyway?"

"I have my ways. Why haven't you fallen love with her, Crater? She's a beautiful girl!"

He turned away. "I wonder how those hills were formed."

"I heard you were at the Earthrise with her quite a few times."

"Could we just walk and not talk? Or is that not possible for you?"

"Oh, I can walk and not talk with the best of them." Three steps later she added, "Yes, with the best of them."

"You only walked three steps before you talked," Crater pointed out, which was the last thing he said before he was shoved down from behind. At the same moment, Maria was shoved down too. When she tried to get up, a heavy boot pushed down on her neck. The next words she heard were in crowhopper, which she didn't entirely understand.

::: FORTY

rater understood the words of their captors. "Should I kill the boy?" a crowhopper asked.

"Not yet," came the answer. "But soon."

Crater's hands were tied behind him, and he was dragged across the dust and roughly thrust atop a spiderwalker where he was lashed aboard with stout cable. Then the rider got aboard and Crater felt the walker undulate as it moved. Hours later he was dragged off the walker and thrown into the dust. Turning his head, he saw Maria lying beside him, her eyes wide and frightened. He wished he hadn't put the gillie in the refrigerator. It might have been helpful.

Before long, another spiderwalker came and stood over them. At first, Crater thought it was going to walk on them, but it carefully stepped along until its thorax was directly above them. Crater couldn't figure why until it drew in its legs and the crowhoppers weaved cables through them. The legs and cables fashioned a cage.

A crowhopper reached inside and untied their hands. Crater and Maria sat up, and Maria impulsively took his hand.

Crater was glad to hold her hand, if that made her feel better, but his focus was on inspecting their metallic prison. After a bit of inspecting, he asked, "How much air do you have?"

"About five hours," she said. "I should have topped off but you acted like you really wanted to walk out on the dust so I put it off."

"But I didn't want to go anywhere," Crater said. "You asked me, remember?"

"I could tell you wanted to talk."

Crater frowned. "I didn't want to talk. I just wanted to see those pointy hills."

She took her hand away. "You send me so many mixed signals, I guess I don't know what to think."

Crater looked at her in consternation. She had five hours of air left, he had around twelve hours, and here they were arguing. To hold on to his sanity, he looked up and studied the thorax of the spiderwalker.

"What are you looking at?" one of the crowhoppers asked. "It's impossible to escape. We're not going to be here very long and you will be well guarded."

"Where are we going?" Crater asked.

"You? Probably nowhere."

Crater considered the situation. The crowhoppers weren't going to kill Maria. She was the reason they'd come to the moon. But Crater supposed they would happily kill him. What was the use in keeping him alive?

With a sigh, Maria lowered her head, pulled her knees up, and wrapped her arms around them in a posture of submission. "Don't give up," he told her.

"I haven't given up," she said. "I'm thinking."

Crater turned his eyes to the crowhopper guard. All he

could see of his face were eyes that looked very tired. He also appeared to be young. "We were all impressed by your cannon," the crowhopper said. "Decan Flaubert—that's him with the three stripes on his helmet—said it was a very nice piece of field expedient battle gear. What did you use for ammunition?"

"Core samples from the nickel asteroid. That was the slippery surface."

"So that's what it was! Flaubert said you did two things right. You built the gun and then you stood your ground behind difficult terrain to cross. Where did you study tactics?"

"Nowhere, but I read a lot," Crater answered. "Let me ask you a question. Why did you bring the crusher along?"

"Flaubert said we would use it to shield us. Who would have thought we'd cross over the crust of a lavatube?"

The crowhopper with the three-striped helmet walked up. "Lucien! Do not talk to these humans!"

"I am bored, Decan Flaubert."

"Well, stop being bored. We're not having any luck with our radio. I sent Absalom to climb that hill with the antenna. Maybe we can establish contact from there."

"Absalom is terrified of heights," Lucien said.

The decan shook his head. "That explains why I have not seen him up there. I have never seen a more worthless trooper unless it's you or Dion. Go find Absalom and carry the antenna up there as high as you can go."

"Yes, Decan!"

Both crowhoppers moved off. Crater looked around and saw no one watching them. "Have you thought of anything?" he asked Maria.

"Yes," she said. "Do you suppose a gillie would help?"

"I suppose one would," Crater said, "but I left them in the refrigerator."

"Did you? Then why is mine in my pocket?"

Why, Crater asked himself, was he not surprised? Of course, Maria couldn't take no for an answer so she'd gone into the chuckwagon and removed "her" gillie from the refrigerator. She was a Medaris and that's the kind of thing a Medaris did. "You stole it," he accused.

"I didn't steal anything. I simply borrowed it."

"Borrowing usually implies permission, which you didn't have." Crater shook his head, then asked, "Has it said anything to you or even come out of its pocket since you stole it?"

"No."

"Then I don't see how it can help."

Another crowhopper walked up and sat on the crater rim again. "What are you talking about? Perhaps I should take your do4u's away."

"Open channel," Crater said to his do4u. "She's scared, of course. I was telling her you're not going to kill her. She's to be ransomed, right?"

The crowhopper shrugged. "Your guess is as good as mine. This entire war is a complete shambles. We attacked Armstrong City with the mission to capture this girl and succeeded only in wrecking the town. Then we were abandoned by our fleet and sent off into this hellish place to catch her. Where were you going with her, anyway?"

"The people with us are settlers. I was guiding them. They're not part of this war. I hope you'll leave them alone."

"I don't intend to do anything except get off this nasty, dusty planet alive. As for your settlers, we have no orders to do anything with them. From what I can tell, we have no orders to do much of anything. By the way, who was your cannon server? By the length of his arms and legs and the way he moved, he looked like a crowhopper, only smaller."

"He's no crowhopper," Crater lied. "Just a funny little fellow. A guide, like me."

"It doesn't matter," the young crowhopper replied.

"Maria is nearly out of air," Crater said. "Can you pump up her tank?"

"Certainly. It wouldn't do for us to let our hostage suffocate, would it? How about you?"

"I could use some air too."

The crowhopper stood. "My guess is if we ever hear from anybody, they'll tell us to kill you."

"My presence is at least keeping your hostage calm," Crater said.

"I noticed she wasn't so scared when she was shooting the other fellows."

"I'm sorry for that," Maria said, mock-whimpering.

"I don't think you are," he said. He cocked his head, listening, then said, "The decan is calling." He made a sound that almost sounded like a laugh. "He's sent Absalom back to camp and the idiot can't figure out how to make the stove work."

"What's your name?" Maria asked.

"Dion, madam."

"You seem young."

"I am nineteen, madam."

"Hey, we're nineteen too!"

"I have to go. Absalom says he's hungry. The stove, you see."

"Don't forget our air," Crater said, but the crowhopper walked away without reply.

Crater and Maria were once more left unguarded and they switched back to their private channel.

"Did you like my acting?" she asked.

Crater didn't have time to compliment her. "Gillie," he said, "do you hear me? Will you come out?"

"It isn't moving," Maria reported after a few seconds. "Do you suppose it's dead? Here. I'll take it out."

Maria plucked the little gillie from her breast pocket but all it did was rest in her hand with its eyes closed, although it had no eyes.

Crater poked it. "Hey, wake up!"

"Don't poke my gillie."

"It isn't your gillie. Gillie, do you hear me?"

"Let me try," Maria said. She stroked its back, though it had no back. "Could you help me, little gillie?"

Hello, the gillie said, perking up. *I am a gillie biocomputer. I was designed by the Macingillie Corporation of the Republic of Calimexica and manufactured . . . well, frankly, I'm not certain where. Many of my kind, however, were manufactured in New Shanghai, Third Republic of East China. I am designed to assist you with communications, administration, scheduling, research, and advice. Whenever you are ready, I would be glad to assist you in any of these endeavors. Do you have any questions for me?*

Maria looked smugly at Crater, then asked, "Gillie, do you know who I am?"

Not really, it said. *Although I know I should. I am uncertain of a number of things, although I am sure I will learn them in due course.*

"My name is Maria High Eagle Medaris. You belong to me. This is Crater Trueblood."

Yes, it said. *I know Crater, although I am not certain why.*

"Listen, Gillie," Crater said, "I need your help."

Excuse me, Crater, but I belong to Maria and I will need her permission to help you.

Crater rolled his eyes. "Tell it to listen to me," he growled.

"Gillie. Do what Crater says. Is that all right, Gillie?"

"If you're going to have one, at least learn how to talk to it," Crater said. "You never ask permission from gillies."

That's fine, the gillie said. *Thank you for asking.*

"This one's apparently different," Maria said, wrinkling her nose at Crater.

Crater bit back a sarcastic retort, then asked, "Gillie, can you access the puter that controls this spiderwalker?"

Gillie must think.

"What's to think about? You either know or you don't!"

"Don't be mean to my gillie," Maria admonished.

Crater dug into a hidden coverall pocket and retrieved a small screwdriver. "When you want something done, always use the simplest tool. Tell me if someone's coming."

"Someone's coming," she said. Sure enough, someone was. The crowhopper called Dion, this time with a bioair tank.

Crater pushed the screwdriver out of sight into the dust, then positioned his backpack to be filled, as did Maria. Both packs were filled and the crowhopper, without comment, went away.

"I wonder why they leave us alone," Maria said.

"Because we're in a cage," Crater said. "Also, we're in a vacuum a thousand miles from nowhere. They're Earthians, after all. They don't know the moon the way I do. Nobody does, really."

"You're full of yourself all of a sudden," Maria accused.

"I'm tired of being a prisoner," Crater said.

He stood up and used the screwdriver to open a hatch in the thorax of the spiderwalker, then peered into it. "That's the puter," he said. "I was hoping it would have a command pad. Don't see one, though."

Gillie has been thinking over your earlier request, the gillie said. *I may be able to help. What do you want done?*

"Can you access this puter?"

Perhaps.

Crater forced back a sigh. "Well, perhaps you can instruct the spiderwalker to use its pincers to cut the cables that bind its legs."

That is a complex command.

"Do it anyway."

"Please do it anyway," Maria amended.

Gillie will try.

Crater watched the gillie, which didn't appear to be doing anything except sitting on Maria's leg. Then the spiderwalker's legs moved against the cables, stretching them, which caused one of them to snap. Crater dodged as it whipped in his direction.

Sorry, the gillie said. *Trying to determine the commands.*

The head of the spiderwalker began to move up and down and it lifted one leg, then the other. "Pincers, gillie," Crater said.

The gillie said nothing, but then the walker lowered its head and snipped apart a cable, then snipped another. The opening was large enough for them to pass through.

"Let's go," Crater said, taking Maria by the hand and stepping through the snipped cables. He unwound them, then tossed them away, then swung up on the back of the walker and helped Maria up. "Get behind me," he said when she tried to sit in front. "I need a shield. They won't shoot you. Probably."

Maria gave it some thought, then settled in behind Crater. Crater urged the walker ahead. It didn't take too many steps before he realized the reason the crowhoppers used that particular walker as a cage. It limped.

::: FORTY-ONE

The spiderwalker's bad leg wasn't so bad it couldn't be used. It hesitated a tick on the uplift but that only caused a slight shudder in the ride. But as time went by, Crater could feel the drag getting worse. Then, without warning, the leg failed completely. The walker walked on but the ride changed to a lurching gait, and before long, other legs were dragging too.

"They're following us," Maria warned. "Just saw them ride over that little hill we crossed a few minutes ago."

Crater studied the terrain ahead, then directed the walker onto a ridge covered with boulders. By their color, shape, and texture, he identified them as basalt. He jumped off the walker and rolled one of them to the edge of the ridge and over. He watched it tumble down, leaving a bright trail in the dust as it picked up speed. About a hundred feet above the bottom, there was a cliff that launched the rock into the vacuum. It flew until it fell into a large crater and kept rolling until it caromed off the far crater lip. "What was that for?" Maria asked from her perch on the walker.

Crater didn't answer because his idea was still forming. He climbed up on the walker and drove it forward, then turned down slope until they reached the interior of the large crater. When he was about a hundred yards from the trail the rolling basalt rock had made, he stopped the walker and rotated its head so that its pincers could reach its dangling leg. Squeezing the handle that operated the pincers, he cut off the leg, which fell off into the dust. After that, he ordered the walker to kneel. Since it was missing a front leg, it toppled over, sending him and Maria flying into the dust. "Crater, what are you doing?" Maria sputtered.

Crater picked up the clipped leg. "Stay here," he commanded.

"What do you hope to accomplish with that thing?" she demanded, still sitting in the dust.

"Stay here, I said."

"Crater Trueblood, tell me what you're doing!"

Crater turned around, although he kept walking backward. "Saving your life. Maybe mine too. It might help if you got on top of the walker so the crowhoppers will be sure to see you."

"Are you crazy? I'll do no such thing!"

Crater didn't have time to argue. Carrying the walker leg, he leaped and bounded until he reached the base of the hill with the basalt rocks. He climbed it and removed the shoestrings from one of his boots, then tore off one of the chest pockets of his coveralls. Using an obsidian rock, millions of them mixed in with the basalt, he sawed the string in two, then tied the two ends to the pocket, thus creating a sling. The remaining shoestring he put back in the eyes of his boot and cinched it tight. He then chose a small lump of basalt, placed it on the cloth patch, then whirled it around and made a practice throw at a boulder a hundred yards away. He struck it dead center. "The rewards of a misspent youth," he said to himself, recalling how he and Petro had made slings when they were kids and pelted miners on the scrapes with pebbles. They'd got their hides tanned for it too.

After stuffing his remaining coverall pockets with basalt lumps, he used the broken spiderwalker leg to pry loose eight big boulders. He carefully rolled them to the edge of the ridge, then sat down and waited in the pale Earthshine.

Before long, the crowhoppers appeared aboard their remaining three walkers. There were two of them on one walker. Spotting Maria, they moved toward her. "Keep coming, boys," Crater said, then used the leg to tip the boulders one by one and send them tumbling down the slope. Just as the small rock had done, they hit the edge of the cliff, went flying, then landed and rolled.

Crater's timing was good. Of the eight boulders, three struck the walkers. One of them, the biggest of the lot, struck the lead spiderwalker dead center, knocking its rider—the decan based on its three-striped helmet—into the dust. He rolled, then got up and waved the other walkers forward. Crater ran down the hill, swinging the sling above his head, then threw the stone with all his might. It struck the decan at the base of his helmet and he dropped to the dust. The remaining two walkers turned around but Crater threw rocks at their riders, hitting two of them. When he came running up, the crowhoppers slid off their walkers, threw down their rifles, and put their hands up.

Maria walked up and picked up one of the rifles. "You could have told me your plan," she said.

"I thought you'd think it was stupid."

"It was stupid, but I'm glad it worked." She inspected the decan. "He's dead. Your rock caught him in his throat. Busted open his pressure sheath. So what do we do with these three?"

"Don't kill us!"

Crater squinted. "Is that you, Lucien?"

"Yes, sir."

"Are you all right?"

"Yes, sir. So are Absalom and Dion."

"That's fine. Here's what I want you to do. Take one of your walkers and go back where you came from. If you follow us, I will kill you. Get off my moon. Understood?"

"Yes, sir!" the three chorused, then did as they were told. They made an odd sight, three black-armored crowhoppers with their helmets drooped low crowded atop a spiderwalker.

After the crowhoppers disappeared over a hill, Maria said, "What do we do now?"

"Catch up with our party."

"You think they went on without us?"

"I'm sure they did. Crescent is second in command and she knows to get the Apps to Endless Dust."

"Crescent is second in command?"

"Of course."

For a reason Crater didn't understand, his question earned him a Maria Medaris frowny face.

::: FORTY-TWO

The first thing Crater needed to do was figure out where they were. The crowhoppers had carried them eastward but, after escaping, the terrain had led them north. He asked Maria's baby gillie to establish contact with a Lunar Positioning Satellite and it did its best, but after a few unsuccessful attempts, he concluded it didn't know how. He decided to head generally west but which way was that?

The landmark he needed presented itself when he and Maria found themselves looking at a steep, flat-topped mountain covered with a white ashy material. "That's the crater Bode, I'm sure of it," Crater said to a sleepy Maria who had been napping behind him, her head resting on his air pack. "See? It looks just like an Earthian volcano cinder cone! It's probably just an impact crater that flattened a hill, but since nobody's ever climbed it to take a look, we don't know for sure. Anyway, if that's Bode, it means we're somewhere between the Mare Vaporum to the northeast, Sinus Aestuum to the west, and Sinus Medii to the southeast, which unfortunately means we're in a bad spot."

Maria yawned, squinted in various directions, then asked, "Why is it bad?"

"It's bad because if we keep going west, we'll have to pass through a whole series of hills and ridges covered with that ashy stuff and it looks slippery. On the other hand, if we go south, we're going to find ourselves trapped in the Sinus Medii by high mountains. There is a pass, however, if I recall correctly. If we can find it, we could turn near Frau Mauro and have a clear path to Endless Dust."

"Frau Mauro?" Maria perked up. "Apollo 14 landed there. Nobody's been back since, as far as I know. Could we visit it?"

Crater was always interested in visiting historical sites, especially if nobody had been there for over one hundred and fifty years, but he doubted it was a good idea and said so.

"Maybe we should just head east and work our way back to Armstrong City," Maria said. "I'm certain our forces have recaptured it by now."

"You forget I'm an outlaw."

"But you saved me! The Colonel will welcome you with open arms. Trust me."

"Maybe so but we're going to Endless Dust. The Apps need my help and I'm not going to abandon Crescent either. Or Ike, for that matter."

Maria tucked her right boot beneath her left leg and leaned back on the spiderwalker to stretch. "You are so hardheaded when it comes to that crowhopper girl."

"No, I'm not," Crater said. "I just know what I have to do."

"All right," Maria said after thinking it over. "I'll go to Endless Dust with you. And you know why? Because you can't do without me."

Crater chose not to argue and aimed the walker generally

southwestward, and for the next twelve hours, in the bluish glow of earthlight, they passed through ragged hills covered with white ash. Closer inspection revealed that there were also odd layers of white pebbles, glass spherical globules, and chunks of gray rock.

Finally, they came to a basin that was black with basalt sands. A fresh impact crater was a few miles ahead and behind it an eroded crater. If the fresh crater was the one he thought it was, a crater named Turner, they had arrived at Mare Insularum.

He woke Maria. "I think that eroded crater ahead is Frau Mauro."

Maria studied it. "I think it is too! Oh, Crater, let's go there!"

Crater was as curious about the site as she was. His recollection was that Apollo 14 had landed in the hills north of the eroded crater. What lay ahead was a corrugated landscape of rilles and hills with massive basalt boulders lying atop black sand mixed in with white pebbles. They crossed several rows of parallel hills, then climbed a steep bank.

At the top, Crater turned on his helmet scope and studied a dark object. "I think that's the lander," he said after a lengthy study. "Who flew on that mission?"

"Al Shepard and Ed Mitchell landed," Maria said. "Shepard was also the first American in space. He flew aboard a Mercury capsule on top of a Redstone rocket. It was a suborbital hop."

"Like one of our jumpcars."

"Except it was good for only one flight and landed in the ocean using parachutes." She thought about that. "I wonder why they didn't just flip it over and land using retros like a jumpcar?"

"Because it took all their propellant just to get up to some decent altitude."

Maria considered that, then said, "I guess people back in the twentieth century thought we'd be living on Mars by now but we're not, except for a research station that's visited every few years to pick up samples."

"The trouble with Mars is it's too far away and there's not much there that the Earth needs," Crater said, "unlike the moon with its Helium-3, Titanium, Thorium, and such. Anyway, before we can live on Mars, we've got to stop fighting these stupid wars."

"We have to resist evil," Maria said.

"I'm all for resisting evil," Crater answered. "But it gets to be wearisome after a time. It seems like as soon as one evil gets stamped out, there's another to take its place. But that's neither here nor there, I suppose. Let's get a little closer to the lander."

The walker descended into a small hollow of dust, climbed another steep hill, went past several badly eroded craters, then up another hill. "It's the lander, all right," Crater said with rising excitement. "And look there, you can see the tracks of that handcart they pulled around. There's what they called Cone Crater. They wanted to climb it but gave up when they were only a few yards from the top because they had trouble judging distances. I've noticed people born on Earth still have the same problem."

Maria grinned eagerly. "Shall we climb it for them?"

Crater grinned too. "Why not!"

They rode the walker to the base of the crater, noting the footprints the ancient astronauts had made up the side and back down again. Not wanting to disturb those artifacts, they left the walker and walked around the base, then climbed up to the rim. It only took a few minutes and they were staring into the famous Cone Crater.

"The dust here is laced with glass beads," Crater said. "There's likely Helium-3 inside them. Too bad they didn't make it to the rim. A sample would have stirred up those old Earthian geologists."

Crater and Maria sat on the rim facing the landing site. "We probably shouldn't get too close," Maria said. "It is a historical site, after all."

"Agreed, but your great-grandfather thoroughly disturbed the Apollo 17 landing site as I recall from my history lessons."

"Great-Granddaddy Jack and Great-Grannie Penny High Eagle were in a desperate situation," Maria pointed out. "They had to use Apollo artifacts to survive. Anyway, that made the site doubly historic, considering it was the first time people had returned to the moon since Apollo."

"And then they kept it secret for about fifty years."

"Not counting a book called *Back to the Moon*, which everybody took to be fiction. And it was, too, except for the moon landing part and the Helium-3 that was brought back. A lot of people claimed that Great-Granddaddy Jack helped write that book but he always said he didn't."

Crater could have said with a Medaris, it was always difficult to tell where the truth ended and a lie started but he let his better angels steer him away. Instead, he said, "Time to get going."

"How much farther to Endless Dust?"

"A couple of days."

"Do we have enough air?"

"The walker has a spare tank of air we can replenish from if we have to. With the amount we got from the crowhoppers, it should be more than enough."

"You know what?"

"What?"

"I'm having fun."

Crater smiled and put his arm around her and hugged her close. He recalled now why he liked Maria so much. Any woman who thought it was fun to fight a bunch of murderous crowhoppers and then visit a historical site was decidedly a very good woman.

FORTY-THREE

Maria and Crater traveled south for a day. To the east, the terminator was a yellowish glow behind the tall hills. When they were just west of crater Davy, the spiderwalker gave a lurch and stopped. Crater inspected its biofuel cell and found it exhausted. "That's it," he said. "It's not going anywhere."

"How far are we from Endless Dust?"

"About fifty miles."

"Can we walk?"

Crater considered the question. "It would take us two days to walk, even if we didn't sleep. Our air's okay but our water is questionable. It would be a close run thing."

"So we walk and hope we make it?"

Crater nodded, although it was an absent nod. He knelt at one of the walker's legs and inspected it. "Interesting," he said. "They're spring-loaded. That dampens the jarring whenever it steps." Maria tossed down the food and water containers. "All right, Mr. Engineer," she said. "You can study the design of spiderwalkers later. We've got a long march ahead of us."

"Maybe not," he said. He produced a utility tool from one of his many pockets and went beneath the walker. He snapped off a cover at the armpit of one of its legs and inspected the joint. Reasoning that the legs had to be replaced occasionally, he found a ball joint that was held in place by a thick rubberized grommet. Two steel plates held it, each bolted down by eighteen screws. Although Crater's utility tool fit the heads of the screws, they were well torqued. Getting them loose would be exceedingly difficult without a power tool.

Crater studied the leg some more and noticed that each joint was designed to be removed. The lowest joint, the one with the foot, had a rotational hinge and only a single large bolt held it. Crater looked around for a suitable rock, spotted one, and carried it over and jammed it up against one of the legs. Then he picked up another boulder and slammed it down on the joint of the leg and broke it off.

Maria was sitting on a boulder, watching. Finally, she asked, "What are you doing?"

"I'm going to make us stilts," he said, testing the spring in the tip of the broken leg joint. He tossed it to Maria. "Look in the walker utility box. There should be a roll of tape in there. Try to figure out how to attach this to your boot."

Although she thought Crater's idea was idiotic, Maria was glad for something to do. While he broke off three more leg joints, she experimented with the tape, then said, "We need something to stand on or the tape will slip."

Crater gave that some thought, then remembered the friction footplates. He found them in another utility box. "I think these will work," he said and tossed them to her.

Maria clamped them on top of the legs. They were perfect. "Sometimes I think you're a genius," she said.

Crater shrugged, then taped his boots to the stilts. With Maria's help, he rose on them, teetered for a moment, then took a step, then another followed by several giant steps. With little effort, he discovered he could cross a hundred yards in a few seconds. He bounded back to Maria, who was busily taping her boots to the stilts. She stood, teetered momentarily, then took a tentative step and fell over.

"Next time hold my hand," Crater suggested.

Maria pulled herself vertical again. Crater grabbed her hand. "Come on. Slow at first."

Maria took a step, lurched against Crater, who held fast, then another and another. "I think I can do it on my own now," she said.

Crater released her hand and Maria began to walk very slowly, then gradually faster. Finally, she bounded on the spring-loaded stilts and covered the entire base of a wide crater with two steps.

"Endless Dust?" Crater asked.

Maria was laughing. "Endless Dust!" she said.

::: FORTY-FOUR

They stilted until they were spent. Crater and Maria sat on a small crater rim about a mile from Endless Dust. To the east, the terminator was getting closer to the crater Alphonsus, its herald a deep red glow. Crater glanced at Maria. He could see how tired she was. "Let's get some sleep," he said. "No reason to arrive exhausted."

Maria gratefully slid down the rim. She looked up at the stars. "I'll be glad to get out of this pressure sheath," she said.

Crater slid down beside her. "So will I."

"I hope there's at least one shower in Endless Dust."

"If there is, Crescent will have it working."

Maria kept staring at the river of stars that poured across the sky. "Tell me about her."

"She tries to be good—which is better than most humans I know."

"I'm sorry I didn't like her at first. I was tired and I was angry. Actually, I've been angry ever since I got space burn and I don't know why."

"You thought I let you down and you were right. I did."

"No, Crater," Maria said. "You didn't. You did your best in a terrible situation. It was a situation that my family put you in and I'm sorry for that."

Her glove crept to his. "Forgive me?"

"Sure."

"I'd like to kiss you."

"We're wearing space helmets."

"That's the part I really don't like about you."

"What part is that?"

"You're too much the engineer. Yes, I know we're wearing space helmets, Crater, but we won't always be wearing them, will we?"

"No, we won't," he said, then closed his eyes. "We're supposed to be sleeping."

Maria agreed and it wasn't long before she was asleep. Crater followed soon afterward. His sleep, however, didn't last long. He woke to see someone standing over him. Crater instantly recognized who it was.

"Hello, Crater," the figure said, then sat down on a nearby boulder. He had a friendly smile, an impish nose, and a lock of brown hair that fell across his forehead. He also wore a Soviet pilot's green g-suit and black boots.

"Yuri Gagarin," Crater said. "Or I should say, respectfully, General Gagarin."

"None other than the exalted first man in space," he replied in a thick Russian accent. "The rank was honorary, of course, since I never commanded anything including myself. Am I what you expected?"

"You're shorter."

"Five foot four inches in my boots. If I had been any bigger, I wouldn't have fit in that little capsule. It is one of the reasons

I was chosen. That and my natural flying abilities, of course, not that such skill was needed. My only responsibility was to keep breathing during my flight. Everything was automatic except for the last part when I jumped out of my craft and parachuted the rest of the way to the Earth." An expression of regret passed over him. "It is too bad I never parachuted again. Had I enough altitude, it might have saved me that day my MiG crashed. But that is history and this is today and the future. I want to thank you for bringing my bones to the moon."

"I was glad to do it," Crater said. "I heard Czarina Sofia erected you a very nice tomb. She also commissioned a mural showing the first Russian triumphs in space."

"It was the Soviet Union that did it, not Russia," Gagarin corrected. "Russia alone would have never done it. We needed a relentless empire to go charging off into the cosmos."

"Maybe for you but not us, buddy," someone said, coming out of the shadows. "All we needed was a good kick in the butt from you commie goons and we showed the world what free men could do. Especially those of us in the United States Navy."

Gagarin rolled his eyes. "John Glenn was a Marine and Neil Armstrong was a civilian," he said. "Sit yourself down, Alan, and try to get off your high Navy horse for once."

Out of the sun, the terminator having crossed during Crater's nap, stepped another small man, this one dressed in a snowy white Apollo moonwalker's suit, the red neck ring empty of its helmet. He had a sardonic, toothy grin. "Just like a commie to begin with the insults," Alan Shepard said with a chuckle. "Well, the first free man in space and the fifth man on the moon just walked into the room. How many times did you fly out of earth orbit, Yuri? Let's see. Oh yeah, none!"

"True, but I was first into space."

"Aw, I'd have beat you if those crazy Germans up in Huntsville hadn't been so nervous about their little Redstone rocket."

"Without those crazy Germans, you'd have never gone anywhere. But even if you'd launched before me, it would have been zoop-zip, up and down, just a hop. I would have still been the first in orbit. As it was, I was both the first in space *and* the first in orbit. That's something you Americans couldn't abide. Especially you, Alan."

Shepard lost his grin. "What you slaves to central planning couldn't stand was that free men beat you to the only place worth going in the solar system—the moon."

Gagarin smirked. "Yes, aboard spacecraft belonging to your federal government. You wish to talk about central planning? Without it, you'd have gone nowhere."

"That spacecraft was built by private industry, buddy," Shepard sniped back. "And the lowest bidder at that."

Crater was thinking of what to say to the two pioneer spacemen to stop them from arguing when Shepard laughed and slapped Gagarin on the back. "How you doing, Yuri?"

Gagarin's shy smile was genuine. "Fine, Alan. Pull up a boulder."

Shepard rolled a boulder beside the Russian and sat down. They basked in the view. "Amazing, isn't it?" Shepard said. "Wish you could have seen it when you were alive."

"I'm glad you did, Alan," Gagarin replied.

"Well, Crater," Shepard said, acknowledging him for the first time, "you've done pretty well for yourself out here. I'm proud of your resourcefulness. Those stilts? Looks like something I would have come up with."

"He's a fellow pilot, you know," Gagarin said.

"Is he now?" Shepard nodded to Crater. "Pilots are a special club. We might try to kill each other during combat but get us together, we're all brothers of the sky."

"And space," Gagarin added.

"And space," Shepard agreed. "So now that you're nearly at Endless Dust, what are you going to do, young man?"

"I'll see about my people, sir. Make sure they're all right."

"Very good," Gagarin said. "They are doing well, by the way."

"That they are," Shepard added. "That little crowhopper of yours saw to that."

"Thank you for telling me, sirs," Crater said. "But do you mind if I ask you how it is you're here? I don't mean to be disrespectful, but aren't you both dead?"

They looked at each other, shrugged, then nodded. "We have been dead for a very long time," Gagarin said.

"Still, you knew who we were," Shepard said.

"I read about you in history books. And I saw photographs of you."

"How about us, Crater?" came another voice, one that Crater had never heard but knew instantly.

Four people walked out of the shadows. Two of them were his foster parents, Bill and Annie Hawkins, both killed on the scrapes of Moontown. Another he recognized from old photographs to be Paul Trueblood, his father, killed in a lander accident. The woman who'd spoken was Juliet, his mother, who had died in childbirth. *His* childbirth. Crater stood to behold her, a beautiful woman dressed in a white robe.

"Is it really you?" he croaked.

"Yes, my sweet boy. It's me."

The Hawkins couple stood back and let the Truebloods gather him in. "We are proud of you, son," his father said. "Especially how you took our invention for making water from dust from concept to reality."

"The Colonel is trying to steal it from me," Crater replied.

"Yes, we know," his mother said. "But the main thing is you're perfecting it and after you do, people will be able to live on the moon and have water for themselves and their families."

Crater was so afraid his mother would disappear. "I'm sorry you died," he said.

"We're sorry too, son," all four of his parents said. "But we were never far from you."

Crater discovered he was crying, the tears flowing liberally but slowly down his cheek due to the low gravity of the moon. "I sometimes get mad at all of you," he confessed. "For dying on me and leaving me alone."

"The crowhoppers say death is life and life is death," Bill Hawkins said. "And they're right."

"Look at it this way," Juliet Hawkins said. "When we were alive but working on the scrapes, you couldn't see us, could you? You were home but where were we? Out of sight. But you could imagine us. When you were tempted to get into the candy box, you knew I wouldn't like it so you didn't do it. Well, how many times in your life, without seeing any of the four of us, did you stop before you did something to think whether we would approve?"

"A lot," Crater admitted. "You all taught me in your own way how to figure out the right thing, then do it."

"So we died," his father said.

"But we were not dead," his mother said.

"Death is life," Bill said.

"Life is death," Juliet added.

"Well," Shepard said, standing, "this is all getting a little metaphysical for me. Yuri? You coming with me?"

"Sure thing, Alan. What are we flying today?"

"How about you landing the LEM—that would be the Lunar Excursion Module for you non-Apollo punks—on the moon? Let's see how much of a real pilot you are! Are you up to landing backward in a little rocket with paper-thin walls and a computer with the memory of the first handheld calculator?"

"If you Americans can do it, this Soviet citizen can, I assure you!"

They started walking off, then both turned back. "Good luck to you, Crater," Gagarin said.

"Do good, boy," Shepard said. "Remember, it's not the smartest pilot who's best, it's the one who pays the most attention."

"Yes, sir," Crater said. "I'll remember that. Thank you for coming by."

Crater watched the two old astronauts walk away until they entered the black shadow of a huge boulder, then he turned back to his parents, only to find them gone too. "Mom?" he called out. "Dad?"

He heard his birth mother's voice. "We've not left you, dear. We never will."

Another tear started to slowly travel from Crater's eye to his cheek. "But I want you where I can see you."

"Then just look," she answered, then said no more.

Crater heard a noise in his do4u and it scared him. It sounded like he imagined a frightened animal might sound. He turned and saw Maria curled up in a ball and shaking as if she were freezing. Crater worried that her space burn had returned. He knelt beside her and pulled her into his arms "Maria, what's wrong?"

Her shaking stopped and her eyes opened. "Crater, did you see her?"

"Who?" he asked.

"Her. She was—" She stopped, her mouth open. Then she closed it and her eyes blinked as if she'd traveled somewhere else. Finally, she said, "Nobody. Did you sleep okay?"

Crater considered telling Maria about his visitation but decided against it. There would be another time. "Yes. Do you think you can make it to Endless Dust?"

Maria picked up the stilts. "Will we need these?"

"I think we're close enough now to walk in."

"Then I'm ready."

Crater stood on the edge of the hill and shielded his eyes against the new sun. "Let's go," he said and down the hill they walked through the endless dust to the town of the same name.

::: FORTY-FIVE

t Endless Dust, Crater and Maria saw evidence that the Apps had arrived. Scrap and other garbage was raked and shoveled into piles. The window on the only observation tower was clean, not a speck of dust on it. Parked near a dustlock was a truck and an empty trailer, a chuckwagon, and a fastbug. Crater switched his do4u to Crescent's private channel. "Crescent, it's Crater and Maria. We're here." When there was no response, Crater tried again with the same lack of result.

"I think our do4u batteries are nearly fried," Crater said. "Ask your gillie to call."

Maria coaxed the little gillie out of her coveralls pocket. "Call Crescent," she said.

Gillie doesn't know who Crescent is, it said. *In fact, I'm not sure who you are.*

"Your gillie is defective."

"It's young, that's all," Maria defended.

Crater's backpack was nearly exhausted and so was Maria's. They needed to go inside. The hatch was a standard one. When

Crater opened it, Maria said, "I've got to get out of this suit!" and pushed past him and climbed inside.

Crater followed, pulled the hatch shut, pressurized the airlock, opened the inner hatch, and switched on the lights. In the next chamber, showers beckoned. "Yes!" Maria cried and sat down on a bench and pulled off her boots. When she saw Crater hesitating, she said, "Look, Crater, you're a boy, I'm a girl, and all that. But I need a shower and you do too. You don't look at me and I won't look at you. Deal?"

Crater nodded, and within minutes, they were both under the showers, their biolastic sheaths being scrubbed in conditioning units, their coveralls in the dustlock laundry, their do4u batteries in recharge. The showers were hot and, most importantly, wet, and they scrubbed off all the nastiness that the biolastic suits, as marvelous as they were, had left behind.

Stepping from the shower, Crater rummaged around and found a cabinet with clean coveralls. Maria held out her arm from behind the door of the cabinet and Crater handed her a pair. She dressed while Crater did the same on the other side of the door. "Are there any boots or shoes?" she asked.

Crater found slippers and handed over a small pair to Maria.

The final hatch opened into a well-lit tubeway. Crater and Maria padded down its glistening mooncrete deck and inspected the various tubes. All were empty of life.

"Where is everybody?" Maria asked.

Crater held a finger to his lips. Having lived underground all his life in mooncrete tubes, he knew what to listen for. "They're this way," he said and led Maria through a hatch marked LIVING QUARTERS 1.

They were greeted by the warm, lustrous aroma of baking

bread. Clarence and Eliza looked up from the table on which they were kneading dough. "Crater and Maria! Thank God you made it through." Wiping their hands on their aprons, they hurried around the table and greeted them with hugs.

"You're all right?" Crater asked.

"We are wonderful," Eliza said. "Endless Dust is a great place."

"A little elbow grease will put it to rights," Clarence said, "and it already feels like home. We can't wait to send for the other Apps."

"Where are Jake and Trudelle?" Maria asked.

"On the scrapes with Crescent and Ike," Eliza answered. "We take turns. Sometimes they're out there while we work on the interior. Then we swap."

"Did you find a crusher?"

"Yes, and a loader and a shuttle car," Clarence said. "Are you hungry?"

"I'm starving," Maria said.

In minutes, Eliza pushed across two plates of warm bread painted with biovat butter. She also had mugs of what smelled like real coffee. Both Maria and Crater set upon the food and drink. Afterward, Maria smiled, patted her stomach, and said, "I think I may have died and gone to heaven."

"Is my gillie still in the chuckwagon refrigerator?" Crater asked.

"We brought it inside," Eliza said. She opened a big lunasteel refrigerator and plucked out the gillie.

Crater held the gillie in his hand and it looked at him without eyes. *Do you have a question for me?*

"Yes. Are you well?"

Gillie is healthy. Gillie is ready to serve. Why is there another gillie in this room? I hate it.

Maria dug her little gillie out of her coveralls pocket and held it on her palm. It said, *Why is there another gillie in this room? I hate it.*

"Gillie," Crater said, "this gillie came from you. You divided and produced it."

That is not possible, both gillies said in unison. *I hate this gillie.*

"You can't hate each other," Crater said.

I hate it, Maria's gillie said.

I hate it, Crater's gillie said. *I will kill it.*

"You can't kill it," Crater admonished.

Yes, I can. I can smite it with many weapons. I am stronger than it.

"That's ridiculous," Crater said.

I can produce lightning. The gillie shot an electrical crackle of energy that briefly turned the kitchen blue.

"Bad gillie!" Crater admonished. "Get up on my shoulder and start paying attention."

The gillie, looking ashamed, although it could look no way at all, wriggled onto Crater's shoulder. Maria, tsking, put hers in her coveralls pocket. "Let's go outside," Crater said.

"Once more into the dust." Maria sighed.

In the dustlock, Crater and Maria pulled on their refurbished and replenished suits and boots, pulled on fresh backpacks, donned their helmets, then entered the airlock. As it was depressurized, Maria said, "My mother visited me out there."

The airlock pressure numbers reached zero. Crater put his hand on the hatch lever. "I'm listening," he said.

"She told me to be kind to my father. He can't help the way he is."

Maria had never told him about her father. "What way is he?"

"He's never liked me. He can be cruel."

"I didn't know that. Would you like to tell me more?"

"Maybe later."

"I had visitors too," Crater said. "Yuri Gagarin and Alan Shepard plus my parents, both sets."

"You dreamed them," Maria said. "While I was talking to my mother, you never woke."

"I was awake," Crater insisted, unwilling to let the visit be so casually dismissed as a simple dream. "It was you who slept."

They looked at one another. Maria said, "I'm about to show a great deal of courage, Crater. I love you."

"I love you too," Crater replied.

"What happens now?"

"I guess we go outside and help my clients."

"We should kiss first."

"Once again I have to point out we're wearing space helmets."

"Ever the practical engineer." Maria sighed, then followed Crater onto the dust.

::: FORTY-SIX

While Maria took up patrol in the streets, Crater headed for the scrape by following boot prints. There, he spotted Jake, Trudelle, and Crescent beside an old crusher. Crescent saw him first. "I am happy to see your face," she said. "We need help with this machine."

"I'm happy to see your face too," Crater said. "What's wrong with the crusher?"

Jake and Trudelle hugged him. "What happened to you? Is Maria all right?"

"We were captured by crowhoppers but escaped. We're both fine." He inspected the crusher. "We had one like this on the Moontown scrapes. It is a Doubleturn 4752 model. None better, although parts might be hard to find."

"There are parts in the maintenance shed. Ike is making an inventory."

Crater checked the tension on the crusher's gears and chains. He opened its electronics and its fuel cell boxes. All seemed to be in order. Then he traced the wiring harness and found a break in one of the cables. "There's your problem," he said. "Likely a rock was thrown up and worked around until it cut this line. It happens."

"We didn't know to look there," Jake said. "You're a wonder, Crater."

"I like tinkering on machines," Crater answered.

A call to Ike soon had him trotting up with a replacement line. "Is this a help?" he asked.

"Yes, Ike, it is a help," Crater said. "Thank you."

After Crater replaced the line, the crusher rumbled to life. Trudelle shoveled in rock. From the other end came gravel. "There's Thorium there," Jake said. "I just know it."

At dinner that night the discussion turned to ghosts. Crater looked up sharply. "Did you say ghosts?"

Jake nodded sheepishly. "Since we arrived, each of us has been visited by dead people."

"My mother," Clarence said.

"Both my parents," Eliza said.

"A man I was cruel to," Jake said, "and died before I could say I was sorry."

"My first-grade teacher," Trudelle said.

Crater turned to Crescent. "Have you seen dead people?"

"No," Crescent said.

"How about you, Ike?"

Ike blinked. "If it would help, I will say I have seen them but I haven't."

Crater's gillie interrupted. *The skies are filled with them*, it said.

"With ghosts?" Crater asked.

No, it said. *Warpods*.

Maria picked up her rifle. "Let's go."

Outside, Crater and Maria looked up and saw a fleet of warpods and a host of silvery torpedo-shaped craft. Streaks of light indicating missiles lit up the sky.

"Are we winning?" Maria asked.

"I'm not even sure who *we* are, but the warpods are getting the worst of it."

Warpods are sent by the Unified Countries of the World, Crater's gillie said, adding, *I have penetrated their puters.*

Teach me, Maria's gillie demanded.

Perhaps, Crater's gillie responded.

Crater kept watching until the warpods and the silvery crafts wandered off, their jets flaring. "Whatever's happening up there isn't about us," he said. "It's good we're out of it."

Maria nodded. "What about the ghosts the Apps saw?"

"What about them?"

"You were visited by your parents and two dead astronauts. I was visited by my mother. They were ghosts too."

"There's no such thing as ghosts. There has to be a rational explanation."

"Why do we always have to be rational? For instance, were you rational when you told me you loved me?"

"You said it first."

"Yes, I did. You never would have said it if I hadn't. What is it about love you're afraid of?"

"I'm not afraid of love. I'm afraid of you!"

Crater wished he could put his hand over his mouth but his helmet kept him from doing it. It was out there anyway. He was afraid of her. He had always been afraid of her.

"Look, Crater, I'm a girl," Maria said. "Some would say I'm a woman. In olden times, girls my age were getting married, having babies. But no matter what you call us, we females can say anything we like about love because in the end, we're the ones who pay the price for it. Did you say you were afraid of me?"

"I might have," Crater allowed.

"Why?"

"I don't know."

Maria frowned. "You know what I think your problem is? You don't know what love is."

Crater didn't want to talk anymore with Maria because she made everything he felt feel convoluted and wrong. "I hope they've got some extra fuel cells in the maintenance shed," he said. "I'm afraid there may be a crack in the loader's."

"You're not going to change the subject!" Maria snapped. "You said you loved me and then you said you were afraid of me. Very well. We need to solve this!"

Crater felt a trickle of sweat on his forehead. "We're in the middle of a war, we're staying at a dilapidated, abandoned town populated by ghosts, and you want to know what I intend to do about being in love with you?"

"And afraid of me. Love is the most important thing in the universe. Fear shouldn't enter into it."

Crater dug deep, then said, "I'll think about it."

It clearly was not the answer Maria wanted to hear. Her face clouded over and she shook her head, then walked away, back to the dustlock.

Crater wanted to shout after her, to tell her to come back, that he really was going to give it some thought. He loved her. He was afraid of her. It was all kind of the same.

But he didn't. After glancing up to make sure the sky was still clear, he headed to the maintenance shed where he hoped to find a fuel cell to replace the one on the loader.

::: FORTY-SEVEN

day passed, then another, and another, and before Crater could imagine it, an entire week had gone by. The time passed so quickly because there was so much to do. He rose each morning with a list of things to do in his head. He adjusted the biovats and refreshed their solutions, cured the balky environmental puters, showed the Apps how to change out the scrubbers on the air systems, and realigned the solar tower that provided energy to the underground tubes.

On the scrapes, Crater soon had the crusher crushing, the loader loading, the shuttle shuttling, the scraper scraping, the conveyors conveying, and the solar dishes boiling the scrag. The dust piled up, and samples taken revealed a big percentage of Thorium and Titanium, just as the Apps had hoped. There was still a problem with the separators, but Crater had an idea how to fix them. Give it a month of refinement and Crater thought Endless Dust might actually have a product ready for market.

If there was a market. Although he asked the gillie to keep

checking, it was apparent all the comm-sats were down. There was no news from the outside at all.

Although he provided most of the engineering, Crater hadn't done everything alone. The Apps had worked hard to learn and so had Crescent. Maria, as befitted a Medaris, was especially strong in management skills and devised an efficient schedule matrix for the puters to process, which provided everyone their daily tasks. Crater was pleased she seemed happy in her work. The way she cheerfully engaged him in conversation made him hope she had forgotten all about her challenge to him to prove his love for her and explain why he was afraid of her and what he was going to do about it. She'd even developed an apparent affection for Crescent. In fact, they were tubemates, ate together at meals, and seemed often to be engaged in deep conversations. About what, Crater didn't know, although sometimes he'd look up and find them both looking back at him. That seemed odd. Ike was adopted by the App women, who held him in high regard. He was at their beck and call. As for the ghosts, Crater was too busy to worry about them.

Crater bunked in a tube by himself. Every night he was satisfyingly exhausted and crawled into his bed, eagerly looking forward to both sleep and waking up the next day with more tasks to be accomplished. One night, however, he woke to find someone standing beside his bunk. It proved to be Captain Jake Teller, the convoy commander who had mentored Crater the first time he'd crossed the moon. Crowhoppers had struck the captain down just before they'd reached Armstrong City and safety.

But now here was Teller wearing a Medaris Convoy Company tunic with the MCC logo, the same one he'd been wearing the first time Crater had met him. He looked smart in his uniform, but he did not appear to be pleased. "So this is where you ended up," he said. "In a nasty little town as a glorified mechanic. I hoped you'd do better."

Crater sat up in bed. "It's not my fault, Captain. There's a war on and I got chased over here. Maria's with me too."

"You like it here, don't you?"

"Yes," Crater answered. "There's always something to do and I'm needed."

"Needed! Maybe for a month or two and then what? Are you going to marry that little crowhopper girl? That's about your only choice. Maria certainly isn't going to stay here."

Teller waved his words aside before Crater could speak them. "You are such a disappointment," he said before sighing. "I'm not really surprised. Deep at your core, young man, you're soft as butter. Soft! I did everything I could to teach you to be tough and hard. I tried to teach you that if you want your dreams to come true, you have to fight and not let anything get in your way. Do you know what your biggest obstacle is?"

"You just said I was soft," Crater said resentfully, "so I guess that's it."

"No, that's not it. Your biggest obstacle is the fact that you're satisfied with being less than you can be. You think helping these people is just as marvelous as being in charge of your own destiny. Don't deny it!"

"I want to help them. What's wrong with that?"

Teller laughed a mean laugh. "Nothing except you don't care if you ever leave. This nasty place is fine with you. Maria is made for bigger things. If you want her, you've got to be willing to grow, to strive, to become a titan of industry."

"You've made your point, Captain," Crater said, "but tell

me this. You're dead, yet here you are standing beside my bed acting like you're alive. You were the most rational man I ever knew. How do you square that in your head?"

The captain's expression fell. After an apparent moment of confusion, he said, "There are more things in heaven and earth, Horatio, than are dreamt of in your philosophy."

"I didn't know you read Shakespeare," Crater said.

"There are probably a lot of things you don't know about me," Teller said, then vanished without walking into the shadows or fading away or anything. One second he was there, the next he was gone. If he could do that, he wasn't real and Crater vowed to remember that. The next thing Crater knew, he was waking up and it was morning. He stared at the rough mooncrete walls of his tube and made a promise. "You're right, Captain Teller," he said, "there is much more here than is dreamt of in any of our philosophies and I'm going to find out what it is."

Crater had noticed a trail leading toward Alphonsus Crater. He took Maria aside. "I'm going up there," he said.

"But you're supposed to show the Apps how to inspect and change out the rollers on the conveyor belt today."

"That can wait."

"If you expect me to go with you, I'm not. I'm teaching Trudelle how to operate my matrix program. If you insist on going, at least take Crescent."

"You and she seem to be getting along well," Crater accused.

"We're women. I'm the spoiled granddaughter of the richest man on the moon. She's the product of a Petri dish and trained to kill upon command. We have a lot in common."

::: FORTY-EIGHT

rater and Crescent, armed with rifles, climbed along the worn path to Alphonsus. "What do you think they were doing up there?" Crescent asked.

"Could be a number of things," Crater answered. "Sightseeing or maybe prospecting or maybe they put their dead there. Lots of possibilities."

They remained silent as they continued to climb until Crescent said, "Look over there. We couldn't see it because of the way the slope is folded, but there is another trail. It looks like it was for vehicles."

"Hauling something up or something down," Crater said after using his helmet binoculars to inspect the trail. "Gillie, any readings so far?"

Yes, but I can't tell what it is. Not radio signals. Something just out of range.

They continued to climb. Atop the lip of the crater, they beheld the floor of Alphonsus. It was much like the floor of any crater, a circle of dust, except there was a small, rectangular building at its center. All paths led to it. Crater sat down on the lip. "Let's just watch it for a while."

Crescent sat beside him. After watching for a few minutes, Crater said, "Is it my imagination or is the dust in this crater slightly pink?"

"I noticed that too," Crescent said. "And over there, where the rim has collapsed, it looks almost red."

Crater led the way down into the crater, then around its edge to the collapsed rim. There, he discovered the soil wasn't red at all. "There's a thin layer of what appears to be a red gas here," he said. "But that's impossible. In this vacuum, it ought to be instantly dispersed."

Crater looked back toward the building. "It's flowing from there. The crater's tilted so gravity pulls it down here. Then it seems to fall through the gap." Crater climbed up on the rubble of the collapsed rim. "There's Endless Dust just below. This stuff's flowing its way. I can see little pockets of it now that I know to look."

"How can a gas flow in a vacuum?" Crescent asked.

"Normally, it can't," Crater said, going down on one knee and pushing his hand into the pinkish stuff. "So maybe it's not a gas at all. Certainly, the way I can swish it around makes it appear to be more like a liquid. But it's not sublimating. Gillie, any ideas what this stuff is?"

Gillie believes this may be a type of extremely dense filamentation plasma with nitrogen, oxygen, carbon, and a variety of other complex components.

Crater absorbed that, then asked, "Is there anything like it anywhere else?"

Yes. The observed universe is mostly plasma. Stars are filled with it.

"But like *this?*"

The gillie frowned in concentration, although it couldn't frown, then said, *Gillie will hypothesize. This may be a naturally forming plasma unique to this place.*

"You mean something's making it?"

Yes. There is likely a heat source. Since there are no known heat sources in the interior of the moon, this is an unknown factor.

Crater turned toward the building. "The answers seem to lie there. You don't have to get any closer if you don't want to, Crescent."

Crescent cradled her rifle. "Let's go," she said. "I'm as curious as you are."

They walked to the building, and along the way Crater noticed that their boots created swirls in the pinkish matter. "We kick it around but it still stays low to the ground," he said. "Whatever it is, the gillie is correct. It's extremely dense."

As they neared the building, Crater saw it was made of mooncrete. Several thin pipes protruded from its roof. He studied the pipes and realized the plasma, if that was what it was, was coming from them. There was a hatch with a key pad. "Gillie, what's the code?" Crater asked.

Gillie has already unlocked it, the gillie replied.

Crescent pulled open the hatch and climbed into an airlock. Crater followed and closed the hatch. Immediately, they heard air hissing as automatic pressurization occurred. When it stopped, Crescent opened the inner hatch into a standard dustlock with a single shower. Crescent opened the next hatch that led into a dressing room.

Air is good, the gillie said.

They took off their helmets and breathed in. The air was indeed good and fresh.

The next hatch led into an interior mooncrete tube but unlike one they'd ever seen. It was circular and on the inside circumference were portholes. Crater looked into one of them but saw only darkness.

"There are stairs leading downward," Crescent said.

It was a circular staircase made of lunasteel. Crescent and Crater walked down it to another circular mooncrete tube with more portholes. This time when Crater looked into the porthole, he saw a pinkish glow.

"Another set of stairs over here," Crescent said.

When they emerged from the next circular staircase, they were startled to arrive in what appeared to be a living tube. There was a bed, a small kitchen, and some overstuffed chairs. Even more startling, sitting in one of the chairs with his boots up on footstool and an old-fashioned book on his lap was a man who was apparently asleep. On second glance, Crater realized the man was an Umlap.

Crescent warily approached the Umlap, then pushed his shoulder with the muzzle of her rifle. The Umlap jerked awake, saw Crescent, and dived behind his chair. "I surrender!"

Crescent pointed her rifle at him. "Come out with your hands up!"

"I don't think that's necessary, Crescent," Crater said. "It's all right, sir. We're not here to hurt you. We're here with a party that's moving into Endless Dust."

The Umlap poked his head above the chair, looked at Crater, then at Crescent. "But is that not a crowhopper?"

"I was a member of the Legion," Crescent answered. "But now I'm not."

"Crowhoppers tell lies."

"Stand up, please," Crater said. "I'm Crater and this is

Crescent. I know General Nero and Perpetually Hopeful, his wife. You work for them, am I right?"

The Umlap's eyes narrowed. "You know Perpetually Hopeful? She is a most interesting woman."

"She is intelligent and beautiful," Crater said.

"For an Umlap, I would agree." The Umlap smiled, which meant he was not happy with what he'd said, then added, "Umlap men have difficulty praising Umlap women."

"A weakness," Crescent said.

"I don't mind praising other kinds of women," the Umlap replied, "although I would have to think long and hard about you, sweetcakes."

When Crater saw Crescent tense, he stepped between her and the Umlap. "What's your name?" he asked.

The Umlap frowned, meaning he was pleased to answer. "I am Places Bad Bets," he said.

"Well, Places Bad Bets, why are you here?"

"Because I placed a bad bet as usual. It was between me and another Umlap named So Often Wrong to decide who took this job. We did rocks, paper, scissors and I lost. For once, So Often Wrong was right. Yes, I work for General Nero, although I haven't had a signal from him in a very long time."

"There's a war on," Crater explained. "Signals have been disrupted."

"Pah! He's just forgotten about me." He nodded his head toward the portholes. "So what do you think of that?"

"I don't know what to think. What is it?"

The Umlap waved Crater over for a closer look. He turned on a spotlight. "Life," he said. "Moon critters."

Crater looked and saw rocks covered with brown scum. "What kind of moon critters?"

"Bacteria, fed by the heat and gasses coming from below."

Crater was incredulous. "How can heat and gasses come up from the moon? The planet's been dead for a very long time."

"According to the General's scientists, at the bottom of this hole is a natural fusion reactor. Somehow a fault developed in this crater a long time ago. Maybe it's a vertical lava tube. Nobody really knows. But enough Helium-3 dust fell into it that a low-grade fusion process got started. That created heat that caused the rock to heat up, gasses and a weird kind of plasma were released, and then bacteria began to grow."

"Where did the bacteria come from?"

The Umlap scowled happily. "The chief scientist in Cleomedes said maybe from rocks tossed up here from asteroid impacts on Earth. Or maybe from rocks zipping in from just about anywhere. Anyway, I'm keeping watch on it for General Nero. He thinks if we can understand it, maybe every moon colony can have one and draw power from it. Maybe even a kind of atmosphere can be created where we won't have to wear pressure suits. Who knows what might be done with it? We're just keeping it secret for now."

Crater was always astonished to discover the secret ways of men like General Nero and Colonel Medaris. What had been discovered in Alphonsus crater would turn a lot of theories and beliefs on their heads. If fusion power on the moon was a natural process and life could live around one of its vents, then who knew how big a population the moon might support? And if his invention to recover water could be made to work on a large scale . . . Crater's mind was racing with all kinds of possibilities. Was there a chance for terraforming? Was it possible with nearly unlimited energy and bacteria pumping out plasma that, given time, an Earth-like environment could form?

"It boggles the brain," Crater said.

"Not mine," Makes Bad Bets replied. "It's just a job keeping tabs on this scraggy hole in the ground. Of course, no one bothers me much so that's nice."

Crater remembered he'd come to Alphonsus to solve a mystery. "Do you ever see things?" he asked. "Or have realistic, colorful dreams?"

"Umlaps don't dream much. If we do, we forget them pretty quick." Makes Bad Bets stretched and yawned. "Say, why don't you stay for lunch? I have turnip paste."

"Some other time," Crater said, trying to sound grateful. "But come to Endless Dust anytime you like. The people there would be happy to make you breakfast, lunch, dinner, or just a snack."

Pleased, the Umlap scowled deeply. "I'll do that!"

Crater and Crescent climbed the stairs, then passed through the dustlock and the airlock and back outside, closing the hatch behind them. "Sometimes, Crescent, I think there's nothing more that can surprise me but then something happens that does. Life on the moon. Who can believe it?"

Crescent wore a confused expression. "But there's been life on the moon for years. What's the difference if there's bacteria?"

She had a point so Crater struggled for an explanation, then said, "People didn't bring the bacteria. It's here all on its own. It doesn't need us to keep it going. It's something of a miracle."

"Brown scum is a miracle? If you say so."

"I say so, Crescent, but if you don't understand, that's okay. We all have different ways of looking at things. Yours is as good as mine."

They trudged silently through the pinkish swirls of the plasma that rolled along the surface of the crater floor, then up the rim and back down the hill to Endless Dust. Before they reached the hatch, they saw them. Three crowhoppers holding rifles were beside the chuckwagon.

::: FORTY-NINE

rater studied the crowhoppers with his helmet scope. Then Maria and the Apps walked into view. They were also armed. It appeared to be a standoff. "They haven't seen us," Crater said. "Crescent, you work your way around the observation tower. I'll go to the left around the maintenance shed. When I give you the signal, we'll blast them. Be careful not to hit our people."

"There's no reason to attack," Crescent replied. "Look closer. The men of the Legion are not holding their rifles in an offensive position. Their barrels are pointing toward the dust."

Crater saw that Crescent was correct. "Gillie," Crater said, "connect me with Maria and the others."

Crater heard Maria say, ". . . no place for you here. Move on."

Jake spoke up. "I don't know. They look strong. We might be able to use them."

"Don't go wobbly on me, Jake," Maria growled. "These are dangerous creatures. They are trained to kill. You can never trust them."

"But Crescent shows us every day that isn't true," Clarence said.

"Clarence is right," Eliza said. "If there is a better woman than Crescent, I have yet to meet her."

"Crater," Crescent said on their private channel, "I don't feel well. My heart hurts."

Crater looked at her with concern, then tried to read her face. "Maybe you should lie down."

"No, it will pass. It is already better. It was silly of me to mention it. I think what Eliza said is what made my heart hurt. Does that make sense? An emotional response. I'm sorry if I upset you."

"Well, it's true what she said. There is no better woman than you."

"It is all your doing," she accused. "I try for you. I have a strong emotional attachment to you. Maria said it's love but I was taught by the Trainers that love isn't real but Maria said it's always real. It's not always right but it's always real."

Crater's engineering practical brain was well aware that there was a serious situation in Endless Dust that could end up in a firefight. Yet the part of his brain that carried his emotions, perhaps that "softness" he was accused of having too much of, told him to focus on Crescent for just a little while. "Crescent," he said, "I have a strong emotional attachment to you too. I want you to always be part of my life. You are like a sister to me. Is that all right? Can we be brother and sister?" He wanted to add, "Or did you expect more?" but he left those words unspoken. Some words didn't need to be said.

Crescent arranged her lips into a brave smile. "I'll be the best sister ever. And if Maria becomes my sister-in-law, I'll love even her, I promise."

"Hey, you two!" Maria's voice boomed in their ears. "We

have a situation down here or did you fail to notice? What are you talking about, anyway?"

Crater and Crescent hurried down the hill. At the chuckwagon, the three crowhoppers—Lucien, Absalom, and Dion—still held their rifles pointed dustward. "What are you doing here?" Crater demanded. "Didn't I tell you to get off my moon?"

"We got lost so we followed your tracks," Lucien said. "We want to surrender."

"Then put your rifles down."

The three youths looked at each other, then leaned their rifles against the chuckwagon. Crater waved his rifle at them. "Move away."

They walked away. Absalom said, "We are hungry and thirsty and we promise to fight no more forever."

"He is telling the truth," Crescent said.

The three Legionnaires stared at her. "What are you?"

"I am a female member of the Legion. I did not surrender. I was captured."

"What Legion?" Lucien asked suspiciously.

"The Phoenix."

Lucien's eyes widened. He bowed and said, "It's an honor."

The other two also bowed, but Crescent looked away from them.

"What are we to do with these fellows?" Maria demanded. "We can't let them stay!"

"We'll not turn them out," Jake said. "So we must take them in." He pointed at the three. "*If* you promise to work very hard for your keep."

"If we can live, we will work," Lucien said, the other two now ex-Legionnaires nodding in agreement.

"Then you're hired," Jake said. "Let's go inside and get you settled. Crescent, will you join us?"

Crescent raised her chin. "You were poor excuses for Legionnaires," she said.

"No argument from us," Absalom replied.

Maria shook her head as the three crowhoppers, Crescent, and the Apps headed for the dustlock. "Keep close watch!" she called after them. "They're still dangerous!"

When there was no reply, she turned to Crater. "Amazing. How can they trust them?"

"It's their town," Crater said. "Let them do what they want to do. Anyway, I think the fight is out of those crowhopper boys."

Maria looked doubtful. "So what did you find up there?"

Crater told her. "That means there may be natural fusion in Aristarchus too!" she chirped. "Grandfather owns that!"

"We should channel the plasma back underground," Crater said. "It's probably causing our hallucinations. It seeps into the enviro systems."

Maria nodded. "What a crazy world this is."

"Or moon in this case," Crater said.

"What do we do now?"

Crater shrugged. "All comm links are down. We're a thousand miles from nowhere."

"You're saying we're stuck."

"For now."

Maria walked across the dust, shaking her head. "So many things are happening out there and we're missing it all."

"Then let's not miss what's happening here."

"I'm not missing anything."

"If you're always thinking about being somewhere else, you're missing everything."

Maria walked on, then stopped and looked up at the sky, empty of everything but stars. "Since there have been people, we've always looked up and hoped that someone would come down and save us."

Crater walked up beside her and took her hand. "I don't want to be saved. I just want to be here with you."

Maria studied Crater, then melted. "Finally. You said exactly what I've always wanted to hear."

She took his hand and leaned in until their helmets touched. "We should kiss. I know, I know. We're wearing space helmets."

"We could take them off in the airlock."

She grinned and pulled Crater toward the hatch, to go inside and kiss and then join the Apps, and the new crowhopper hires, and Crescent who was now Crater's sister, and Ike who was very helpful.

Crater's heart sang with all the possibilities.

::: FIFTY

want to ask you something," Crater said to Lucien after dinner.

"Yes, of course," Lucien said. He was out of his armor and in a civilian's tunic and leggings.

Crater walked him away from the others. "Why did you bow to Crescent?"

"Have you not noticed the pendant she wears? It means she's from the Phoenix Century. She said so too."

"I heard her say that but I don't know what it means."

Lucien blinked. "Of course you don't, sir. Only we Legionnaires would know that. My apologies. Phoenix Centuries are deserving of special honors. That's why I bowed to her."

"There's more than one Phoenix Century?"

"There have been several. Crescent is from the newest. She is the only survivor. Such courage as hers is unequaled."

"She's brave in a fight," Crater allowed, "but I'm not following you."

"I'm not speaking of battlefield courage, sir. Crescent is

courageous with every breath she takes. They are limited in number, you see. She is programmed to die."

When Crater saw Crescent washing dishes, he joined her to dry them. They worked in silence until he said, "I know about the Phoenix Century."

She kept washing.

"Why didn't you tell me?"

"What was there to tell? Life is death. Death is life. It does not matter."

"It matters to me. How much longer?"

"I am nineteen. Like you. A coincidence, no? A year. Maybe a little more, maybe a little less. Twenty-one is the oldest any Phoenix Legionnaire has ever reached. I have felt it coming. When I said my heart hurt, I think it was truly an emotional response when I realized these people from the mountains really do care about me and want me to be part of their family. But it was also more than that. It was a signal from my body to expect the end."

"I don't understand why they made you this way."

She put down the dish she was washing and looked at Crater. "A force that is well trained and has nothing to lose is deadly. Look at those three over there. They love life because they think they're going to live forever. They're not. Nobody is. Those of us in a Phoenix Century accept death as natural and soon. What matters if it is today on the battlefield or tomorrow in our beds?"

"There must be something that can be done. When the war stops, I'll take you to a doctor."

Crescent shook her head, her lips arranged into a sad

smile. "There are no doctors who can change a genetic program deep within every cell of my body. No, Crater. I thank you, but there's nothing you can do."

Crescent picked up the dish and finished washing it, then handed it to Crater to dry. "Centurion Trabonnet told me to return to the steppes and breathe its air again," she said. "But I think I will stay here. Here, I am happy."

"I'll stay with you," Crater said.

"I don't think Maria will like that."

"It's my choice. She'll respect that."

Crescent's smile changed from sad to happy. "I would like to see your face every day."

"You will."

::: FIFTY-ONE

fter the work was done for the day, the residents of Endless Dust usually gathered at various tables and played whatever games interested them. Ike and the three ex-Legionnaires preferred cards (Lucien, Absalom, and Dion owed the Helper approximately ten million johncredits), the Apps and Maria preferred Monopoly (Maria played as if it were real money and got upset if she lost), and Crescent and Crater played chess (Crescent usually won but was teaching Crater the finer points of the game). Afterward, Crater and Maria liked to go up the spiral staircase into the observation tower to bask beneath the stars. The tower windows provided a view in every direction, even overhead where the mighty river of the galaxy greeted them. It had been weeks since the battle of warpods and the silvery ships. The sky was at peace. The comm-sats were still down. Endless Dust had become their world.

One evening, as they rested on cushions and Maria snuggled into his arms, Crater decided it was time he told her the results of his thinking about their future. "I know we're only nineteen . . . ," he began.

Maria snuggled in deeper. "Almost twenty," she said dreamily. "Time goes so fast here, we'll be thirty before we know it."

"You like it here," he said.

"I like being with you."

"I think we should get married."

She sat up. "Did you just say what I think you said?"

"Yes. You're happy here. I'm happy here. We want to be together. It would be the right thing to do."

"Very logical, Mr. Engineer."

"It is. That's why I reached this conclusion. We're needed here, Maria. After the war, the other Apps will come. We can show them everything they need to know to thrive."

"But the Apps own Endless Dust. We'd only be renters."

"No, we wouldn't. I talked to them. They want us to stay. If we do, we have a full share."

Maria frowned. "Clearly, you've been talking about us with the others."

"Not much," he said, then nodded. "Okay. Some."

She nodded toward the looming crater to the northwest. "What about Alphonsus? Eventually, General Nero will come to see about his bugs in the ground."

Crater shrugged. "Let him. Endless Dust doesn't have anything to do with that. We'll just mine our Thorium and Titanium and mind our own business."

"You really mean it, don't you?"

"I really do."

With a shout, Maria threw herself into his arms and kissed him hard. "All right, Crater," she said.

"All right what?" He grinned.

She didn't answer. Instead, an odd expression crossed her

face. "What's that?" she asked. "A dust storm? But how could there be a dust storm on the moon?"

Crater climbed to his feet, astonished to see dust blowing past the tower until he saw what was causing it. A silvery ship, its jets kicking up dust, was landing. It didn't land tail-first like a jumpcar but horizontally on landing skids. Crater had never seen a ship like it. It was cylindrical and had nubs with pods he guessed were weapons of some type. It was, he judged, around seventy feet long. A military landing craft. "We're being invaded," he said.

Maria activated her do4u to send out the alert to the others, then followed Crater down the stairs. Within minutes, the residents of Endless Dust burst from the airlock and took up defensive positions. Lucien, Absalom, and Dion rolled up the cannon Crater had built. Its ammunition was Titanium slugs, guaranteed to punch a hole in just about anything.

They held their fire, waiting to see what was going to happen. Finally, a hatch opened in the ship and a ramp unfolded. Then a man walked down the ramp or, more accurately, swaggered. Crater recognized the swagger. "Petro!"

"Hi, chump!" Petro said. "And Maria. Long time no see, doll." He took note of the cannon and the rifles aimed in his direction. "Whoa! Guess I should've rung the doorbell or something."

"Where've you been?" Crater blurted.

Petro pointed to the sky. "Flying for the Colonel and the Lunar Council. Like this taxi? You should see the ship I took off from. Faster than grease. It can fly circles around warpods. And our kinetic energy weapons knock them to pieces."

"We saw you up there," Maria said. "We hoped you were on our side."

"You were in Armstrong City when I last saw you," Crater said. "You were saying something about prospecting—"

"A cover story. The Colonel recruited me to fly for him. He knows the future King of England can do anything. I worked my way up to the exalted rank of commander. Got my own battle cruiser. The war's all but over and we're going to win." He pointed skyward. "There were some fantastic battles up there. You missed them all, you down in the dust. Endless Dust, they tell me this place is called. Well, I'm here to pick you and Maria up and fly you away. Maybe there will yet be a few skirmishes for you to win a medal or two. Come aboard and we'll get out of this scrag hole."

"You want us to leave now?" Crater asked.

"That's why I'm here. And by the way, Crater, the Colonel said all was forgiven. You saved Maria. You're pardoned of all crimes. Come on!"

"I don't know ..."

Maria walked up to Crater. "Of course you know. Your destiny—our destiny—was never here, Crater. Deep in your heart, you have to accept that. And we'll be together. That's what you said you wanted, right?"

"But ..."

"You want your answer? Here it is. Yes, yes, yes! I'll marry you." She hugged him. "I love you more than anything. But let's go. There's a grand life out there for us!"

Maria climbed onto the ramp and went to Petro, taking his hands in hers. "Thank you for coming after us."

"The Colonel made it my top priority now that we've chased the warpods away. You won't believe all that's happened."

Maria laughed with delight. "How's Armstrong City?"

"The dome's sealed. The new maintenance shed is abuilding. Those crowhoppers really did a number on it."

Maria smirked. "Oh, yes, they certainly did."

"Crater, Maria, what's going on?" Jake asked. The other Apps, the ex-Legionnaires, Crescent, and Ike were standing in the street, their rifles lowered, the cannon abandoned.

Petro peered at them. "Guess I should be introduced," he said.

Crater named them, then said, "This is my brother, Petro."

"Nice to meet you, folks," Petro said. "Sorry to take Crater and Maria away, but there's a lot of people in the outside world who've been worried sick about them."

Maria was already halfway up the ramp. "Come on, Crater!"

Crater climbed up on the ramp, looked Petro in the eye, then hugged him. "Thanks for coming after us."

"Hey, what's a brother for? Anyway, Mom would have killed me if I hadn't. But, honestly, Crater, we've got to go. I'm a commander, not an admiral. I'm already overdue."

Crater walked off the ramp, back into the dust, then turned around. "I'm not going."

Crescent took a step forward. "No, Crater. Maria's right. You must go."

Crater kept his eyes on Maria, who had turned around at the hatch. "I'm staying," he said.

"Your choice, buddy." Petro chuckled. "You were always a chump."

Petro stopped momentarily beside Maria, then climbed through the hatch and went inside.

Maria walked halfway down the ramp. Tears were streaming down her face. "Please, Crater. Please."

"You go on," Crater said. "They need you out there."

The ramp began to slowly rise. Maria looked over her shoulder, back toward the ship, then, holding the handrails, walked to the ramp's end. All she had to do was take a single step and she would be back on the dust. Crater closed his eyes and willed himself to keep them closed. In a short while, he felt the brush of dust blowing past him as the silver taxi jetted skyward. He waited a little longer, then opened his eyes, there to see his future.

::: Reading Group Guide

1. The characters are three years older now than they were in the first book, *Crater*. How have they changed?

2. The Colonel says during the battle in chapter one, "Kill them all. Remember they're only crowhoppers. It isn't as if they are real humans." So why did Crater disobey the Colonel and take one as a prisoner? What trouble does it immediately bring him?

3. Crater often does what others want him to do, even when he doesn't like it. Does this make him weak? Do you like him better when he goes against authority?

4. Maria has grown to be a tough businesswomen who is used to getting her way. Do you like her this way? How does she change during the story, and is it in a good or bad way? What lessons does she learn? Why do you think she has feelings for Crater?

5. Crescent was genetically engineered to be a warrior who kills on command. Yet she is still human. Once she starts living in a different culture, how does she change?

6. Absalom, Dion, Lucien, and Carillon are crowhopper warriors who seem a little different than the others. What is this difference? Did you like or sympathize with them? What do you think will happen to the three young crowhoppers who stay in Endless Dust?

7. What do you think about the odd phenomena of lights and movement that has been observed on the moon for centuries? Do you think we should find out what is actually happening there? What do you think about what Crater and Crescent found in Alphonsus crater?

8. Would you like a gillie of your own? Why do you think the two gillies hate each other?

9. The Apps in Endless Dust are about to be joined by their family and friends. When others find out about the rich minerals they have found there, do you think they will be able to keep their simple life, or will outsiders come in and change everything?

10. What do you think would happen if a huge deposit of gold was found on the moon?

11. Crescent is a crowhopper of the Phoenix Century. Discuss what this means to her.

12. At the end of the novel, Maria is given the choice to stay in Endless Dust with Crater or leave. Which do you think she did?

::: Author's Note

My fascination with the moon began in Coalwood, West Virginia, when five other teenaged boys and I famously built rockets. To see what we were aiming at, we constructed an observatory atop the coal company clubhouse, which was actually a hotel for bachelor miners not unlike the Dust Palace I describe in *Crater* and *Crescent*. On top of this three-story building, we had a small telescope, given to us by one of the company junior engineers, and there we studied the heavens. I was naturally very interested in looking at the planets and stars, but I had a problem. When I took off my glasses and pressed my eye against the telescope eyepiece, I mostly saw blurs, no matter how much I fiddled with the focus knob. Happily, when I moved the telescope to look at the big, bright moon, I could see everything! After the other boys wore themselves out marveling at the rings of Saturn and the bands of Jupiter, none of which I could make out very well, I usually just looked at the moon and, before long, I could even imagine myself traveling through its mountain passes and into its craters and across its great basins. The near side of the moon became as familiar to me as my little town.

As recounted in my memoir *Rocket Boys*, my fascination with the moon led me to suggest to the future President John F. Kennedy when he visited the coalfields that maybe the United States ought to go to the moon. He apparently agreed with me, since that's what we did. I also told him I thought we should go up there and just mine the blame thing because, as a West Virginia boy, I didn't see much value in living anywhere that couldn't be mined. Whether he agreed with me on that, we will never know. I am fairly certain other presidents didn't. For that matter, it's clear they didn't like us going to the moon at all, because as soon as we got good at flying up there, the plug was pulled on the entire enterprise. I try not to take this personally, although it's difficult. The present president (circa 2013) won't even consider it. In fact, he said in a speech at Cape Canaveral that since we'd been there already, it didn't make any sense to go back. He even laughed when he said it, as if it were all a big joke. As you can imagine, that made me smile like an Umlap.

Despite the ignorance and small-mindedness of some politicians, most people who pay attention know the moon is loaded with treasure just waiting to be mined. Besides the Helium-3 this series is named after, there's thorium (which my settlers in this novel are after), plus aluminum, calcium, nickel, magnesium, silicon, titanium, and a whole lot more. We also know that the moon is vastly wetter than we thought when we went there the first time. Crater's invention, or something like it, may one day be able to extract enough water to support a new civilization of hardy pioneers and miners. As for the gold found in the sample taken by Crater from the nickel "lake," this is a real possibility. In fact, scientists believe that all the gold embedded in Earth's crust was delivered here by asteroids. If that is so, certainly the moon, battered as it was and is by asteroids, should hold a fair lot of gold. The only way to find out if I'm right, of course, is to go look.

Another mystery explored in this novel has to do with the baffling lights and movement seen on the moon for centuries called lunar transient phenomena, or LTP. There are many reports of monks staring at the medieval moon and thinking maybe they saw evidence of angels up there. On the other side of the world, ancient Chinese astronomers wondered if there were dragons spitting fire on the moon. Such sightings have continued. Just as the gillie apprises Crater, the Russian astronomer Nikolai A. Kozyrev in 1958 spent an hour watching what he concluded were eruptions inside Alphonsus Crater that produced white and pink flares. In 1963, astronomers at Lowell Observatory recorded red, pink, and orange lights at Aristarchus Crater. When German astronomers spotted a bright glow at Aristarchus while the first men were walking on the moon, Neil Armstrong was asked to look over that way. He did and reported "an area that is considerably more illuminated than the surrounding area [with] a slight amount of fluorescence." Reports of LTP continue to come in from professional and amateur astronomers across the world. All this means something odd is happening on the moon. What it might be, only guesses can be made. Whatever it is, it's cool and prodigious. It's my recommendation, of course, that we take a closer look by going there.

This novel also explores other phenomena, which has little to do with the moon and more with the human condition. This includes such tendencies as bullying and discrimination.

Crescent, the crowhopper girl, is clearly different from the humans in Moontown, not only because of her outward appearance but because of her culture. Crater, for reasons he doesn't entirely comprehend but probably due to his fundamentally good character, first refuses to kill Crescent and then defends her from Moontown bullies. He also tries to understand why she is the way she is. Crater's actions, of course, are good and admirable. No one should be hurt or disliked just because of how they look and where they come from. This is not to say, I hasten to add, that the crowhopper culture, as I have presented it, is one to be admired, nor do I believe it is necessary to admire any and all cultures. My point is everyone is an individual who usually has nothing to say about their physiology or the culture into which they were born. Therefore they should be respected as individuals and, if need be, defended from bullies. There is probably nothing more exalted in the eyes of our Maker than to defend the weak and fight for people (and animals) who lack the ability to fight for themselves.

A troubling scenario in this novel has to with Ike the Helper. We have reached a stage in our scientific knowledge where it will soon be possible to design people with certain desirable physical and mental characteristics. In a way we've always had this ability, although it took a lot longer and was vastly more hit or miss. What I'm referring to is the tendency of people to pick mates based on perceived positive qualities. The offspring of such choices may or may not be born with those characteristics but, if kept up over generations, the evidence shows they can be enhanced. Some royal families took this to the extreme and inadvertently reinforced such negative traits as hemophilia and mental disorders. The situation brought forth in this novel is what happens when what is usually thought to be a negative characteristic is deliberately sought.

Ike the Helper is an example of a person designed in a laboratory to be functional and teachable but with less than "normal" intelligence. There is only one reason for Ike to exist and that is so he can be a slave or, euphemistically, a "Helper." In *Crescent*, the demonstrators outside the Helper store in Armstrong City aren't fooled by this twist of a word, but others eagerly adopt it, rationalizing that if the intelligence of anyone is low enough, and if they are sold as a product, they don't qualify as fully human. Crater also isn't fooled, but he struggles with the morality of the situation. After all, Ike *wants* to help! He's been taught to be helpful since he was a child, and if he isn't allowed to help, he is unhappy. If we ever allow real "helpers" to be created, we will find ourselves in a moral quagmire, and I'm not certain how we'll get out of it. It is up to writers, however, to worry about such things through our stories. If my readers think about the implications of Ike the Helper and Crescent the Legionnaire, then I've done a portion of my job.

All I know for sure is the future is out there and it will be either very good, or about the same, or awful, depending on what is done with the present. Since I tend to be an optimist, I think there's a greater chance that it will be very good, but I suppose it might not be. Actually, however it works out is really kind of up to you.

— Homer Hickam

::: About the Author

Homer Hickam is the author of the #1 *New York Times* bestseller *Rocket Boys*, which was made into the acclaimed movie *October Sky*. He is also the author of *Torpedo Junction, The Keeper's Son, The Ambassador's Son, Sky of Stone, Back to the Moon, Red Helmet, Crater,* and many other books. He is married to Linda Terry Hickam. Homer loves his cats, hunts dinosaurs when he can, and shares his time between homes in the U.S. Virgin Islands and Huntsville, Alabama. Visit homerhickam.com for more information.